FOREIGN POLICY
AND THE
BLACK
(INTER)NATIONAL
INTEREST

SUNY series in Afro-American Studies
John R. Howard and Robert C. Smith, editors

FOREIGN POLICY AND THE BLACK (INTER)NATIONAL INTEREST

edited by

CHARLES P. HENRY

State University
of New York
Press

#42889721

Published by
State University of New York Press, Albany

© 2000 State University of New York

Production by Susan Geraghty
Marketing by Patrick Durocher

Printed in the United States of America

For information, address State University of New York
Press, State University Plaza, Albany, N.Y., 12246

Library of Congress Cataloging-in-Publication Data

Foreign policy and the Black (inter)national interest / edited by Charles P. Henry.
     p. cm. — (SUNY series in Afro-American studies)
   Includes bibliographical references and index.
   ISBN 0-7914-4697-2 (hc : alk. paper) — ISBN 0-7914-4698-0 (pbk. : alk. paper)
     1. United States—Foreign relations—1989—Citizen participation. 2. United
States—Foreign relations—1989—Social aspects. 3. United States—Race
relations—Political aspects. 4. Afro-Americans—Politics and government. 5.
Afro-Americans—Civil rights. 6. United States—Race relations. 7. Blacks—Politics and
government. 8. Blacks—Civil rights. 9. World politics—1989– 10. Race
relations—Political aspects. I. Henry, Charles P., 1947– II. Series.

E840.F6754 2000
327.73017'496—dc21
                                                                99-057708

10 9 8 7 6 5 4 3 2 1

*To the memory of
Floyd Holbert, Bertram Gross,
and Erskine Peters*

CONTENTS

ACKNOWLEDGMENTS

This work is the product of my search for recent relevant reading materials for a class I taught on "Human Rights and U.S. Foreign Policy" in the spring of 1998. I discovered that there were few, if any works, that examined Black foreign policy interests since the end of the Cold War. This vacuum seemed ironic given the rise in racial and ethnic conflict worldwide and recent scholarship concerning the clash of civilizations/cultures, and I decided to make a contribution to this discussion by calling on friends and colleagues in the academy and in the political world to add their voices. I wish to thank Robert Smith, an old friend and colleague, who introduced the project to SUNY Press and a special thanks to the former editor of the Afro-American Series at SUNY, Clay Morgan, the current editor, Priscilla Ross, and to Cheryl Redmond.

The following contributions have been published before in similar forums. I am grateful to the publishers for their permission to make use of the following essays: James Jennings' "The International Convention on the Elimination of All Forms of Discrimination: Implications for Challenging Racial Hierarchy," previously appeared in the *Howard Law Journal*, vol. 40, no. 3 (1998); Charles Henry and Tunua Thrash, "United States Human Rights Petitions before the United Nations," was published in *The Black Scholar*, vol. 26, no. 3–4 (Fall-Winter 1996).

INTRODUCTION

Black Global Politics in a Post–Cold War World

Charles P. Henry

> I don't believe we can have world peace until America has an "integrated" foreign policy.
> —Martin Luther King Jr.

In a *Playboy* essay, Martin Luther King Jr. contended that our disastrous experiments in Vietnam and the Dominican Republic had been a result of racist decision making. "Men of the white West," said King, "have grown up in a racist culture, and their thinking is colored by that fact. . . . They don't respect anyone who is not white."[1]

King's 1967 break with American foreign policy on Vietnam marks a watershed in African American views on such policy just as Vietnam itself represents the beginning of the end of the bipartisan Cold War consensus on anticommunism. Our mistakes in dealing with Vietnam and by extension China seemed, indeed, to be those of a nation who saw most of Asia as a threatening, "yellow" monolith controlled by Mao Zedong's little red book. If we had had diplomatic relations with "Red China" or had known a little about the historical antagonism between China and Vietnam, we would have seen that both countries were more concerned about domestic development than an international Communist alliance. As Malcolm X was fond of pointing out, the French defeat at Dien Bien Phu in 1954 was a decisive defeat for colonialism, demonstrating that a relatively small group of disciplined guerillas could win against a larger, stronger, conventionally equipped army of a major power (with United States support). Instead of withdrawing, our segregated foreign policy making process led us in the oppposite direction.

King was not the first African American leader to oppose the war in Vietnam. Malcolm X, the Student Non-Violent Coordinating Committee, Muhammad Ali, and even Coretta Scott King and James Bevel of the Southern Christian Leadership Conference (SCLC), had preceded him in public opposition to the war.[2] No national leader, however, of King's status had taken the position that King set forth in his sermon at Riverside Church in New York on April 4, 1967 (exactly one year before his assassination). In his remarks, King presented seven reasons for opposing U.S. policy:

1. Spending on the war was draining funds for domestic programs;
2. Young Black men were being killed at an extraordinarily high rate in integrated army units yet still faced segregated schools at home;
3. It was morally inconsistent for him to urge nonviolence at home while America applied violence abroad;
4. Winning the Nobel Prize gave him the responsibility to work for peace everywhere;[3]
5. He opposed all forms of imperialism;
6. America needed a radical revolution in values that would lead it to place human rights above American profits;
7. He opposed the war because he loved America and wanted to see it become a "divine Messianic force" not a world policeman.[4]

The King reflected in the Riverside sermon is not the King widely celebrated in January. It is this King, however, that much of the Third World identifies with. The Riverside sermon was a beautiful blending of domestic and international policy. The struggle for civil rights and the "War on Poverty" had indeed been gutted by the priority given to Vietnam. Blacks were paying a high price both in terms of program funding and lives lost. Yet King's remarks were almost universally condemned by African American leaders. Figures King had worked closely with such as Whitney Young of the Urban League, Roy Wilkens of the NAACP, and UN Undersecretary Ralph Bunche were quick to condemn him for linking the domestic Black agenda to foreign policy. Yet King's action inspired a host of younger leaders such as Ron Dellums to see domestic policy in a broader context. Lyndon Johnson bluntly said that King had no authority to speak on issues of foreign policy and closed off his access to the White House.

By the time of the Tet offensive in 1968, a much larger number of establishment figures had joined King in opposition. The "containment strategy" of George Kennan, which had governed U.S. foreign policy since its enunciation in 1948, was now fractured beyond repair. Such influential elite figures as Reinhold Niebuhr,[5] Arthur Schlesinger, Hans Morganthou, and John Kenneth Galbraith were now arguing that the communist world was polycentric and Vietnam was not vital to our national security. Thus, Vietnam represented the beginning of a process that would end with the fall of the Berlin Wall in 1989, that is, the removal of anticommunism as the guiding principle of U.S. post–World War II foreign policy.

As of today, no strategy or ideology has replaced "containment theory" and "anticommunism" as the decisive influence in U.S. foreign policy. Anticommunism was a perfect policy in that it combined elements of idealpolitik and realpolitik. Idealists supported it because of its opposition to the violation of individual political and civil rights that was widespread in the Soviet bloc. Realists approved of its emphasis on geopolitics protecting our economic and cultural interests in Western Europe and our strategic interests in the Pacific. Without anticommunism, U.S. foreign policy was a ship without a rudder.

Under Henry Kissinger's leadership, both the Nixon and Ford administrations advanced a foreign policy primarily along realist lines. The balance of power emphasis of these two administrations was briefly replaced by the human rights idealism of the Carter administration. Recognizing the utility of anticommunism over détente, Ronald Reagan rode to victory on the revival of superpower confrontation. Unlike the Johnson administration, which split Black leadership, Ronald Reagan made it clear that African American interests could not be the "national interest."

Pioneer Black scholar and diplomat Elliott Skinner has delineated several factors that tend to exclude African Americans from the foreign policy making process. First, most societies have made decision making in foreign policy an elite process reserved for monarchs, presidents, and at most a few high-ranking advisors and legislators. Second, those persons who had access to the foreign policy elite were themselves drawn from the same socioeconomic status, race, and gender groups as Ronald Palmer discusses in his contribution. In short, foreign policy makers trusted those who looked like themselves. Third, in democratic societies external pressure on decision-making elites has been influential because public opinion is especially ill-informed in the area of foreign relations. Immigrant or ethnic groups with close ties to their land of origin have an opportunity to fill the information vaccum and lobby on behalf of their native land. African Americans, in general, lack specific and affective ties to particular African nations. Finally, United States foreign policy has traditionally given low priority to relationships with Caribbean and African nations.[6] Percy Hintzen's contribution to this volume is an exhaustive treatment of U.S. foreign policy in the English-speaking

Caribbean that views Caribbean independence as subservient to U.S. Cold War interests. Central to his discussion is the role of U.S. government in undermining any radical assertions of independence in the post–World War II era. This led to American support for anticommunist Afro-Ceole nationalism as an alternative to socialism or communism. Ron Walters' contribution emphasizes the marginalization of Africa in foreign aid and trade prior to 1993. Even with the switch from public sector development assistance to private sector–driven trade and investment, Africa suffers in comparison to other regions both in terms of amounts and limitations on the recipients of the investment.

The following table of key events in U.S. foreign policy from an African American perspective demonstrates the very limited effectiveness of Black influence.[7]

KEY EVENTS IN U.S. FOREIGN POLICY
FROM A BLACK PERSPECTIVE

1794–1800—The Haitian Revolution led by Toussaint L'Ouverture.

1815—Paul Cuffee returns 38 African Americans back to Africa.

1820—The establishment of Liberia for freed African American slaves.

1884–85—The Berlin West African Conference divides Africa among the colonial powers.

1919—The first of five Pan African Congresses led by W. E. B. DuBois

1935—The Italian-Ethiopian War

1946—National Negro Congress Petition on Human Rights presented to UN

1947—U.S. Armed Forces desegregated

1950—Ralph Bunche wins the Nobel Peace Prize

1955—The Non-Aligned Nations meet in Bandung, Indonesia

1957—Ghana becomes the first postcolonial African nation

1967—Martin Luther King Jr. publicly opposes Vietnam War

1977—Andrew Young becomes U.S. Representative to the UN, TransAfrica is formed, the Sullivan Principles are established.

1984—Jesse Jackson raises South Africa as a presidential campaign issue.

1986—Comprehensive Anti-Apartheid Act is passed over Reagan's veto.

1987—Colin Powell becomes National Security Advisor.

1994—U.S. ratifies the International Convention on the Elimination of All Forms of Discrimination.

1998—President Clinton visits five African nations.

The Haitian Revolution marked the first successful colonial revolt led by slaves in the New World. Inspired by the ideals of the French Revolution, Toussaint L'Ouverture and his generals defeated Napoleon's finest troops, leading Napoleon to not only give up on Haiti but to also sell the Louisiana territory to Jefferson. While great efforts were made to suppress news of the Haitian Revolution in the United States, including laws banning the importation of slaves from the Caribbean, Toussaint quickly became a hero in America's Black communities. However, as Lorenzo Morris points out in his contribution, United States endorsement of Haitian leaders today carries baggage that hinders rather than helps their popular appeal. Prior to 1815, wealthy Black Massachusetts shipowner Paul Cuffee petitioned Congress to provide him with funds to take a group of educated African Americans back to Africa to "Christianize" and "civilize" their brethren. When Congress—by a narrow vote—refused, Cuffee used his own funds and ship to return thirty-eight free Blacks to Sierra Leone. Cuffee's efforts inspired the formation of the American Colonization Society (ACS) in 1816 whose members included many of the nation's most prominent political leaders and whose goal was the removal of free Blacks from the nation. Most free Blacks vigorously opposed the ACS program. In 1820, the nation of Liberia was established by eighty-six African Americans with U.S. government support. While the United States supported the removal of free Blacks to the African continent, it refused to recognize Liberia as an independent nation until 1847. The historic ties of the United States to Liberia are presented as the context for current democratization efforts promoted by the United States in the contribution of Keith Jennings and Celena Slade. As in Haiti, U.S. support of Liberian leaders is now seen negatively by rank-and-file Liberians. By contrast, the United States quickly recognized the colonial division of Africa that occurred at the 1884–85 Berlin Conference.

The Treaty of Versailles in 1919 not only gave hope to a new generation of liberal internationalists in the United States but also inspired W. E. B. DuBois to seize the opportunity to hold the first of a series of Pan African Congresses. The purpose of the Congress, held over the objection of U.S. officials, was to lobby for a timetable for self-rule in the colonies and to place those colonies ruled by the defeated Axis powers under the mandate of the League of Nations. While the Pan African Congresses represented a Black elite, Marcus Garvey moved rapidly during the same period to popularize the uplift of Africa among Black masses worldwide. Italy's invasion of Ethiopia in 1935 symbolized the failure of the League of Nations to deter aggression against a member African nation and opened the door for the fascist aggression of World War II. Italy's action, which may be seen as partial revenge for Italy's defeat at Adowa in 1896, led to the mobilization of Ethiopian support groups in the United States and clashes between African Americans and Italian Americans in cities like New York.

Immediately after the formation of the United Nations and its new Commission on Human Rights, African Americans began to use this new international forum to expose racial discrimination in the United States as the Charles Henry and Tunua Thrash contribution discusses in detail. The 1946 petition of the National Negro Congress was quickly followed by a longer 1947 petition sponsored by the National Association for the Advancement of Colored People (NAACP) and a 1951 genocide petition submitted by the Civil Rights Congress led by William Patterson and Paul Robeson. The period after World War II also witnessed the desegregation of the United States Armed Forces in 1947 and the first Black Nobel laureate, Ralph Bunche, who won the Nobel Peace Prize in 1950 for his mediation of the conflict in Palestine. However, by 1947, the postwar optimism that had seen Black liberals and leftists united with Africans and West Indians in opposing colonialism abroad and Jim Crow at home had begun to erode under the pressure of McCarthyism. Many Black liberals joined White liberals such as those in the new Americans for Democratic Action in promoting a united front against communism while charging that the greatest internal threat to American leadership of the "free world" was racial discrimination.[8]

During the height of the Cold War, "Third World" nations gathered in Bandung, Indonesia to form the "nonaligned movement." Congressman Adam Clayton Powell Jr. attended the conference and Richard Wright reported on the proceedings. The struggle for the allegiance of these nonaligned nations would help force the removal of Jim Crow laws in the United States, most notably in the 1954 Supreme Court decision *Brown v. Topeka Board of Education*, and present an alternative to communism and capitalism.

Ghana's independence in 1957 marked the beginning of the end of colonialism in Africa and had reverberation in the United States. Kwame Nkrumah, Ghana's leader, had been educated in the United States, but in the 1950s and 1960s a younger generation of African Americans began to turn to African leaders and intellectuals like Nkrumah, Sekou Toure, Amilcar Cabral, Jomo Kenyatta, and Julius Nyerere for guidance. A number even took up residence in countries such as Ghana. While African countries became popular assignments for Peace Corps volunteers, Allen Caldwell describes a kind of counter–Peace Corps in his contribution on Kenya. With the help of transnational philanthropy, Black youth in Baltimore are being sent to Kenya to receive a quality of education they cannot find in inner-city American schools.

King's Riverside speech in 1967 condemning the war in Vietnam stood in sharp contrast to the inclusion of King's lieutenant, Andrew Young, in the Carter administration a decade later. Young was named U.S. ambassador to the United Nations and quickly gained the respect of Third World delegates. During the same period, Reverend Leon Sullivan of Philadelphia, a member of the board of directors of General Motors, set forth a voluntary code of principles for companies doing business in South Africa. Young and Sullivan—along with the formation of a new lobbying group of African issues, TransAfrica—represent the emergence of an "insider" strategy for the first time in regard to Black influence on U.S. foreign policy.

This strategy quickly disappeared as the Reagan administration began a policy of "constructive engagement" with the apartheid regime in South Africa. Reagan's policies, both domestic and foreign, help generate support for the presidential campaign of Jesse Jackson in 1984. While Jackson had minimal impact on domestic policy, he was successful in introducing into the presidential debate the issue of U.S. foreign policy toward South Africa. To the dismay of the foreign policy establishment, he also had success as a citizen diplomat in the case of U.S. airman Ronald Goodman, who had been captured by the Syrians. In 1986, Congress passed the Comprehensive Anti-Apartheid Act over the veto of President Reagan. As Winston Nagan points out, this act was the first time U.S. foreign policy officially condemned institutional racism.

With the dissolution of the Soviet Union, new challenges emerged in foreign policy that this volume explores. With the end of the Cold War Black liberals and leftists were again free to join ranks in a worldwide assault on racial domination. However, there are currently no figures on the Black left comparable to Paul Robeson and W. E. B. Dubois and a Black right has emerged to compete for the "national interest." Already this period has produced the first African American to achieve elite decision-making status, Colin Powell, who was named national security advisor in 1987 and the late Ron Brown played a decisive role in developing Black and other business ties with Africa as Clinton's secretary of commerce. By 1994, the United States had ratified the Convention of the Elimination of All Forms of Racial Discrimination, and James Jennings explores its implications in his contribution. As recently as 1998, President Clinton gave new prominence to Africa as he undertook a five-country tour.

Many of these key events demonstrate that racism at worst and ethnocentrism at best have been at the center of U.S. foreign policy. As Lauren demonstrates, the spread of democracy in the nineteenth century was integrally linked to a rise in racism. Moreover, this racism grew with the development of science, not in spite of it.[9] Thus, such concepts as manifest destiny, the White man's burden, eugenics, and racial hierarchy are central to the development of the "national interest" of the elites that controlled U.S. foreign policy.

While recent scholarship has devoted more attention to the influence of culture,[10] it is absolutely essential to acknowledge what Martin Luther

King pointed out in 1967—that we have been blinded by our bias. The frantic search for a new worldview or guiding principle for U.S. foreign policy must include a multicultural perspective if the blunders of "anti-communism" are to be avoided in the future.

Perhaps the closet equivalent to "containment strategy" in today's foreign policy debates is Samuel P. Huntington's suggestion that world politics has entered a new phase in which the fundamental source of conflict will not be primarily ideological or primarily economic but cultural. The Harvard professor's 1993 *Foreign Affairs* article received a great deal of attention because it seemed to accurately reflect the alarming rise in ethnic, racial, and religious conflict that followed the fall of the Soviet Union. While Huntington's "clash of civilizations" thesis was widely debated in academic circles and even given a domestic spin by some,[11] his views were not reflected in U.S. foreign policy and generated little if any interest among U.S. minorities. Yet if, indeed, a "kin-country" syndrome is at work in such U.S. foreign policy decisions as the Gulf War and if cultural differences exacerbate economic conflict with such countries as Japan, then the cultural conflict thesis deserves more attention for several reasons.

It is widely acknowledged that the East-West conflict of past years has been replaced by North-South conflict. However, the use of geography obscures the real role that race and economics play in the international arena. As Abdul Aziz Said suggests, security is no longer a function of geopolitics but of technology. The old terminology of balance of power and national interest do not adequately explain the politics of global capital and global issues.[12] Moreover, the conflict involves not only the governments of the developed versus less developed nations but non-governmental organizations (NGOs) as well. In the human rights field, for example, NGOs in Third World nations routinely criticize U.S. and European human rights organizations for focusing on political and civil rights while ignoring the right to development. As geo-economics replace geopolitics, entire continents such as Africa and nations as large as India are left out of the discussions over "economic zones." No more than twenty or thirty national and international actors have any significant impact in this arena according to Edward Said and they are overwhelmingly White.

With the lack of an identifiable enemy after the Cold War, the Great Powers of the international system have begun to work together to protect their own—generally economic—interests. Neorealism and neoliberalism have converged around technology and trade. In this new international system some 80 percent of the world's population finds itself on the global periphery. No better example of this marginalization can be found than the disparate treatment of the genocide committed in

Rwanda as compared to the "ethnic cleansing" of Bosnia and Kosovo. As President Clinton so tellingly stated, the stability and peace of Europe are strategic priorities for U.S. interests.

As great as the horror of Rwanda and central Africa is, the more pernicious threat is the burden of debt and economic marginalization crushing Africa and to a lesser extent the Caribbean as revealed in the contributions of Walters, Morris, Hintzen, and Jennings and Slade. Structural adjustment programs imposed by international financial institutions (IFIs) on African and Caribbean countries can cause real incomes to fall as much as 50 percent. Given that 40 percent or more of the people in these countries already live below absolute poverty levels, the result is denial of education and health services, malnutrition, and premature death.[13]

While the World Bank recognizes that "programs of action can be sustained only if they arise out of consensus built on dialogue within each country,"[14] it has yet to engage in such dialogue when imposing structural adjustment programs. In fact, the imposition of such programs requires draconian measures on the part of the state that work against an open democratic system. And although African states are pictured as authoritarian regimes controlling all aspects of life, they are in fact weak with few central services and partial territorial control. No African state approaches the level of government services or control over police and military that resides in the government of the United States or any other industrialized country.

What is needed is stronger not weaker government. But this stronger government must be accountable to voters. Moreover, this government must be the product of an active civil society. Government reflects civil society rather than opposing it. Mere privatization of public power that shifts into private hands the many coercive functions that once belonged to the state is likely to increase the class disparities in African society rather than decrease them. Further, if we expect social change in African states and the Caribbean, it is likely to come from social movements— as it has in the United States—rather than political parties.

The complex dynamics involved in constructing an open and vigorous civil society in Africa are seen in the politics of the African Growth and Opportunity Act. As Walters points out, the bill contains no debt relief, no funds for development, imposes conditionalities without discussion, has weak labor and human rights standards, and shrinks the public sector. Thus this bill, which comes from an administration dedicated to promoting democracy in Africa, simultaneously weakens the state and African leadership while undercutting support for elements of civil society including labor groups, human rights groups, and those groups that would benefit from development funds. Fareed Zakaria's controversial article "The Rise of Illiberal Democracy" actually calls for a moratorium on U.S. democracy projects while we work to consolidate democracy in those countries where it already exists by developing constitutional liberalism.[15] Zakaria's suggestion that we endorse "liberal autocracies" in less developed nations brought an immediate response from Assistant Secretary of State John Shattuck and USAID Administrator J. Brian Atwood. They challenged Zakaria's contention that U.S. democracy assistance only focused on elections and that such elections can increase social tensions and destabilize societies.[16]

As Keith Jennings and Clena Slade illustrate in the case of Liberia and Lorenzo Morris in Haiti, the North American–West European model of development is largely inapplicable in the Third World, where cultural practices and economic conditions are quite different from our own. Morris asks, for example, is it possible to decommission a military and turn them into a civilian police force in a country with no history of civilian control over the military? Clarence Lusane interrogates the role of democratization in limiting the drug trade, arguing that it may have negative as well as positive consequences. Is it any wonder then that lacking strong governments that can control drug smuggling or vibrant civil societies that give civilians status and power, many African and Caribbean states fear domestic disorder and welcome international order. That is, for many less developed countries the realist focus on the sharp boundary between domestic order and international anarchy seems reversed.

This fear of domestic disorder explains the willingness of some African leaders to accept even the limited recognition that the African Growth and Opportunity Act represents internationally. However, it does not explain the split among African American leaders over the bill. As Walters explains, the "two line" struggle historically reflected by African American activists in regard to Africa disappeared with the fall of apartheid in South Africa. What has emerged is a more conservative political framework that to some extent mirrors domestic policy such as welfare reform. This conservative political framework has led to the replacement of aid with trade as discussed by Walters and the privatization of the sanctions regime as outlined by Nagan.

The rise in ethnic, racial, and religious conflict reflects a return to stable and traditional roots at a time when technological change and the loss of an ideological compass leave entire groups searching for roots. As Robert Kaplan has demonstrated, those societies best able to cope with change are those where strong traditional values have been institutionalized.[17] Even in the United States, which has its own culture wars,[18] ethnic, racial, and religious identity serve as a ground for the pragmatism of U.S. foreign policy. It seems clear, for example, that in an era when U.S. foreign policy is driven primarily by economic interests, President Clinton's 1998 trip to Africa served primarily as a symbolic reminder to African Americans that his administration would not ignore Africa.

The search for new foreign policy paradigms must be undertaken with a critical eye on race and culture. Americans have tended to insist on using U.S. beliefs as a model because of the success this nation has enjoyed. Rather than tolerating differences, we have tried to transform other countries into our image.[19] Even as we acknowledge the unique interweaving of religious and civil traditions that characterized the civil society tradition in the United States—setting it off from those of other nation-states and giving the unity of natural law documents and religious themes their particular saliency in eighteenth-century America— we continue to insist that other nations follow our lead. At the same time, we must acknowledge that an emphasis on race or ethnic identity can have negative consequences. Foreign policy debates often obscure the fact that states are political entities while nations represent a cultural grouping. Most nation-states reflect the domination of and expansion of one cultural group over others. The dominant group's interests become the national interest. This is as true of the United States as it is of developing societies. "In America, that paradigm of modern society," says Adam Seligman, "the private is invested with a public nature in an attempt to constitute its value in the face of what is conceived to be a neutral public arena . . . it is precisely due to its 'Protestant' nature that in America the locus of morality and ethical value is in the individual and not in the public realm."[20]

As we move into the next millennium, it is apparent that nonstate actors will play an increasingly significant role in international affairs. Not only are national minorities more likely to see their issues as international issues, as the contribution of James Jennings suggests, but transnational social movements will become important proponents of global issues or defenders of common interests that challenge transnational corporations. The nonprofits or third sector will continue to grow and new links between civil society actors in this country and abroad will be established, as Allen Caldwell demonstrates in the field of education. Yet, as Caldwell demonstrates, the success of almost all transnational campaigns depends on how the issue of nationalism is engaged. Advocacy networks in the North function in a cultural milieu of internationalism that is generally optimistic about the promise and possibilities of international networking. For network members in developing countries it is a much more difficult process to justify external intervention or pressure in domestic affairs of fragile or weak states. To be truly effective, these networks must become sites of cultural and political negotiation rather than mere enactors of dominant Western norms.[21] These networks represent the "two line" struggle of the future without which the success of democratization and development in the African and the Caribbean is doubtful.

NOTES

1. James H. Cone, "Martin Luther King, Jr." in Peter J. Albert and Ronald Hoffman (eds.), *We Shall Overcome* (New York: Pantheon, 1990), p. 208.

2. John Bracey reports that efforts to get the issue of Vietnam addressed at SCLC's unity rally at Soldier Field in Chicago in 1966 were in vain and young protesters were hustled out of the stadium. Public lecture, University of California at Berkeley, May 1, 1998.

3. There had been serious talks about King going to Nigeria to negotiate an end to the Biafrian War before his death.

4. See Martin Luther King Jr., "The Trumpet of Conscience," in James M. Washington (ed.), *A Testament of Hope* (New York: Harper & Row, 1986), pp. 634–40.

5. It is interesting to note that the theologian Reinhold Niebuhr had a profound impact on both Martin Luther King Jr. and on U.S. foreign policy-makers. It was Niebuhr's attack on the Social Gospel movement that introduced King to the notion that love must be linked to power to bring about social justice. Niebuhr's work also challenged the liberal internationalism of the post–World War I period with Niebuhr arguing that altruism was almost totally absent in relations between states and providing a moral base for "containment strategy." See Kenneth L. Smith and Ira G. Zepp Jr., *Search for the Beloved Community* (Valley Forge, Pa.: Judson Press, 1974), pp. 71–98, and Robert W. McElroy, *Morality and American Foreign Policy* (Princeton: Princeton University Press, 1992), pp. 12–15.

6. Elliot Skinner, *African Americans and U.S. Policy toward Africa 1850–1924* (Washington, D.C.: Howard University Press, 1992), pp. 1–16.

7. See, in general, John Hope Franklin and Alfred A. Moss Jr., *From Slavery to Freedom* (New York: McGraw-Hill, 1994) and Paul Gordon Lauren, *Power and Prejudice* (Boulder, Colo.: Westview Press, 1996).

8. See Penny M. Von Eschen, *Race against Empire* (Ithaca, N.Y.: Cornell University Press, 1997).

9. Ibid., pp. 34–53.

10. See, for example, Richard J. Payne, *Foreign Policy Begins at Home: Cultural Influences on U.S. Behavior Abroad* (Albany: State University of New York Press, 1995) and Howard J. Wirada, *Ethnocentrism in Foreign Policy* (Washington, D.C.: American Enterprise Institute, 1985).

11. James Kurth, "The Real Clash of Civilizations" *Washington Times,* October 4, 1994.

12. Abdul Aziz Said, *Ethnicity and U.S. Foreign Policy* (New York: Praeger, 1981), p. 6.

13. Claude Ake, "Rethinking African Democracy," in Larry Diamond and March F. Plattner (eds.), *The Global Resurgence of Democracy* (Baltimore: Johns Hopkins University Press, 1996), p. 73.

14. See ibid. and also Lloyd Sanchikonye (ed.), *Democracy, Civil Society and the State: Social Movements in Southern Africa* (Harare, Zimbabwe: SAPES, 1995).

15. Fareed Zakaria, "The Rise of Illiberal Democracy," *Foreign Affairs*, November/December 1997, pp. 22–41.

16. John Shattuck and J. Brian Atwood, "Defending Democracy," *Foreign Affairs*, March/April 1998, pp. 167–70.

17. Robert D. Kaplan, "The Coming Anarchy," *Atlantic Monthly*, February 1994, pp. 44–76.

18. See, for example, James Davison Hunter, *Culture Wars* (New York: Basic Books, 1991) and George Lakoff, *Moral Politics* (Chicago: University of Chicago Press, 1997).

19. Payne, *Foreign Policy*, pp. 10, 14.

20. Adam B. Seligman, *The Idea of Civil Society* (Princeton: Princeton University Press, 1992), p. 134.

21. See Margaret E. Keck and Kathryn Sikkink, *Activists beyond Borders* (Ithaca, N.Y.: Cornell University Press, 1998).

PART I

Global Issues

CHAPTER 1

The African Growth and Opportunity Act: Changing Foreign Policy Priorities toward Africa in a Conservative Political Culture

Ronald Walters

In the era of Republican approaches to government, United States policy toward Africa has experienced a significant shift from an emphasis upon public sector–sponsored development assistance to private sector–driven trade and investment. One of the more interesting aspects of this shift is that it represents an example of "political convergence" between Republicans and a sector of the Democratic Party, but also involving many Black Democrats as well. Nevertheless, the shift prompted a political conflict initiated by the difference of opinion between those who favored it, for whatever reasons, and many Africa-oriented groups and politicians who favored the maintenance of economic development strategies. We will examine the nature of this conflict, emphasizing the arguments of the opponents in an effort to understand why a "bipartisan" piece of legislation that ostensibly promised much to the continent of Africa, might instead be considered to be detrimental.

THE FIRST ITERATION: REAGAN's TRADE AND INVESTMENT APPROACH

In 1985, when the American government was led by a Republican president and the Democratics controlled Congress, the Congress attempted

17

to reduce the amount of foreign aid to Zaire from $6.4 million to $4.0 million, in order to discipline a government widely regarded as corrupt, both politically and economically. However, the secretary of state, George Shulz, nevertheless opposed it.[1] This was symptomatic of the Cold War framework in which American policy toward Africa was making use of the Zaire regime and the strategic positioning of this country in its anti-Soviet policies in Angola, South Africa, Mozambique, and Zimbabwe and in Eastern Africa as well.

Where the Reagan administration did support increases in African economic assistance and no immediate political interests were at stake, it was in an attempt to stimulate the emergence of private enterprise as markets for the sale of American goods. In fact, when the administration came into office, Africa was suffering from a famine and officials registered considerable dismay that in light of the economic assistance that the United States had previously provided, Africa was not strong enough to defend itself from the ravages of the drought. The answer, for them, was not to repeat the economic development assistance approach, but to assert that private enterprise could help to pull Africa out of its economic morass. The program designed for this purpose would be called the Economic Policy Initiative, and it would be designed to act as further leverage with African countries for them to support the increasingly stringent private sector "conditionalities" (political or economic conditions constructed as requirements for eligibility to participate in a funding program) being implemented by the International Monetary Fund and the World Bank. These international agencies had for some time supported an export orientation to African agriculture and desired stronger private market management to this sector of African economies in order that it might earn greater foreign exchange. The achievement of this objective required changing the attitude toward socialism resident in the political transition to independence of many African governments to that of capitalist-oriented economics. The administration selected the countries of Zaire, Senegal, Ghana, Mali, Uganda, Madagascar, Somalia, and Zambia to participate in a five-year, $500 million program that it trumpeted as the "new" approach to African economic solvency.[2]

Some of those who opposed the United States dictating what the policies of African countries should be, such as well-known African American economist Robert Browne, a former Carter administration appointee as director of the Africa Development Bank, regarded this program as a "new form of colonialism."[3] Others, such as Congressman William Gray, head of the Congressional Black Caucus (CBC), felt that the amount of funds were insufficient in light of the commitment of $8.4 billion made to Central America. Indeed, by 1990, Central America received thirty-four times the per capita aid to Africa.[4] Moreover, Africa aid was later reduced in order to provide funds for former Soviet governments as, during the mid-1980s to late-1980s period, economic support funds, for example, were slashed from $452.8 million to $58.9 million.[5] These reductions in economic development funds and the underlying attitudes that fostered them were continued under George Bush.

THE SECOND ITERATION:
CLINTON's PRIVATE SECTOR INITIATIVES

The Setting

A major impetus for the thrust in the direction of private sector–led development strategies was the feeling among African officials that the declining economic assistance from the West together with their mounting debt contributed to a growing marginalization of Africa in world economic relations, as indicated by Michael Clough's work *Free at Last: U.S. Policy toward Africa and the End of the Cold War* (New York: Council on Foreign Relations, 1992). In fact, Carol Lancaster captured the sentiment of many African observers with her statement that "the 'marginalization of Africa' is not just speculation. Not only are foreign governments closing embassies and cutting back aid flows but Africa's role in the world economy is also shrinking." She went on to state that the percentage of African exports and imports of total world trade dropped significantly between 1965 to 1992, from 4 percent to 2 percent.[6]

What can be clearly seen above is the sharp difference in the aggregate resource flows to Africa in the period of the Cold War prior to 1993, especially in terms of net private capital. Then, as also indicated, net official capital flows fell sharply by 48 percent in 1996 alone.[7] Also, the advent of the Republican-controlled Congress in 1995 led to policy proposals for FY 1996 of deep cuts in African economic assistance. In fact, the Africa AID budget experienced: the loss of "earmarks" for the Development Funds for Africa and Reductions in the amounts; a 33 percent reduction in funds for the African Development Foundation; and a nearly 50 percent reduction in the U.S. International Development Assistance (IDA) replenishment, a major source of multilateral funding for Africa programs.[8]

Nevertheless, in the period after 1993, some countries began to experience significant levels of economic growth. Therefore, what made the sudden economic interest in Africa possible was not simply Republican ideology or past marginalization, but that the new signs that some parts of the continent were experiencing significant rates of economic growth and political progress made the plausibility of reasonable profits appear to change the former image of Africa as merely an aid case. Thus, the evidence of a new image presented itself in that twenty-five countries had experienced elections since 1990; and signs of an economic recovery were found in the rise in output for the fourth consecutive year since 1994. Africa grew by 2.6% in 1994, 3.2% in 1995, 4.4% in 1996, 3% in 1997, and was forecast to grow at 4% for 1998.[9] United Nations data on thirty-eight countries indicated that in 1997, fifteen of these countries achieved rates of at least 5%, among them eleven reached 6%, with several over 7%, such as Angola, Ethiopia, Rwanda, and Uganda. Moreover, the return on the rate of investment had reached 33.3% compared to 14% in Asia.

In this period, American export sales to Africa had increased by 13.5 percent between 1995 and 1997, reaching $6.1 billion, indeed achieving levels of trade with West Africa that were greater than those with the former states of the Soviet Union combined. The vaunted "Afro-pessimism" that saw the former European colonial powers withdrawing from Africa economically was represented in the declining terms of trade between them. The African Caribbean Pacific (ACP) countries' share of the European import market declined from a level greater than 7% in 1975 by half to 3.5% in 1995 and even then, 47% of ACP export to the European market originated in just twelve countries.[10] In fact, the serious decline of ACP trade preference has been the result of European countries expanding their global economic competition, courting markets in Asia, Latin America, and Central and Eastern Europe.

Thus, the stage was set for the presentation of the McDermott proposals with the release of a report on U.S. trade and investment policy for Africa in June of 1996. McDermott, a Democrat, launched a bipartisan coalition on trade and investment that had three pillars: the accomplishment of a U.S.-Africa Free Trade Area by 2020; the creation of a U.S.-Africa Economic Cooperation Forum; and the establishment of a U.S.-Africa Trade and Investment Partnership modeled on APEC (the Asia Pacific Economic Cooperation association).

H.R. 1432: The African Growth and Opportunity Act

The idea of the "African Growth and Opportunity Act" was presented by Rep. Jim McDermott (D-WA) in the spring of 1996. The congressman noted that American policy toward Eastern Europe in the post-Soviet era was being shaped by fundamental economic directions and his observation was that similar planning for the African continent was not occurring. Furthermore, he held that Africa was adrift in this era and that the previous emphasis upon development assistance for Africa "did not constitute a policy."[11] This position was consistent with that of the Clinton administration, which had begun to link the national interest of the United States in this era closely to the economic security of the United States through its effective participation in global economic affairs, led by the private sector.

One year later, in the spring of 1997, the legislation H.R. 1432 was introduced by Rep. Charles Rangel, a member of the Congressional Black Caucus (CBC) and the ranking minority member on the House Ways and Means Committee, and a key Republican sponsor, Rep. Phillip Crane (R-IL). On April 29, 1997, the House Trade Subcommittee heard twenty witnesses, including an amazing array of supporters from both the right and left ideological spectrum, leading off with Rep. Newt Gingrich, Speaker of the House, followed by David Dinkins, former mayor of New York City and chairman of the Constituency for Africa, and Jack Kemp, former Republican vice presidential candidate and head co-chair of Empower America.[12]

Fully "fleshed out" by now, the bill contained the original three emphases of the McDermott proposals and added the following:

1. A $150 million equity fund and an $500 million infrastructure fund
2. An Export-Import Bank initiative to expand loans for private projects
3. The elimination of trade quotas on textiles
4. The renewal and expansion of GSP (General System of Preferences) for trade to Africa and to allow an additional 1,800 products that are currently excluded to be traded from Africa for ten years.

The Development of Opposition

Opposition developed to H.R. 1432 in late 1997 and the spring of 1998, led by a coalition of forces represented by labor, humanitarian organizations headed by Public Citizen, progressive Africa-oriented organizations headed by TransAfrica, and some members of the Congressional Black Caucus, headed by Congressman Jesse Jackson Jr. The bill was initially also opposed by Rev. Jesse Jackson Sr., the president's special envoy to Africa, and Rep. Maxine Waters, head of the CBC, both of whom later supported it due to substantial pressures from the White House. There were a series of factors that came to represent the broad basis of objections to this bill as presented below.

A. The bill did not mandate debt reduction. There was strong feeling that African leaders could not provide the leadership or maintain significant participation in the trade and investment regime if their economic resources were devoted to serving the crushing level of debt. In 1997, total debt in sub-Sahara Africa was $223 billion, an amount that represented 90 percent of GNP of those countries. Of this amount, the U.S. proportion is relatively small at $4.5 billion; however, American leadership was felt to be important in creating a climate for movement on significant measures to reduce the debt by the European countries and multilateral financial institutions to whom most of the debt was owed.

The World Bank and the International Monetary Fund had created a strategy for Highly Indebted Poor countries (HIPC) to pay down the debt of the most severely indebted countries, which also maintained the highest levels of poverty. But this did not take into consideration the fact that for moderately poor countries such as Zambia, serving the debt amounted to *five times* the health budget and thirty times the budget for education, or that in Zimbabwe, seven hundred people were dying from AIDS per week.[13]

The bill did not protect or mandate an increase in DFA. The principle supported by many groups was that economic assistance was complimentary to trade and investment and that, given the poverty of Africa, the trade and investment thrust could not be successful without maintaining development assistance funding at significant, even enhanced levels. In this sense, Secretary General Rubens Ricupero, at the United Nations Conference on Trade and Development (UNCTAD), said that a report of his organization called for Official Development Assistance (ODA) to be "increased, as foreign direct investment (FDI) was not a substitute but only a complement to ODA."[14] Thus, the report called for significant increase in public investment in physical and human infrastructure" in order to "help lay the basis for recovery of private investment and a process of diversification."

Accordingly, there was language in the bill that stated that it recognized the importance of development assistance, but it did not go so far as to either increase levels of assistance or to explicitly recognize that higher level of development assistance was crucial to trade and investment objectives.

The bill continues the emphasis on "conditionalities." Opponents felt that the bill violated the political sovereignty of African countries by placing emphasis on so many critical conditions for eligibility, such as:

- No trade with Libya, Cuba, or Iraq
- Cuts in government spending, privatization of governmental services

- Eliminating barriers to trade such as government protection for national industries and reduction of business taxes and regulations
- Liberalization of trade and movement toward the World Trade Organization (WTO) regime
- Movement toward democratic institutions and practices.

Countries such as South Africa strongly objected to the political and economic conditions contained in the bill on the grounds that, should the South African government accede to such conditions, it would violate the confidence of countries such as those named in the bill, when they supported the Black South African struggle for majority rule and the United States government did not. Moreover, the UNCTAD report referred to above also indicated that those countries that liberalized their trade fastest showed the lowest levels of growth, while those that liberalized slowest maintained the protection of their fragile economies from the strong influences of global market forces such as prices and trading regimes.[15] This finding was supported by another expert observer:

> African societies typically lack a sizeable independent formal business sector with the capital and experience to seize quickly the new opportunities opened up by the reforms. Trade liberalization exposes them to foreign competition; removal of government regulations loosens their monopoly holds on domestic markets; and the reduction in government contracts and other public resources means a cut in revenues.[16]

At the same time, movement toward the WTO is fraught with difficulty, as African countries have resisted the economic conditionalities as well as their expansion to noneconomic sectors beyond trade issues.[17]

The bill did not mandate any labor or human rights standards. The UN Reports find that real wages on the continent are depressed to the point that further reductions are unlikely to stimulate competition. However, the current level of wages makes it attractive for some investors to build economic enterprises where they do not have to raise wages too far above the mean to attract workers and to do so without providing labor rights guarantees. For example, in Vietnam, workers in the Nike plant that manufactures tennis shoes earn $73 per month whereas the minimum wage is $40 per month.[18] Although this wage is nearly 100 percent greater than the average, because of its very low level, it provides manufacturers with a significant margin of profit, yet does not raise the average wage to levels that would allow for substantial changes in the conditions of life for workers. This fact leaves African workers open to considerable exploitation, given the distance between the sale price of

the product and its manufacturing costs and the lack of social investments by the companies to provide "added value" to the workers' lives.

Accordingly, organized labor opposed a similar regime of trade
expansion in the North Atlantic Free Trade Association (NAFTA),
which, together with the World Trade Organization, has relatively weak
labor rights regimes to protect workers' right to organize in the plants
for higher wages and to protect their jobs from foreign imports in
selected industries.

Therefore, the AFL-CIO opposed H.R. 1432 on these grounds and
also that the "African content" definition in the bill, at only 30 percent,
may create an incentive for other countries such as China to provide the
other 70 percent of content in textile apparel and tranship such goods
through Africa bound for the U.S. market. The further importation of
such goods would further depress the already devastated textile industry in the United States with lower priced goods, thus causing workers
to lose the remaining jobs in this industry. At present the level of textile
trade from Africa to the United States is only 1 percent of total trade in
textiles and the United States Trade Representative (USTR) data indicate
that the level would have to reach 3 percent before any damage to U.S.
jobs would occur.[19]

Without strong labor rights, it should be noted, the bill would have
the same effect as the largely failed Caribbean Basin Initiative, which
gave American firms access to the cheap labor of the Caribbean but
stimulated little economic development in the region. On the other
hand, it should be noted that some of the countries that have challenged
the enhancement of labor rights most vigorously have been countries
such as Egypt and Tanzania, feeling that they would lose their comparative advantage in the low-wage structure of the continent.[20]

**Lacks any measures to assure African leadership and direction and to
ensure that poor households benefit from investment.** In order for
Africans to exercise leadership and direction over the degree and focus
of trade and investment, there needs to be expanded financial capability, business development and training centers, and effective instruments
for international trade and investment. Indeed, Jennifer Whitaker con-
cludes in her analysis of African economic development prospects that
"further prospects for progress in Africa will depend upon infusions of
technical assistance and training from the advanced nations."[21] Moreover, United Nations data indicates that only four countries in Africa
are connected to the Internet, whereas about 120 cities have such facilities available. This means that there must be a substantial growth of
communications technology in order to facilitate global transactions.
Communications infrastructure conceived in relationship to the entry of

Western firms into the former Soviet Union, are absent in Africa and where such regional economic organizations as the West African Common Market and the Southern African Development Coordination Conference (SADCC) have sought to enhance their capability to promote private sector economic activity, funding for this purpose has been largely absent.

Therefore, if African leadership does not have the human, financial, and technological capacity to lead in this area, they would be subject to the much larger and much more sophisticated planning and financial capability and thus the leadership of large corporations.

The effect of shrinking the public sector. The above statement suggests that the lack of ability in governments, or in the private sector in most African countries, to lead in the trade and investment field, together with the requirement that government play less of a role, presents several problems for Africa's fragile economies and political systems.

One of these problems is the protection of consumers' economic interests and the reduction of poverty. Unregulated markets and private sector activity as the primary engine of economic growth has traditionally been unsuccessful at reducing widespread poverty. Some evidence for this is found in the fact that despite higher levels of aggregate GDP for the continent, it has had scant impact on the reduction of malnutrition. World Bank data finds that, for example, "Sub-Sahara Africa (SSA) has had an aggregate malnutrition rate of nearly 30 percent for the last decade. While malnutrition prevalence has decreased significantly in most other developing countries in the last decade, it has been nearly static for SSA."[22]

Market activity throughout the Third World often sets prices for goods at such a level that lower-income classes cannot participate and are often relegated to inferior goods. Indeed, World Bank economists indicate that growth rates of 6–7 percent per annum for a considerable period of time are necessary to reduce poverty and even then, "relying on aggregate income growth as the sole means for reducing poverty in Africa will effectively postpone significant poverty reduction for the poorest for up to 50 years."[23]

In addition, market deregulation reduces the ability of governments to continue to regulate the quality of goods, monitor prices, and adjust fiscal policy such that the fruits of economic activity are distributed to the poorer parts of the populations. On the other hand, Mamadou Dia, recognized that "the combination of the patrimonial state and the absence of the rule of law puts the average entrepreneur at the mercy of the political elite and bureaucracy. Property rights are not legally protected and wealth can be confiscated or reduced through selective manipulation of the formal rules and regulations."[24] In any case, it is far from certain, given the role of authoritarian governments in the evolution of private sector development in the "Asian Tiger" countries, that strong governmental leadership is not a necessary ingredient. The problem is not only strong leadership, but that which has entrepreneurial goals. Dia would suggest that a set of central tasks are: reconciling indigenous institutions with transplanted ones, developing accountable and skilled management, and funding what he regards as the "missing middle" of capital formation. All of this would appear to require strong state leadership at the outset if the Asian model is at all relevant.

Lobbying

The attack. The first significant opposition to the bill was that which TransAfrica transmitted to Rep. Rangel by letter in early February of 1997, containing the concerns of its president, Randall Robinson. In this letter, he asserted that provisions in the bill would: contain government's role in African economies; open African economies too much through the privatization of critical public facilities; and grant foreign investors new rights without the governments being able to effectively regulate such activity.[25]

Organized labor began to contact its allies in the Black community to oppose the legislation and, in a repeat of the debate over the NAFTA legislation, urged Rep. Rangel to "include adherence to core labor standards (as defined under Section 502[a][4] of the 1974 Trade Act, as amended) among the eligibility requirement listed under section 4; provide for funding and enforcement for mechanisms to prevent illegal transhipment of goods through Africa; require that all workers employed producing goods granted market access under the bill be local citizens; and provide support for some of the nonlabor matters previously mentioned.[26]

Thus, in late February some members of the Congressional Black Caucus began to follow the lead of labor and registered their concern over the legislation, as six members, led by Rep. Sanford Bishop, sent a letter to Congressman Rangel expressing their view that the legislation should be changed to protect American jobs. They pointed out that 50 percent of the nation's textile workers were minorities and that 80 percent of them were women.[27]

Rangel responded to organized labor and its allies by releasing a letter to Robinson on February 25, asserting that Robinson had "misread the bill," and that it did not mandate eligibility requirements, but merely established the preferences of the U.S. government, that in fact, there would be separate negotiations with each country over the terms of the trade agreement and these would be governed by existing law. In any case, a key point of difference was over the shift in the strategy from development to private sector support and to this, Rangel responded: "You further assert that 'the bill's backers describe it as a radical shift in emphasis from sustainable development strategies to a private sector and market incentives approach.' I must admit that I have never heard the bill described this way by its supporters. Rather, they talk about a shift from dependence on foreign assistance to a private sector and market incentives approach *so as to create* a sustainable development strategy."[28]

One week later, Rangel answered the AFL-CIO, repeating essentially the points raised in his reply to Robinson, that many of the proposals in the bill would be administered flexibly and would be subject to the president's determination. However, with respect to the key concern on the transhipment of goods, he said only that, "I am pleased to report that in the full Ways and Means Committee markup of the bill on February 25, we were able through a Chairman's amendment to strengthen considerably the textile transhipment and enforcement provisions of the bill." The lack of specificity, however, did not mollify labor.

An interesting coalition in opposition to the bill developed between Randall Robinson and Ralph Nader, head of Public Citizen, who published a joint commentary in *The Washington Times*, repeating many of the points of opposition presented above. However, they added: "The potential effect of the Crane Bill is ominous, particularly as we observe how the imposition of similar conditions by the IMF on Asia is resulting in growing instability, lower growth rates and the purchase at fire sale prices of natural resources and productive capacity by a few immense foreign corporations. Because economic and political pressure on sub-Sahara Africa is enormous, some African governments have not made public their misgivings. We must not replace European colonialism that long burdened Africa with a new colonialism of servitude to external corporate interests."[30]

By early March, both TransAfrica and Public Citizen were in full revolt. Public Citizen posted a position on its "Global Trade Watch" website that was in full opposition to the bill, urging opponents to vote against it because it was a "job-killer" and comparing it to NAFTA.[31] The posted position was supported by a list of twenty organizations headed by TransAfrica, and others in the religious, environmental, social justice, and human rights community. The same day, TransAfrica released an open letter to "Members of Congress" calling the Crane Bill "lethal medicine for Africa," identifying specific changes in language focused on eliminating section 9(e) related to the "conditionalities" under which a country would be eligible to participate in the bill, requiring binding labor rights and increasing the African content to 50 percent and African ownership of 55 percent of the economic activity, strengthening aid programs for Africa, and binding debt relief.[32]

The counterattack. The Clinton administration began its counterattack by distributing a list of talking points issued by assistant secretary of state for African affairs, Susan Rice.[33] The points were essentially an added defense of the points raised by Rangel and continued several others that placed a strong reliance on the view of African ambassadors and their countries in the following language: "Africans need this bill. They don't want a handout. They want the hand of a partner. And they've said so. The African Ambassadors to Washington have repeatedly urged Congress and the President to enact this legislation." The use of African legitimacy as a counter to various arguments was also a key staple of Rep. Rangel, who traveled to Africa as head of the Presidential Mission on Economic Cooperation to Africa from December 6 to 17, 1997. The Rangel mission, which contained five members of the CBC (Rep. William Jefferson, Rep. Carrie Meek, Rep. Sheila Jackson-Lee, and Rep. Carolyn Kilpatrick), other congressional staff, non-governmental organizations, private sector individuals, and executive branch representatives, visited Ethiopia, Eritrea, Uganda, Botswana, Mauritius, and Cote d'Ivoire. In his report to the president at the end of the mission, Rangel indicated that he had "received strong positive feedback from the countries we visited that they fully supported these new U.S. initiatives to move from a purely donor-donee relationship to one based more on economic cooperation and increased trade and investment. They had "received a strong message from every country [they] visited that enactment into law of H.R. 1432, the African Growth and Opportunity Act, will be a key catalyst in getting U.S. business to do business with viable countries in Africa and is therefore essential. Everything must be done to ensure passage of this legislation early next year."[34]

Thus, the African Diplomatic Corps in Washington was substantially supportive of the bill and spoke for itself in the lobbying process. For instance, in early March 1998, the ambassador of Djibouti, Roble Olhaye, who was also dean of the African Diplomatic Corps, wrote to Randall Robinson informing him that they had indeed been consulted on the details of H.R. 1432 and supported the legislation. He, furthermore, assured Robinson of his sensitivity to the fact that the bill was drafted to the advantage of large corporations and continued: "We believe that the legislation is drafted in such a way so as to allow African countries themselves to determine what should be the proper balance between foreign corporations and indigenous African economic interests and still be eligible to receive the benefits of the legislation."[35]

The point of assurance was a rejoinder to Robinson's concerns and that of others regarding whether African governments, ravaged by debt and declining resource flows from the major industrial countries, were in any credible position to reject the prospect of additional economic activity of either a public or private derivation.

Also in early March, the assistant secretary general of the Organization of African Unity, Ambassador Vijay S. Makhan, released a document boldly entitled, "Political Support for the African Growth and Opportunity Act, H.R. 1432 (Crane-McDermott-Rangel Bill)" which reaffirmed the support of the organization for the legislation. In addition, the communication contained a point-by-point refutation of the three issues raised in the original letter of concern from Randall Robinson to Rep. Rangel, indicating that with regard to the conditionalities, that thirty African countries had undergone reforms that had created sentiments against deficit financing of budgets; that privatization was not so much of an issue since most governments had already sold off many nonperforming parastatals; and that the bill itself would not establish new rights for corporations, since many countries had revised their investment codes to attract foreign investors.[36] Ambassador Makhan left no confusion as to the lobbying purpose of his letter as he said: "I trust that this letter would assist in securing the passage of this Bill as it is, in Congress."[37]

Finally, the role of some of the other Africa-oriented nongovernmental organizations was important as either supportive or appositive to the bill. For example, the Constituency for Africa (CFA), led by David Dinkins and Mel Foote, executive director, was the lead private organization promoting the bill. The CFA held a series of "town meetings" around the country and as a part of its regular program, provided grassroots education on the purposes of the bill. In fact, a major such town meeting held in Denver, Colorado, was hosted by Mayor Wellington Webb, the major purpose of which was to place the new emphasis on trade and investment as an agenda item on the table of the G-7 Summit meeting of heads of the major economic powers in the summer of 1997.

In the preparations for this meeting, it became clear that many of the nongovernmental organizations such as Amnesty International, the Washington Office on Africa, Bread for the World, and others opposed the bill. Nevertheless, the Denver town meeting was held June 13–14, the week before the G-7 meeting, and it touted the advantages of trade and investment with Africa. Then, a subsequent town hall meeting was held in July 1997 that also featured Mayor Webb and Rev. Jesse Jackson and that discussed essentially the same message.[38]

Passage

On March 11, H.R. 1432 passed the House, 233–186. The balance of the Democratic Party voted against it, but many Democrats voted for the bill, including twenty-four members of the Congressional Black Caucus (twelve against). Rep. Jesse Jackson Jr. led the opposition on the floor. Earlier in the month, he had also joined the public opposition to the bill with the letter to Rep. Philip Crane that emphasized the strong provisions in the bill that, in his opinion, weighted the balance substantially in favor of foreign corporations doing business in Africa "unfettered" from the proper kinds of collateral investments in the social sector.[39] Direct social sector investment from private corporations was important to progressives, since it had constituted the critical conditionalities fought for as a requirement for American corporations electing to do business inside South Africa before Black majority rule.

Jackson also found that in attacking the bill on the floor, he confronted some of his own colleagues who were defending it, as the following exchange suggests:

MR. JACKSON: I would ask the gentleman, is he aware in the bill of any African countries losing foreign aid they are now receiving unless they adopt the economic reforms dictated in this bill?

MR. [DON] PAYNE: Mr. Chairman, I am glad the gentleman brought that question up. This bill is separate from aid. The Development fund for Africa was an earmarked area that this year is funded for about $700 million, and $30 million has been allocated or recommended by the administration to go into the aid. Therefore, the answer is no. This is a separate entity, and it will not take aid from any country that does not conform to the bill.

Secondly, I might say that a country that does not comply with governance and human rights, with transparency and basic human rights, will not be invited to be in the rounds, just as NATO expansion has been done.

MR. JACKSON: Mr. Chairman, if the gentleman will continue to yield, is the gentleman aware of any African countries being forced to cut corporate taxes, privatize, and shrink their government services, or grant expanded rights to foreign investors under the bill?

MR. PAYNE: To my knowledge, I know of none. If the gentleman knows of any information that I am not privy to, I would certainly appreciate it, but to my knowledge it does not negatively impact on what is going on in those countries. There will be IMF requirements which already are in many countries.[40]

This exchange was a delicate dialogue prompted by Jackson's challenge to the conditionalities in the bill, which were answered by Payne in a way which suggested that although some have interpreted them as advisory, they in fact were binding. Thus, Rep. Maxine Waters proposed to amend the bill to eliminate the necessity for countries to comply with all of the conditions.[41] As the amendment failed, her next attempt was to ensure that the $700 million appropriation for the DFA remained in force for the next nine years, accomplishing a form of earmarking.[42] This amendment too failed under the reasoning put forth by Rep. Royce (R-CA) that, "since the bill does not require a cutoff of aid to Africa, the aid floor is unnecessary."[43] Rep. Waters then offered another amendment that proposed that the president had the discretion with respect to the issue of conditions of eligibility to participate in the bill. However, this too failed.

Therefore, the issue of the conditions of eligibility to participate remained rather firm as the bill was passed into law, opponents having lost measure after measure of "perfecting" elements that would make the bill acceptable for them to support. Nevertheless, twenty-four members of the CBC supported the bill and twelve finally opposed it.[44]

Next Steps: Senate Prospects

After H.R. 1432 passed the House, the focus of the process passed to the Senate and at this writing (April 1998), the Senate has not taken up the measure. However, the landscape of its politics is littered with the residue of both, the existing proposals offered by TransAfrica and Public Citizen. Bread for the World has drafted a bill to shore up Development Assistance, focusing on rural finance, agricultural research and extension, and food security, entitled, "Africa: Seeds of Hope"—H.R. 3636, which was introduced on April 1, 1998, by Reps. Douglass Bereuter (R-NE), Lee Hamilton (D-IN), Cynthia McKinney (D-GA), Eva Clayton (D-NC), Tony Hall (D-OH), and James Leach (R-IA).

Although the White House had based its policy direction on this thrust by making it the basic element in its 5-nation Africa trip taken March 25–April 3, 1998, and is thereby heavily invested, it has offered no bill of its own, preferring to support the general direction of the House bill, monitor the debate, and weigh in at the appropriate time. That time would appear to be in Senate consideration of the bill, since in the Senate, S. 778 has attracted only four (4) cosponsors and there is a stronger unified support base for the bill, all of which means that it could fail. Otherwise, the administration has already begun to implement aspects of the proposals within the capability of the executive, such as installing a Special Trade Representative for Africa in the USTR and committing the $150 million and the $500 million to OPIC to administer should the authorizing legislation pass.

An Integrated Approach

Whether or not H.R. 1432 becomes law, the route to a much stronger thrust in trade and investment is one that is balanced by a strong development assistance role. The concept of a balanced policy was not envisioned at first by the proponents of the bill, who touted it as "trade not aid," appearing to deprecate the role of economic assistance for development and the domestic version of a "handout" as "dependency." Rep. Sheila Jackson-Lee, for example, said that "this bill is not trade and not aid, it is trade and aid," in an attempt to reconcile the two approaches.[45]

We have referred above to the view of the UNCTAD that economic assistance is complimentary to trade and investment, because it provides the infrastructure within which the private sector can succeed. Indeed, even some of the most radical opponents of capitalist strategies recognize that "the public sector should be the *facilitator* while the private sector plays the central role of main actor."[46] And although the bill expresses the desire to support governments dedicated to eliminating poverty and establishing accountable government and calls for the continuance of development funding—things that opponents share—it does not go far enough. It does not mandate a balanced strategy that alone would achieve the goals of trade and investment; it does not mandate debt relief; it does not mandate labor standards that would spread the fruits of such economic activity to the common person. That is the critical evaluation that is at the heart of the opposition to the bill: does it seek to empower all Africans or merely create an African version of a small middle-class elite?

Here, there might be a recognition that given the persistent level of poverty, disease, and debt, and the lack of dynamic growth, which is the case with most African countries, perhaps the trade and development model will be relevant to only the handful of countries with which U.S. companies will ultimately seek to partner. For the others, the urgent necessity for measures to make them economically viable as partners must entail making greater economic resources available and lessening the entanglement of crushing levels of concessional debt. So, while one side of the policy seeks to take advantage of those already positioned to participate, the other side of a balanced policy would seek to enhance the position of others to do so.

CONCLUSION

One source of the dynamics that makes possible a "bipartisan" approach favoring the new shift to private sector–oriented policies toward African economic development is lodged in the larger political culture of conservatism. This has contributed to a "political convergence" not only over Africa policy, but over crime, welfare reform, and other issues where the interest of African descendant peoples have been involved. In this sense, we have a typical political formulation: the president, the Republican Party, and a faction of the Democratic party provides the winning coalition on an issue that has traditionally been defined by Republican interests.

In this case, the fact that the sector of the coalition within the Democratic Party also includes the majority of the Black Congressional Caucus, which itself was split, constitutes a difference in the typical formulation. This might be explained by the difference within the Black and progressive community over ideology as expressed in former conflicts over U.S. policy toward Angola or South Africa, where clear sides were drawn with respect to those who supported either the left or the right. This difference was expressed formerly as a "two-line struggle."[47]

The left in these cases supported the strongly people-oriented socialist regimes of the MPLA government of Angola or the African National Congress of South Africa, while the right supported the UNITA rebels in Angola and the White minority regime of South Africa. This mirrors and tends to explain the continuation of the ideological conflict at a time when American policy is focused globally on economic security, through the deployment of the conservative economic tools of the private sector.

The left, sensitive to the profound level of economic disadvantage on the continent, favors enhanced levels of economic assistance to Africa, debt forgiveness, policies that more equitably distribute the returns from economic activity, democracy, and human rights. The right, on the other hand, favors free trade approaches and private direct investment from which it might benefit due to its position of economic advantage.

This abbreviated discussion using the symbolic terms of "left" and "right" also masks, however, other divisions of class and culture. Over time, a class of Africans and African American bureaucrats and business-oriented associates have emerged within the African policy debate, and they possess a much stronger business orientation to world and African affairs. Thus, the ideological divisions are also expressed, to some extent, by a generational divide about problem solving on the African continent and the collusion between the new African American business elite, desperate African politicians, and pragmatic African American politicians helps to legitimize this "new" approach in the eyes of U.S. foreign policy decision-makers.

However, like the older aspects of what was considered to be two separate lines of strategy that were each righteous roads to the solution of African dependence, both were necessary then and are necessary now. In any case, the deep splits within the Democratic Party coalition with respect to the bill, assures that, given this environment, it would appear that the bill that emerges will carry a decidedly Republican stamp.

NOTES

1. Joanne Omang, "Shulz Cites 'Major Concerns' on Foreign Aid Bill," *The Washington Post*, March 26, 1985, p. 11.

2. Leon Dash, "New U.S. Plan Would Help Free-Market African States," *The Washington Post*, May 7, 1984, p. 1.

3. Ibid.

4. Peter J. Schraeder, *United States Foreign Policy toward Africa: Incrementalism, Crisis and Change* (Port Chester, N.Y.: Cambridge University Press, 1994), p. 251.

5. Ibid.

6. Carol Lancaster, "United States and Africa: Into the 21st Century," Policy Essay no. 7, Overseas Development Council, Washington, D.C., 1993, p. 11.

7. Christina Katsouris, "Sharp Fall in Resource Flows to Africa," *Africa Recovery*, vol. 11, no. 2 (October 1997), p. 1.

8. "US/Africa Assistance Falls; Additional Cuts Expected," The *Washington Notes on Africa*, vol. 21, no. 3 (Winter 1995–96), p. 10.

9. Henk-Jan Brinkman and Carl Gray, "Fourth Year of Positive Growth in Africa," *United Nations Office of Communications and Public Information*, vol. 11, no. 3 (February 1998), p. 1.

10. "Trade in the New World Order," *The Courier*, Journal of the Africa, Caribbean and Pacific Organization, November–December 1997, p. 58.

11. Press Release, Remarks by Rep. Jim McDermott (D-WA), Overseas Development Council, Conference on African Economic Recovery, June 12, 1996, Washington, D.C.

12. *West Africa*, May 19–25, 1997, p. 800.

13. "AIDS Claims 700 Lives a Week in Zimbabwe," *Electronic Mail & Guardian*, March 21, 1998. References the *Sunday Standard of Zimbabwe*, Misa, March 16, 1998.

14. "UNCTAD Secretary-General Calls for Action to Sustain African Economic Recovery," UNCTAD, TAD/INF/2727, Press Release, October 21, 1997.

15. "UN Secretary General Calls for Action to Sustain African Economic Recovery," op. cit.

16. Lancaster, "United States and Africa," p. 40.

17. Tim Wall, "Africa Resist New Trade Conditionalities," *Africa Recovery*, January–April 1997, p. 9.

18. "Taking a Look inside Nike's Factories," *Time*, March 30, 1998, p. 52.

19. "Likely Impact of Providing Quota-Free and Duty-Free Entry to Textiles and Apparel From Sub-Saharan Africa," U.S. International Trade Commission, Publication 3056, September 1997.

20. Tim Wall, op. cit.

21. See Jennifer Seymour Whitaker, *How Can Africa Survive?* (New York: Council on Foreign Relations, 1988), p. 78.

22. "Nutritional Status and Poverty in Sub-Sahara Africa," *Findings*, Economic Management and Social Policy, No. 108, International Bank for Reconstruction and Development, April 1998, p. 1.

23. Peter Svarre, "Growth Alone Won't End Poverty, says World Bank," *Africa Recovery*, January–April 1997, p. 31.

24. Mamadou Dia, *Africa's Management in the 1990s and Beyond: Reconciling Indigenous and Transplanted Institutions* (Washington, D.C.: The World Bank, 1996), p. 44.

25. Letter, Randall Robinson, president, TransAfrica, to Rep. Charles B. Rangel, February 10, 1998.

26. Letter, Peggy Taylor, director, Department of Legislation, AFL-CIO, to Rep. Charles B. Rangel, February 24, 1998.

27. Lorraine Woellert, "Black Caucus Divided on Africa Trade," *The Washington Times*, February 26, 1998, p. A4.

28. Letter, Rep. Charles B. Rangel, Committee on Ways and Means, to Randall Robinson, President, TransAfrica, February 25, 1998.

29. Letter, Rep. Charles B. Rangel, House Ways and Means Committee, to Ms. Peggy Taylor, Legislative Director, AFL-CIO, March 2, 1998.

30. "A Force March to Congress' Tune," *The Washington Times*, March 11, 1998, p. A11.

31. "Global Trade Watch," *Public Citizen*, March 4, 1998. Internet: www. citizen.org/gtw

32. Letter, Randall Robinson, President, TransAfrica, to Members of the House, U.S. Congress, March 4, 1998.

33. AF/Fo, March 4, 1998.

34. Letter, Rep. Charles B. Rangel, Head of Presidential Mission on Economic Cooperation to Africa, to President Bill Clinton, December 17, 1997. This communication was followed by a more detailed report of January 17, 1998.

35. Ambassador Roble Olhaye, Republic of Djibouti and Dean of the African Diplomatic Corps, to Randall Robinson, President, TransAfrica, March 4, 1998, cc: The Honorable Congressman Charles B. Rangel.

36. Ambassador Vijay S. Makhan, Assistant Secretary General of the Organization of African Unity, to Rep. Charles B. Rangel, March 10, 1998. cc: Rep. Phil Crane, Rep. Jim McDermott, Mel Foote, Constituency for Africa, Mrs. Rosa Whitaker, Assistant U.S. Trade Representative for Africa.

37. Ibid.

38. The writer serves as Vice President of CFA and in March of 1998 made a public statement in opposition to the Bill. See "The Second Rape of Africa?," *The Washington Informer*, March 5–12, 1998.

39. Letter, Rep. Jesse Jackson Jr. to Rep. Philip Crane, March 10, 1998.

40. "African Growth and Opportunity Act, *Congressional Record*, House of Representatives, p. H1042.

41. Ibid, p. 1065.

42. Ibid, p. 1070.

43. Ibid. p. 1515.

44. See House of Representatives, Roll Call no. 47, March 11, 1998.

45. African Growth and Opportunity Act," *Congressional Record*, House of Representatives, March 11, 1998, p. H1052.

46. Tajudeen Abdul-Raheem, ed., *Pan Africanism: Politics, Economy and Social Change in the Twenty-First Century* (New York: New York University Press, 1996), p. 156.

47. See Ronald Walters, *Pan Africanism in the African Diaspora* (Detroit: Wayne State University Press, 1993), p. 74.

CHAPTER 2

Transnational Philanthropy and African American Education

Allen Caldwell

INTRODUCTION

This chapter is concerned with both historic and contemporary attempts by American transnational philanthropic actors to undertake action in the issue-area of international education for sub-Saharan Africans and African Americans. Additionally, this essay will be comprised of three brief case studies that individually were—or, presently, are—situated in sub-Saharan Africa. The three case studies themselves are each drawn from different and distinctive time periods. The first two examples are historic, while the third is contemporary. The first case study reviews an attempt by one American transnational philanthropic actor to influence educational policy in the then newly founded republic of Liberia. The second case study reveals the efforts by American transnational philanthropy to export the Tuskegee-Hampton model of industrial education for Blacks in the southern states of the United States to Blacks in English-speaking sub-Sahara Africa between World War I and World War II. And the final case study highlights a recent undertaking of American transnational philanthropy to educate African American adolescent males from inner-city Baltimore in the east African country of Kenya.

In writing this chapter, I have adopted a transnational theoretical approach because it represents the most appropriate model from which to investigate the work of American transnational philanthropy in the issue-area of international education. This appropriateness stems from the definition of transnational relations that underwrites transnational theory. Briefly, that definition is as follows: the "regular interactions

37

across national boundaries when at least one actor is a non-state agent or does not operate on behalf of a national government or an international organization."[1] With transnational relations being defined as such, the success or failure of the activities undertaken by a nonstate actor becomes contingent upon satisfying two preconditions: First, the domestic structure, the "normative and organizational arrangements," of the target state (the state in which the nonstate actor implements its project or program), and how effectively the nonstate actor builds effective coalitions within that domestic structure will, in part, determine the impact of the nonstate agents' proposed activities.[2] Second, and more broadly, the "degrees of international institutionalization, i.e., the extent to which the specific issue-area is regulated by bilateral agreements, multilateral regimes, and/or international organizations"[3] will assume a prominent role in determining the success or failure of the activities of a nonstate agent.

As will be illustrated below, the application of transnational theory to analyze past and present international education efforts of American transnational philanthropy in sub-Saharan Africa—from its activities in Liberia in the middle of the nineteenth century, to its intrusion into British sub-Sahara Africa between World I and World II, to its present-day efforts in Kenya—will allow me to uncover some of the clues that thwarted their earlier attempts to significantly impact education policy in both Liberia and in English-speaking sub-Saharan Africa. What is more, through the utilization of this theoretical framework it may be possible to anticipate potential pitfalls that could eventually undermine the current attempt by American transnational philanthropy to educate African American adolescent males from inner-city Baltimore in Kenya.

LIBERIA

The primary American transnational philanthropic agent who attempted to impact educational policy in the country of Liberia was a Black American himself, Alexander Crummel. For nearly two decades, from 1853 to 1872, Crummel, working with and through a host of missionary associations, attempted to construct a national education system for the young nation. Crummel's intention to create an education system for Liberia, however, went far beyond the technical confines of merely teaching and learning. Beyond instructing and imbuing what he considered the truly heathenish adults and youth of the nation with an education steeped in the ecclesiasticalism of the Episcopal Church, Crummel's scheme to create an educational system served to underwrite his double-billed political vision for Liberia, not to mention for Blacks the world over. First, Crummel intended to use education as one, of several, means for nation-building. He believed that if he could educate what in his eyes were the native heathen population, his second, and, in the long term, more globally significant political vision would be realized: that Black people were capable of self-government.[4]

Technically, the schematic nature of Crummel's education plan went something like this: if he could increase the number of American Negro immigrants into Liberia he would have, among other things, a well-equipped Black teaching force. This Black teaching force would, in turn, serve as the foundation of Liberian education. And, in time, once a full-scale education system was up and running, with Black Americans teaching the native population what's what, the task of building a nation founded on Christian principals could get underway. Indeed, this eventually would prove to Whites that Blacks were politically capable of self-government. But, in order to realize his plans to staff the country's future schools with a Black American teaching force, Crummel had first to simultaneously convince both domestic and international actors that his scheme was worthy of their investment.[5]

Internationally, Crummel had to persuade two groups of Americans that Liberia was worth an investment of resources and human capital. First, he had to press upon the White hierarchy of the American-based Protestant Episcopal Church, the missionary organization which had sent him to Liberia, that an increase of American Black immigrants, as opposed to White missionaries, would strengthen the presence of the Episcopal Church in Liberia. Still more significantly, Crummel had also to encourage the American Black population, and mainly Blacks from the northern states of the United States, that emigration to Liberia would allow them to fully participate in the making of a Black Christian nation. Within the domestic structure of Liberia, Crummel had to convince the mulatto ruling class of Liberia that his education plans, as well as his broader political agenda, would benefit all Liberians. This, though, would prove difficult. Opposition from the light-skinned, mulatto ruling class toward Crummel—who was a member of the Negro political party, a political party made up of dark-skinned Blacks—had manifested itself over an educational issue. The dispute centered around the location of Liberia College. Crummel and his supporters pushed for the college to be placed outside of the Liberian capital, Monrovia. They argued that a college built within close proximity of the rural, dark-skinned, native population would increase the likelihood that this group would avail themselves of formal schooling. The mulatto ruling class countered that Monrovia represented the ideal location for the school. The battle over the location of the college was won by the mulattos.[6]

Crummel's scheme to create an education system and, then, from there to undertake the dual task of nation-building and self-government in Liberia floundered. When viewing his efforts from a transnational perspective it becomes clear that Crummel's failure to meet one precondition of transnational theory precluded him from meeting the other. First, domestically Crummel, as a nonstate agent, failed to build effective and long-term coalitions with the primary political actors of Liberia. Without the support of the powerful, light-skinned, mulatto ruling class, his efforts were essentially doomed. Second, and regarding international coalitions, Crummel stumbled in two respects. To begin with, he was unsuccessful in his attempts to persuade the Protestant Episcopal Church in America to expand their presence in Liberia. The support of this philanthropic body was critical because it was this group, from the start, that underwrote many of Crummel's activities in Liberia. Failure to build an effective coalition inside this organization proved costly, but not as costly as his other international miscalculation. Crummel's other mistake was his misjudgment in believing that Black Americans, particularly Black Americans from the northern states, would cross the Atlantic to serve as his education frontline workers in Liberia. With the American Civil War about to break out, and many Blacks envisioning their freedom if the northern forces emerged victorious at the conclusion of the campaign, Blacks were unwilling to uproot themselves and start anew in Liberia.[7]

As a result of one precondition not being met, whether or not the other precondition was satisfied is rendered moot. The absence of any effective coalition, on both domestic and international fronts, meant that, in the long term, there was no specific issue-area to regulate. Denied support both within Liberia and the United States, Crummel's plans to build an education system in Liberia eventually crumbled.

ENGLISH-SPEAKING SUB-SAHARA AFRICA

Between World War I and World War II, American transnational philanthropic actors formed an international alliance with the British Colonial Office in London. The immediate purpose of this collaboration between American nonstate agents and British state actors was to create, in the issue-area of international education, education systems throughout English-speaking sub-Sahara Africa identical to the "non-academic education designed for southern American Negroes (the so-called Tuskegee philosophy)."[8] Prior to World War I and during the interwar years, a popular belief among many influential Whites, on both sides of the Atlantic, was that as a result of a shared pigmentation pedigree and "similar dependent statutes," the same education policies and practices could be applied to Blacks in English-speaking sub-Sahara Africa that were applied to Blacks in the American South. The American transnational philanthropic actors who assumed prominent parts in the transference of industrial education to Africa were the Phelp-Stokes Fund, the Carnegie Corporation, the Laura Spelman Rockefeller Memorial, and the International Education Board.[9]

Similar to Crummel's education plans for Liberia, industrial education for Blacks in English-speaking sub-Saharan Africa was designed to accomplish more than just teaching and learning. Taking as their point of departure the "assumptions of evolutionary racial hierarchy"[10] used to justify industrial education for Blacks in the American South, American nonstate agents and British state actors sought to replicate, and reinforce, the racial status quo of the American South in English-speaking sub-Saharan Africa through policies of industrial education. Politically, industrial education was designed in such a way that it reinforced the widely held White notion that Blacks were incapable of self-government. Moreover, if Blacks were indeed incapable of self-government, the reasoning went, then, Black disfranchisement, both in the American South and English-speaking sub-Saharan Africa, was perfectly rational. Economically, with the advent of full-scale industrialization, industrial education trained Blacks to fill pre-ordained slots in emerging, postagrarian labor markets. Industrial education—again, both in the American South and English-speaking sub-Saharan Africa—was intended to train Blacks to fill the menial, low-skilled, low-waged, secondary job market. And, socially, the objective of industrial education was to make race tantamount to class. In the American South, in English-speaking sub-Sahara Africa, and the world over, American philanthropy—and where possible, British Colonial administrators—pressed for industrial education for Blacks as a means to justify their view of the world as a pigmentocracy in which Whites were socially and culturally superior to Blacks.[11]

Technically, the means employed to justify the socioeconomic and political ends of industrial education can be found in the curriculum. The cocktail of classes that constituted the industrial education curriculum emphasized, among other things, the following: "health and hygiene, appreciation and use of the environment, the effective development of home and household, and recreation and culture . . . agricultural training . . . character education" and "vocational rather than literary education."[12] Against the backdrop of the then-emerging industrialization sweeping through many parts of the world, the aims of the nonacademic, industrial education curriculum for Blacks in English-speaking sub-Sahara Africa paralleled its aims in the southern United States; which was to subordinate Blacks—in the political, social, economical, and cultural domains—to Whites. Biracial societies, made up of Blacks and Whites, could function efficiently if Blacks were educated to accept their proper place in the racial hierarchy. One American transnational philanthropist neatly summarized that Blacks could occupy the positions of "junior partners in the firm" of the then-industrializing nations. Of course, he did not need to say what the race of the managing partners in the firm would be.[13]

The attempt by American transnational philanthropic bodies and British Colonial officials to transfer industrial education policies and programs from the southern states of the United States to Blacks in English-speaking sub-Saharan Africa, in the end, must be pronounced a failure. The American and British joint education strategy to build brawn as opposed to cultivating brains in Blacks eventually proved untenable. By examining their efforts through a transnational lens it becomes clear that only one of the theoretical preconditions was actually met.

First, as nonstate actors, the coalition of American transnational philanthropists proved successful in satisfying one precondition of transnational theory: they established and maintained a bilateral alliance with their educational counterparts in the British Colonial Office. As a result, these American nonstate actors, working in collaboration with British state agents, were able to regulate the specific issue-area of international education as it related to Blacks in English-speaking sub-Sahara Africa. Accordingly—and taking as their point of departure the industrial education policies and programs for Blacks in the southern states of the United States that they had previously underwritten—American transnational philanthropists maintained that the most appropriate model of international education for Blacks in English-speaking sub-Sahara Africa was nonacademic, industrial education. Through a close and extended bilateral alliance with British Colonial officials, before World War I and during the interwar years, American transnational philanthropy sought nothing less than the international institutionalization of industrial education for Blacks in all English-speaking nations the world over.

Second, although American transnational philanthropists succeeded in meeting one precondition, they did not satisfy the other—and this proved to be decisively fatal. The other precondition stresses that the nonstate actor must penetrate the normative and organizational arrangements of their target state(s) and build effective coalitions within that state in order to be successful.

As previously highlighted, American transnational philanthropists did build effective coalitions, but their coalitions were disturbingly demarcated: their affiliations only extended as far as the ruling and racial elite. Left out from their educational and political affiliations in English-speaking sub-Sahara Africa were sufficient numbers of representatives from their target populations in their target countries: Blacks who were seeking some type of formal schooling. Their remissness proved costly. Organizationally and normatively speaking, the American nonstate actors proved incapable (or unwilling) of plumbing down into the dark depths of the racially stratified hierarchies of English-speaking sub-Saharan African countries were the attitudes and aspirations of the Black majorities were to be found. If they had, they would have discovered Blacks in English-speaking sub-Saharan Africa opposed to their industrial education policies. In addition to being influenced by W. E. B. Dubois's call for Pan-Africanism as well as the Marcus Garvey's strident demands for a "great Black government,"[14] Black resistance to industrial education in English-speaking Africa was fueled by a fierce desire on the part of Blacks to define and determine the extent and degree of their participation in the social, political, civil, and economic processes of their respective countries. And, most significant for the immediate purpose, Blacks in English-speaking sub-Sahara Africa wanted, and deserved, an education based on an academic curriculum, one that cultivated their mental capabilities rather than their manual capacities.[15] As one Simbini Mamba Nkomo, a visiting African professor of history at Tuskegee, declared: "We feel that . . . there must be an increased emphasis on higher education if Africa is ever to relieve other countries of the responsibility of carrying its leadership."[16]

EMERGING PATTERNS

In 1996, the Abell Foundation, located in the city of Baltimore, opened a school to educate African American adolescent males from inner-city Baltimore. The institution, the Baraka School, is located in a small town (Laikipia) in the east African country of Kenya. The foundation opened its school in Kenya hoping to "save boys from inner-city Baltimore by sending them to school in a setting where they can avoid the pitfalls of violence-addled neighborhoods, family struggles and suffocating peer pressure."[17] As a result of its sponsoring a school across national boundaries, the Abell Foundation is emerging as an American transnational philanthropic non-state actor in the issue-area of international education.

Yet the question arises as to why? Why would an urban-based American foundation choose to open a school for inner-city African American adolescent males in a small, "middle of nowhere,"[18] town in

Kenya? For the Abell Foundation, the answer stemmed from the narrow approaches to urban public school reform adopted by educators in the United States.

In the United States today, the majority of educational reforms applied toward urban public schools address problems at two levels: the school themselves or the educational bureaucracies that the schools are part of. Since problems associated with urban public schools are identified and addressed at either the school or bureaucratic levels, reforms are undertaken to address—among other things—the following: "rigid district bureaucracies, resignation among teachers and school principals, low expectations for students, and ideologies to justify poor student performances."[19] One detrimental result of identifying problems solely within the narrow ranges of the school or education bureaucracy has been that reforms have taken on a maddeningly redundant character, the process has become Sisyphean-like: "repeated cycles of centralizing and decentralizing reforms in education have had little discernible effect on the efficiency, accountability, or effectiveness of public schools."[20] Still, the reformers, like Sisyphus, continue, time and again, to shoulder their rocks of reform up the education mountain, seeking the summit of high student achievement.

Yet reaching that summit has proved elusive—if not all together impossible. The elusiveness is a result of reformer's identifying and addressing the ills besetting urban public schools at the school or bureaucratic levels. If reformers of urban public schools, and all other invested stakeholders, are ever to reach the summit of high student achievement, a reconceptualization of identifying and addressing the problems associated with urban public schools will have to occur. What is required is a more comprehensive approach, one that takes into account context. If conceiving of the reform process is unconfined from—but still inclusive of—the schools and bureaucracy, then, it will be possible to measure "how the cumulative effects of economic and political decisions in the larger urban context have, over time, severely constrained the ability and actions of current actors in central-city schools, including their efforts to achieve meaningful school reform. These effects are embodied in the poverty and social isolation of neighborhoods."[21]

Ideally, urban public school reform in the United States should take into account the inner-city context that the school is part of, but that is in the ideal world. In the real world, however, such a broad approach to fixing urban public schools in this manner is unlikely to happen any time soon. Although this is not the time or place to discuss the matter, the majority of reformers and the reforms they design and promote will, for the foreseeable future, avoid examining the harsh and brutal urban context and how that context impacts the schooling process. To do so, to expand the reform process to embrace the inner-city context that urban schools are embedded in, would constitute a Herculean-like task instead of a Sisyphean one—and, thus far, school reformers, educational bureaucrats, academic researchers, and all other invested parties have not shown the necessary commitment to approach, on a sufficient and sustained basis, inner-city school reform in this manner.

From the perspective of the Abell Foundation, the staples of reform that were fixated on the schools and the educational bureaucracy in Baltimore were viewed as markedly short-sighted—if, that is, the true objective was to enhance the quality of education for the city's African American adolescent male population. Beyond merely tinkering with the schools and bureaucracy, the foundation felt it essential that efforts at inner-city public school reform grapple with the formidable problems associated with the urban context: the political-economy of the ghetto, poverty, and social and racial isolation, to name just a few. However, and much to the foundation's dismay, a more comprehensive approach to urban public school reform in the city of Baltimore was not adopted. Therefore, since educational reformers in Baltimore would not innovate, the foundation decided that it would. If members of their target population, young African American males in the seventh and eighth grades from inner-city Baltimore, were to remain isolated in beleaguered urban public schools and neighborhoods, then, the foundation would underwrite their departure from both the schools and neighborhoods.[22]

Originally, the foundation wanted to place young African American males, in the seventh and eighth grades, in boarding schools, but this strategy was abandoned for two reasons: first, it proved simply too expensive. And second, since many boarding schools begin at the ninth-grade level, the foundation concluded that the one- or two-year delay in implementing their interventions might irreparably harm the students. For the earlier the interventions into a young person's life, the better the likelihood they will be effective. Waiting until their target students reached the ninth grade was not a risk the foundation was willing to take. With viable options dwindling, the foundation sought out affordable schools in the developing world. After a protracted and thorough search, the foundation was able to lease a sizable piece of land from a private owner in Kenya.[23]

Although it would be premature at this early stage to proclaim the Baraka School a lasting success, it can already boast of several significant achievements. First, reading scores among the students have risen, on average, four years. Behavioral problems have been successfully addressed and overcome. Of the eighteen participants who made up the first group, only one decided not to return. And this year, school enrollment has expanded to forty students (half of them seventh-graders, the other half eighth-graders). Significantly, the context in which the school is located is having a positive effect on learning outcomes.[24] "The school sits in the shadow of Mount Kenya, and the 150 acres of grounds are dotted with yellow and orange flowers, mango and guava trees, olive trees and gorgeous bougainvillea. All over the empty green spaces, birds flirt and chirp. Butterflies float and dip. . . . 'In the city, they feel like they have to act tough,' said Kate Walsh, head of the Baraka School project and education program officer for the Abell Foundation. . . . 'Here, they don't have to act tough. They can be little boys.'"[25] Indeed, the Baraka School is proving itself so successful that the city of Baltimore has agreed to partially subsidize the costs of the students living and learning in Kenya.

As a transnational philanthropic actor in the issue-area of international education, the Abell Foundation has impacted urban public school reform. By internationalizing the solution to inner-city school reform, the foundation is helping to transform what to date has been a narrow, technical dispute into a debate about policy. What's more, the overall impact of the foundation's program may not be limited to one small school in the middle of Kenya where a few Black male students from the city of Baltimore go to school, the possibility exists that similar (or, perhaps, identical) efforts at educating inner-city youth may be adopted: "if this experiment in Kenya works, the foundation plans to build other such schools around sub-Saharan Africa and in the Caribbean. Already education activist and other philanthropic groups have contacted Baraka officials about how to start similar schools."[26]

A sufficient and sustained expansion of the Abell Foundation's experiment could possibly result in the institutionalization of the Baraka School model. But the path to institutionalization is filled with theoretical pitfalls. In order to avoid these pitfalls, American transnational philanthropic nonstate agents and their counterparts in the central governments of the identified target countries will have to successfully regulate the specific issue-area of international education—here, in the form of Baraka-type schools serving urban youth from America. For that regulation to be a success, the two preconditions of transnational theory will have to be satisfied.

First, within the targeted developing countries, American transnational philanthropic actors, as nonstate agents, will have to penetrate the domestic political structures of the individual developing countries where Baraka-type schools are to be established. Once that is accomplished, American transnational philanthropic actors can attempt to build effective coalitions within the domestic structure of the individual target states. Due to the specific issue-area, the American nonstate actors will have to build coalitions with political actors from the ministries of education in the target states.

Second, only after establishing and maintaining effective coalitions can bilateral agreements—here, between American nonstate actors and developing-country state actors—regulating the specific issue-area be formulated. Regarding Baraka-type schools in developing countries, successful regulation that will define and determine the establishment and operations of such schools will include but not be limited to the following: Property issues: will foundation sponsored Baraka-type schools rent public or private land? Legal concerns: will there be restrictions on how many American teachers can work in the school? local teachers? will American teachers and local teachers receive equal pay? what jurisdiction applies to students? as minors, U.S. laws or the laws of the target country? School policy: will local adolescents be permitted to enroll? if so, what percentage of total enrollment can they comprise? how many American students will be permitted? Student discipline: it's unlawful for a teacher to physically strike a student in this country, but not in other countries, what rule applies?

If the Baraka School model is to be institutionalized—by the Abell Foundation and other American transnational philanthropic actors— American transnational philanthropic nonstate agents will have to satisfy the two preconditions laid forth in transnational theory. If effective coalitions are built and regulatory concerns hammered out, the Baraka School model can exist on a lasting and enduring basis. However, if these contemporary actors fail to meet both preconditions, if they follow in the footsteps of their philanthropic forefathers by making theoretical missteps, then, the past will undoubtedly repeat itself.

CONCLUSION

This chapter has investigated the historic and contemporary activities of American transnational philanthropic nonstate agents, operating in the specific issue-area of international education in sub-Saharan Africa. It has been theoretically suggested that the success or failure of the activities sponsored by American transnational philanthropic nonstate agents is determined by whether or not the nonstate agents satisfactorily meet the two preconditions of transnational theory. Those two preconditions are: the ability to build effective coalitions within target states and the extent to which the specific issue-area is regulated by bilateral agreements.

There is a caveat, though. It seems that when operating in the specific issue-area of international education, American transnational philanthropic nonstate agents are more likely to succeed in meeting both preconditions only when they refrain from subordinating education to a larger, more complex, political agenda. As was highlighted in the first two case studies, American transnational philanthropic nonstate agents attempted to achieve political ends through the means of education, and both times their efforts failed. This, notwithstanding the old adage, that all education is political. Across countries and contexts, when education is blatantly subordinated to politics it cheapens the learning process and, worse, cheats the learner.

To avoid that devaluation, for both the process and the individual, when American transnational philanthropic nonstate agents undertake activities in the specific issue-area of international education perhaps they would do well to remember this: a large part of the education process is to "make human beings who will live life to the fullest, who will continually add to the quality and meaning of their experience and their ability to direct that experience, and who will participate actively with their fellow human beings in the building of a good society."[27] When education is subordinated to politics, this rarely happens.

NOTES

1. Thomas Risse-Kappan, eds., *Bringing Transnational Relations Back In* (Cambridge: Cambridge University Press, 1995), p. 3

2. Ibid. p. 6.

3. Ibid.

4. J. R. Oldfield, *Alexander Crummel and the Creation of an African-American Church in Liberia* (Lewiston: Mellen Press, 1990), pp. 62–63.

5. Ibid., pp. 59–74.

6. Ibid., pp. 79–111.

7. Ibid., pp. 59–74.

8. Edward H. Berman, "Educational Colonialism in Africa: The Role of American Foundations, 1910–1945," in Robert F. Arnove, *Philanthropy and Cultural Imperialism: The Foundations at Home and Abroad* (Boston: G. K. Hall & Co., 1980), p. 179.

9. Ibid., pp. 179–80.

10. Kevin K. Gaines, *Uplifting the Race: Black Leadership, Politics, and Culture in the Twentieth Century* (Chapel Hill: University of North Carolina Press, 1996), p. 38.

11. Ibid., pp. 32–38.

12. Edward H. Berman, *Educational Colonialism in Africa* (Arnove, 1980), pp. 186–88.

13. Ibid., p. 194.

14. Kenneth James King, *Pan-Africanism and Education: A Study of Race, Philanthropy and Education in the Southern States of America and East Africa* (Oxford: Clarendon Press, 1971), p. 223.

15. Ibid., pp. 128–49, 252–59.

16. Ibid., p. 221.

17. Stephen Buckley, "Way Out of the Inner-City," *The Washington Post,* July 24, 1997, p. 1.

18. Ibid., p. 1.

19. William Julius Wilson, "Forward," in Anyon Jean, *Ghetto Schooling: A Political Economy of Urban Educational Reform* (New York: Teacher's College Press, 1997), p. ix.

20. Richard F. Elmore, "School Decentralization: Who Gains? Who Loses?" in Jane Hannoway and Martin Carnoy (eds.), *Decentralization and School Improvement: Can We Fulfill the Promise* (San Francisco: Jossey-Bass, 1993), p. 34.

21. Wilson, "Forward" from *Ghetto Schooling* (New York: Teachers' College, 1997), p. ix.

22. Allen F. Caldwell, Interview with Abell Foundation, January 1998.

23. Ibid.

24. Ibid.

25. Buckley, *The Washington Post,* July 1997, p. 24.

26. Ibid., p. 24.

27. Lawrence A. Cremin., *Popular Education and Its Discontent* (New York: Harper & Row, 1989), p. 125.

CHAPTER 3

We Are the World:
Race and the International
War on Drugs

Clarence Lusane

The [illegal drug] problem has assumed such a global nature that
it cannot be dealt with by individual countries.
—Giorgio Giacomelli, Director General,
UN International Drug Control Program

INTRODUCTION

President Bill Clinton walks around with drug money in his pocket. For
that matter, so does Attorney General Janet Reno and FBI Director
William Frei. To this list we can add House Speaker Newt Gingrich,
Tipper Gore, basketball superstar Michael Jordan, newscaster Barbara
Walters, and former Drug Czar William Bennett. In fact, we can include
nearly every person in the United States to this list. According to FBI
chemists, who used a portable ion mobility spectrometer to test currency
from all over the United States, including inner cities and Las Vegas
gambling houses, virtually every single dollar bill in the nation contains
traces of cocaine.[1] The fact that no one can avoid being touched by the
ubiquitous nature of illegal drugs underscores the seriousness of the
problem in contemporary U.S. society.

For African Americans, perhaps no other issue has been as vexing as
that of the health and social devastation wrought by the trafficking and
abuse of illegal narcotics. In the national and international "war on
drugs," from the vantage point of the Black community, more often

51

than not it appears that the drugs are winning. How to address this problem has been the subject of heated debate involving discourses ranging from drug legalization, conspiracies of genocide, militarization, and armed community defenses. Too often, however, the issue of drug abuse and trafficking is localized and even among some African Americans seen as a "Black" problem. The fact is that dilemmas of drug abuse and drug trafficking are national and global in scope and affect millions in both the developed and the developing world. While many Black activists, policy-makers, and scholars proclaim accurately that illegal narcotic crops do not grow in Black ghettoes and that drug-carrying planes do not land in the inner cities, a global framework on drugs has either been lacking or constructed along the lines of conspiracy, that is, (credible) allegations that the CIA and other U.S. intelligence agencies consciously allowed their anti-Communist allies to import cocaine and heroin into the Black community. While these charges have merit (see discussion below), they decontextualized African American drug issues from their historical and political frames, and point to solutions that are reductionist (e.g., ban the CIA) or unworkable (e.g., stop the import of all drugs coming into the United States) at worse.

Racism, narcotics, and international politics have been linked since the days of the Opium Wars of the mid-1800s, when China, viewed as backward and exploitable by European powers, unsuccessfully sought to resist the importation of opium into the country by England and France. Since that time, the connection between race, illegal drugs, and political expediency has been dynamic and perpetual. In the contemporary period, narcotics capitalism involves international channels of production, distribution, and consumption; channels that are unregulated and disrespectful of national borders, or class, gender, or race boundaries. It is this constellation of factors, along with broader economic and social deprivations, that ultimately determine the nature and intensity of drug trafficking and drug abuse in the African American community.

This chapter addresses a number of critical global variables that shape and drive the international narcotics industry, and the role that race occupies in that process. It is the thesis of this chapter that the illegal drugs problematic in the Black community can only be addressed when placed in a context that links the local with the global, that is, identification of globalized capitalist economies that bind nations and communities together in networks of drug production, distribution, and consumption; analysis of the specter of global geopolitics that determine global, national, and ultimately local drug policies; and recognition of the global links of criminal enterprises, including those in the Black community. Only by the construction of such a framework will we be able to grasp the wide range of complex, discursive, and intersecting factors that (re)shape these issues, and develop effective policy and political action. African American policy-makers and activists, who are concerned about the drug problems confronting the Black community, can not afford to ignore the international context that qualitatively drive the issue. Framing the problematic of racialized illegal narcotics in a global paradigm opens the parameters by which we can both historicize and analyze a complex and multifaceted issue that manifests most dramatically at a local level but is rooted in international economic and political arenas.

Uncovering the nexus of race and illegal drugs is not only political and theoretical, but also an ideological endeavor. One has to be careful to not present the issue as a problem of the "other"; so thoroughly racialized that we ignore important and similar drug-related issues faced by other communities in regards to the broader politics of abuse and trafficking. At the same time, the disproportionate impact of illegal narcotics on African Americans, particularly in the areas of health and criminal justice, is undeniable and there remains a vested and compelling interest on the part of the Black community to confront and resolve this issue. Walking the fine line between reductionism and only seeing race, and elevatism, espousing the rhetoric of color-blindness while denying the reality of racism, is a difficult but necessary path.

The Black drug crisis intersects with a profound economic crisis, in part, driven by global factors, confronting at least one-third of Black America. Deindustrialization shifted many jobs out of the inner cities in 1970s, 1980s, and 1990s, eliminating many opportunities for African Americans in the relatively high-paying manufacturing sector, particularly males with less than a high school education and lacking other skills. This destabilization reverberated across the social landscape, pushing many into various components of the underground economy.

A VESTED INTEREST

> The war on drugs foreseeably and unnecessarily blighted the lives
> of hundreds of thousands of young, disadvantaged Americans,
> especially Black Americans, and undetermined decades of efforts
> to improve the life chances of members of the urban Black under-
> class.
> —Michael Tonry, "Race and the War on Drugs"

The Black community has a vested and urgent interest in the extirpation of the drug problem. The myriad of contradictions brought by illegal narcotics are wide-ranging, ever-expanding, and painfully deadly. Although the problem manifests at many levels, most critical is the harm wrought on the Black community's health and the criminalizing of a generation of Black youth who are the drug culture's largest victims of violence.

African Americans, especially those most disadvantaged, suffer by the funding priorities that are being diverted to the drug war. Funds that could be spent on social programs such as health care, housing, education, and job training, are being spent on drug education, interdiction, border patrol, eradication, and prisons. In 1997, the federal government spent $16 billion to fight its drug war, up from $4.7 billion in 1987.[2] The nation's health care needs are not only going unmet, but are being exacerbated by the problems brought by illegal substance addiction and abuse, and trafficking. Although the number of African American deaths from the use of legal drugs, such as alcohol, prescription narcotics, and tobacco, are astronomical, illegal drugs also kill. In 1994, there were about 2,800 African American deaths linked to the pharmacological properties of illegal narcotics according to the Centers for Disease Control and Prevention (CDC).[3]

African American Health Costs

Among African Americans, drug use is the main cause for the widening spread of the HIV and AIDS viruses. This is due to the practice among drug users of sharing infected needles, and unsafe drug-related prostitution and sexual encounters endemic within the culture and sociology of drug addiction. CDC researchers have noted that AIDS is the leading cause of death for African Americans between twenty-five and forty-four, and over half of these deaths are injection-related.[4] Although twice as many Whites as Blacks inject drugs, Blacks are four times as likely as Whites to contract injection-linked AIDS.[5]

In 1995, there were over 12,600 new injection-related AIDS cases among African Americans.[6] And the problem is growing. As researcher Dawn Day discovered, "Over 70 percent of all injection-related AIDS cases among African Americans have been reported" in the period 1990–1995.[7] Some have projected that African Americans will be more than half of all AIDS cases in the United States by the year 2001.[8] Already, in one stunning revelation, "in 1996, 85 percent of the children reported with AIDS were African Americans and Hispanic," according to the National Institutes of Health.[9]

On a global scale, for Blacks in Africa and the diaspora, the AIDS and drugs connection is also salient. Drug use in the Caribbean, inter alia, contributes significantly to the spread of AIDS and registers the highest per capita prevalence of HIV in the world, 1.90 percent, outside of sub-Saharan Africa.[10] While the number of AIDS cases has been dropping in the rest of the Americas, it has been growing in dramatic fashion in the region, according to the Caribbean Epidemiology Center. The number of cases, states the center, grew by 13.5 percent in 1993 from the year before, by 19.2 percent in 1994, and 22.5 percent in 1995.[11] Injection-related contamination in the region is relatively low compared to the rest of the world, except in the Bahamas, where 40 percent of reported AIDS cases are linked to illegal drug injection.[12] Rather, the growth of crack cocaine and heroin abuse and addiction has created an atmosphere where unprotected sex-for-drugs and prostitution have increased tremendously in recent years. Overall, there are about 310,000 cases of AIDS or HIV in the Caribbean according the United Nations.[13]

The most tragic circumstances of AIDS and HIV expansion is taking place in the eighty-four nations that comprise sub-Saharan Africa. In that region, the UN estimates that there are 20.8 million cases of AIDS/HIV with a prevalence rate of 7.4 percent, by far the highest in the world.[14] Although most cases are contracted through sexual practices, the ever-growing problem of drug use and trafficking, from Nigeria to South Africa, portends to make a grim situation even grimmer.

African Americans and the Criminal Justice Crisis

It is in the area of criminal justice that the specter of race in the war on drugs is most pernicious. Historically, African Americans have been victimized by a racist and class-biased criminal justice system. The war on drugs, however, has made the situation even worse in the present era. Initiated by President Nixon in the late 1960s, and continued and expanded by Presidents Ford, Carter, Reagan, Bush, and Clinton, the drug war has disproportionately targeted young African American males and resulted in a clogged judicial system that is filling the jails and prisons in unprecedented numbers. The courts, jails, and prisons are filled to overcapacity as the drug war ravages inner-city communities while ignoring drug traffickers and users in surrounding suburbs.

While much of the focus has been on Black men, Black women have not escaped the collateral damage of the drug war. The increase in incarceration for drug offenses for Black males from 1986 to 1991 grew by 429 percent.[15] However, the increase for Black women increased by a stunning 828 percent.[16] Overall, the rate of increase in African American women under some form of justice supervision has grown by 78 percent in the period 1989–1994, the largest of any demographic group, and almost solely due to drug offenses.[17]

Drug possession and trafficking are the primary causes of the phenomenal rise in involvement with the criminal justice system for young African Americans, particularly young African American males. African

Americans are 12 percent of the U.S. population and, proportionately, roughly 13 percent of all drug users according to NIDA. Yet African Americans constitute 35 percent of those arrested on drug possession charges, 55 percent of those convicted on those charges, and 74 percent of those who are given prison sentences for those charges.[18]

As Marc Mauer notes, "Black and Hispanics combined now constitute nearly 90 percent of all offenders sentenced to state prisons for drug offenses."[19] Due greatly to the disproportionate focus on inner-city, low-level dealers, almost one-third of young Black men (32.2 percent) between twenty and twenty-nine are either incarcerated, on parole, or on probation.[20] In a number of cities, the figures are even worse. Half of the young Black males ages 18–35 in Washington, D.C., the nation's capital, are incarcerated, on parole, on probation, out on bond, or being sought on an arrest warrant.[21] This is an increase from 42 percent in 1990. Although the rates of drug use and violent crimes remained fairly unchanged, between 1980 and 1995, the Black prison population grew from 146,900 to 541,900.

One aspect of the racialized drug war that has received the most attention is the 100–1 sentencing discrepancy between the laws regarding crack cocaine and ones regarding cocaine powder. Under the Omnibus Anti-Drug Abuse Act of 1988, possession of five grams of crack cocaine nets a mandatory sentence of five years. For an equal amount of cocaine powder, there is no minimum sentence and, indeed, many offenders receive probation. It takes 500 grams of cocaine powder to receive a sentence of five years.[22] According to the U.S. Sentencing Commission, there are three times as many users of powder cocaine as crack cocaine. But there are far more prosecutions for crack than for powder. Although 91% of those who used cocaine snorted it, 31% smoked it, and 10% swallowed it, most of the law enforcement focus however is on the 31% who smoked the substance according to the 1999 National Household Survey on Drug Abuse.[23] In 1992, of those arrested for federal crack cocaine offenses 92.6% were Black. According to one sampling by the U.S. Sentencing Commission, of the defendants charged with simple possession of crack cocaine in the second quarter of 1992, all were Black.[24]

In 1996, after the U.S. Sentencing Commission recommended that the discrepancy between the two sentences be made more equal, the proposal was rejected in new crime legislation by Congress and President Clinton. One response to the decision to maintain the discriminatory legislation was rioting by federal prisoners, most of whom are in prison on drug charges, in Illinois, Pennsylvania, Alabama, and Tennessee.[25]

In July 1997, Attorney General Janet Reno and Drug Czar Barry McCaffrey joined reformers in recommending to the president that the disparity be lessened to a ratio 10 to 1 (250 grams for cocaine powder and 25 grams for crack). While Clinton endorse their proposal, the Congressional Black Caucus did not. Caucus members argued that *no discrepancy* should exist. Caucus Chairperson Rep. Maxine Waters stated, "It's not good enough. Crack wouldn't be crack without powdered cocaine."[26]

These issues clearly designate the urgency around drugs facing African Americans. The economic, social, and health costs are escalating and demand a critical intervention by policy-makers. While these issues are felt most immediately in local communities, and must be addressed at that level also, the role of global economics and politics are decisive factors in the perpetuation of the national drug crisis.

THE DRUG TRADE AS GLOBAL ENTERPRISE

The benefits of global capitalism are unevenly distributed.
—George Soros

Today's global economy is a capitalist one. So is the global drug economy. The production, distribution, and consumption of the illegal narcotic industry involves functions and processes that are similar to that of other international capitalist industries. Products—commodities—are produced, packaged, and marketed for a global consumer audience. Scholars Patricia McRae and David Ackerman argue persuasively that the international drug trade should be viewed as functioning in the same manner as a transnational corporation.[27] Historian Alfred McCoy makes a similar point when he argues, "Over the past two centuries, narcotics have become major global commodities that operate on fluid laws of supply and demand not susceptible to simple repression."[28] McRae and Ackerman contend that, in a number of instances, economic power accumulated by the cartels have also given them political and social power to the point that they often function as "counter-hegemonic" groups capable of challenging the authority of the state.[29]

Illegal drug trafficking is big business, big global business. In 1995, the illegal trade in drugs represent 8 percent of the world's total exports.[30] According to a June 1997 report by the United Nations International Drug Control Programme (UNIDCP), drug trafficking is a $400-billion-a-year global enterprise.[31] The *World Drug Report* states that nearly 140 million globally smoke marijuana or hashish, 13 million use cocaine regularly, 8 million use heroin, and 30 million use stimulants such as amphetamines.[32] The global drug trade is larger than most industries including automobile, iron, and steel exports.[33] The report notes, "The justification for calling illicit drugs an industry is firstly, that there is a great demand for the product in question, therefore a market for illicit drugs exist, and secondly, meeting this demand involves an extensive and complex process of production, manufacture, distribution, and investment."[34]

Cross-national ownership of drug crops has become a growing problem that makes it even more difficult for communities and local or federal authorities to identify and eliminate criminal enterprises. In California, for instance, marijuana increasingly is under the control of Mexican nationals. Law enforcement officials estimate that between 85 and 90 percent of the state's groves are controlled and owned by Mexicans though primarily operated by U.S. nationals.[35]

For the Black community, addressing the issue of drugs also means being involved in the policy debates regarding economic globalization. Ironically, increases in global trade and development of trade pacts have created greater trafficking control issues. Trade policies, such as the North American Free Trade Agreement (1993), the General Agreement on Tariffs and Trade and the World Trade Organization (1994), and Europe's Maastricht Treaty (1991) have facilitated the spread of drugs. These policies have made not only the movement of money and legal goods more efficient and faster, but also have made the importation and trafficking of narcotics easier as inspection barriers have been eased. Since NAFTA became operational in 1994, according to *Business Week*, 70 percent of the cocaine that comes into the United States and one-half of the marijuana comes through Mexico, and government experts attribute this growth to a vast increase in trucking traffic from Mexico and limited inspections, both derived from NAFTA implementation.[36] As the *Washington Post* noted, Mexican drug groups are "taking advantage of the porous border and the surge in traffic across it brought about by the North American Free Trade Agreement."[37] The problem has become so acute that, in 1997, Congress introduced the "NAFTA Accountability Act," H.R. 978, in an effort to address the problem. In Europe, similar issues arise with the border openings resulting in increasing crime as Castells notes,

> [T]he consolidation of the European Union has handed organized crime a wonderful opportunity to take advantage of contradictions between national legislations and of the reluctance of most police forces to relinquish their independence. Thus, Germany has become a major operational center for the Sicilian Mafia, Galicia is a major staging point for the Colombian cartels, and the Netherlands harbors important nodes of heroin traffic of the Chinese Triads.[38]

In the broadest sense, the growth and harvesting of cocoa leaves, opium, hashish, marijuana, and other crops essential to illegal drug production are also driven by global capitalist economics that have relegated developing nations to producing, under profoundly inequitable circumstances, for the developed world. Narco-governments in Bolivia, Peru, Thailand, Afghanistan, Myanmar, and elsewhere merge illegal and extralegal activities with governmental recognition of the critical, indeed, decisive role of drug dollars in the national economy. The path that links drug production in the developing world with impoverished communities in the developed one travels through a global economy that brutally dictates and limits the economic options for millions.

Economic priorities determine that disproportionately poor Black communities, in the United States and elsewhere, become the target of global drug traffickers seeking to maximize profits with minimum disruption and harassment. As Castells noted, global trafficking enterprises "base their management and production functions in low-risk areas, where they have relative control of the institutional environment, while targeting as preferential markets those areas with the most affluent demand, so that higher prices can be charged."[39] Marginalized Black communities, and other arenas of poverty, in the United States, Nicaragua, Colombia, South Africa, England, Canada, and other nations bear the brunt of a global marketing that seeks the easiest markets to penetrate. Substance abuse and trafficking occur across class and status boundaries, and, indeed, an argument can be made that wealthy communities spend more on illegal narcotics than poor ones. Nevertheless, the capacity to resist the influx of drugs and the resources to fight the health and criminal consequences of abuse and addiction is conditioned through the prism of class and the nexus of race and poverty.

The economically driven drug problems of the African American community has reverberations in the rest of the Black world. Drug profits from U.S. consumers built the international drug conglomerates that are opening new markets in poor Black communities in South Africa, Nicaragua, England, Canada, France, and elsewhere. In sensational fashion, crack cocaine has come to South Africa. Freed from decades of apartheid segregation, the people of South Africa, particularly those in the Black townships, face a new enemy and find that their budding democracy is now threatened by the economics and politics of a global drug trade that has quickly gotten out of control. In August 1996, the very public burning and shooting of a drug dealer in the Cape Town area dramatized that South Africa had arrived in the modern trafficking era. Confronted by a 500–car caravan, drug dealer Rashaad Staggie, one of the leaders of the notorious Hard Livings drug gang, was killed by members of the antidrug group People against Gangsterism and Drugs (PAGAD). The entire incident was broadcast live and divided a nation frustrated with growing street crime and insecurity. While many condemn the vigilantism of PAGAD, its take-no-prisoner tactics also has wide support, particularly among Indians. Crack cocaine trafficking and use, however, is most severe in the Black townships. Nevertheless, a political and racial division has transpired as the Black government finds itself on the defense regarding the drug issue. One consequence of the Staggie killing was the emergence of a united front of drug dealers. About a week after Staggie's death, 150 drug gangs from the Western Cape met and formed an umbrella group called "The Firm," which, in a surreal move, issued a press statement that it would fight back against PAGAD. A shootout happened a few days later between PAGAD and The Firm.

Similar to the conditions facing poor Black U.S. communities, the rise in drug trafficking in South Africa is driven by gruesome economic and social conditions facing millions of Black South Africans. The unemployment rate for Black South Africans, for example, is officially about 48 percent. These dire economic times coincide with a dramatic rise in cocaine imports into the country. In 1992, authorities seized 24 pounds of cocaine, in 1995 that number rose to 411 pounds. It is no wonder that the *Washington Post* called South Africa "one of the hottest new transshipment points and domestic markets in the world."[40]

In Nicaragua, crack is devastating the Black and Indian populations of the Atlantic coast. The bags of cocaine that routinely wash upon the shore, dumped by planes and boats along the trafficking routes that go from South America to the United States, are 90 percent to 95 percent pure, but since at least 1993, that cocaine has been processed into crack and is sold for less than $1 per rock that is starting to result in growing overdose deaths. One Miskito Indian community estimates that as many as half their young men may be addicted to the drug. In 1997, in Bluefields, a largely Black community, police conservatively estimate that there are over a hundred crack houses in a city with a population of only 50,000. In the region, unemployment runs as high as 90 percent in most areas.[41]

Black Canadians have also felt both the pain of a growing drug problem as well as the taking the brunt of that nation's drug war. According to a report issued by a special commission in Ontario, in the period 1986–1993, "the number of Blacks imprisoned in Ontario increased by 204 percent compared with a 23 percent increase for Whites."[42] At the heart of this increase is Canada's war on drugs and its focus "small-scale traders and couriers" in Black areas; a war that has had "an insignificant impact on drug use."[43] The commission found that almost half of the Black youth (18–24) in the Toronto area had been stopped by the police while less than a quarter of White youth had been affronted. The 445–page report noted that "Blacks are 27 times as likely to be jailed before their trials on drug trafficking and importing charges and 20 times as likely as Whites to be imprisoned for drug possession charges," and that "systemic racism" exists in Ontario's criminal justice system.[44] Blacks in Ontario make up only 3 percent of the population but constitute 15 percent of the prison population.[45]

The economics of international drug trafficking are facilitated by the imposition of political interests regarding drug policies. While Western governments have not necessarily benefited financially directly from drug profits in the manner that many developing nations have, it has been the geopolitical maneuvering of Western governments and their intelligence agencies, particularly during the half century of the Cold War, that allowed traffickers to distribute and sell their wares with only minimal disruption.

GLOBAL DRUG GEO-POLITICS

The fact is, if you want to go into the subversion business, collect intelligence, and move arms, you deal with drug movers.
—Gen. Paul F. Gorman, former head of the U.S. Southern Command

The global enterprise of trafficking in illegal narcotics, and the subindustries that accompany it (political and police corruption, money laundering, etc.), are framed by political considerations and priorities that have historically shaped the nature and character of the industry. For most of the twentieth century, the dynamics of drug trafficking were intricately tied to the politics of the Cold War. Beginning with the formation of the Soviet Union in 1917 and the spread of socialist states from China to Cuba, U.S. drug policies were subservient to the political priorities of the war against communism and geopolitical positioning. That these policies would have a negative impact on Black and poor communities was an irrelevant factor to U.S. policy-makers.

Official collaboration between U.S. government entities and known drug traffickers dates back to at least the World War II era. The Office of Strategic Services (OSS), the predecessor to the CIA, made deals with the Corsican heroin traffickers as well as with gangster Lucky Luciano in the U.S. effort to prevent communists from gaining a political foothold in postwar France and Italy. Luciano (and eventually other organized crime figures) had dealt heroin in the United States since 1915.[46] The OSS's Operation Underworld would negotiate a deal that would eventually free Luciano from prison in 1946 in exchange for his role in helping to secure the docks of New York from Nazi sabotage and using his mob contacts in Sicily to attack the Italian Communist Party.[47]

From 1924 to 1944, the U.S. heroin addict population dropped from 200,000 to about 20,000.[48] These numbers would begin to grow again after the war and after Luciano established a worldwide network of traffickers, distributors, and retailers for heroin.[49] The U.S. government "through the CIA and its wartime predecessor, the OSS, created a situation that made it possible for the Sicilian-American Mafia and the Corsican underworld to revive the international narcotics traffic."[50]

Similar alliances led to similar consequences in Southeast Asia. In Laos, beginning around 1960, the CIA created a secret army of 30,000 Hmong tribesmen to fight the Communists in charge of the nation. Hmong Gen. Vang Pao was allowed to use the CIA's Air America planes to traffic opium, the Hmong's major cash crop. This heroin would not only be used to addict thousands of U.S. soldiers fighting in Vietnam, including a disproportionate number of African American soldiers, but it would eventually comprise about one-third of all heroin in the United States by the end of the war in the mid-1970s.[51] By 1989, 73 percent of the world's heroin was being produced in Southeast Asia.[52]

Beginning in the late 1970s, in Southwest Asia, in the area known as the Golden Crescent where Afghanistan, Pakistan, and Iran come together, the United States supported the anti-Communist Mujahedeen guerrillas fighting to overthrow their Soviet-backed government. The covert activities of the CIA in the area would create trafficking lines that did not previously exist. A tremendous spurt in heroin production occurred that would have a direct impact on heroin use in the United States. As researcher Alfred McCoy notes, "As heroin from Afghanistan and Pakistan poured into America throughout 1979 . . . the number of drug-related deaths in New York City rose by 77 percent."[53]

The trafficking surge would also directly impact the Black community. Although heroin in Harlem had traditionally come from Southeast Asia, by the early 1980s, as a result of trafficking routes opened by U.S. intelligence operations in Afghanistan and Pakistan, about 42 percent of the Harlem's heroin was now coming from southern Asia.[54] As McCoy noted, by late 1980, heroin from the region "had captured 60 percent of the U.S. market."[55] Between 1982 and 1985, covering the first Reagan term, the number of cocaine users grew to 5.8 million, a 38 percent rise.[56]

The pattern of exploding narcotics trafficking would be repeated when the Reagan administration made the decision to support anticommunist rebels in Central America. From Honduras to Costa Rica to Panama to Nicaragua, the CIA and other agencies would employ numerous drug traffickers to assist their covert wars against the Sandinistas in Nicaragua and guerrillas fighting to overthrow military and political dictatorships in El Salvador and Guatemala.

Importantly, it was not just the CIA but the entire U.S. foreign policy apparatus that was integrated into carrying out the U.S. covert war in the region. This included all branches of the military, the National Security Agency, and the U.S. State Department. All of these activities and connections would be revealed in the investigations and hearings held by Sen. John Kerry (D-MA) in the late 1980s. The report issued by the Subcommittee on Terrorism, Narcotics, and International Operations of the Committee on Foreign Relations in the U.S. Senate stated, for example, "The U.S. State Department paid four contractors $806,401.20 to supply humanitarian aid to the Contra forces in Central America. All four of these companies were owned by known drug traffickers."[57] It went on to say that the U.S. State Department made "payments to drug traffickers . . . for humanitarian assistance to the Contras, in some cases after the traffickers had been indicted . . . on drug charges."[58]

Although the *Washington Post* attempted to imply that the Kerry report was ambiguous, a careful read of the report expresses fairly clear conclusions.[59] The Kerry report stated, for example, that "on the basis of this evidence, it is clear that . . . elements of the contras . . . knowingly received financial and material assistance from drug traffickers. . . . In each case, one or another agency of the U.S. government had information about the involvement."[60] The Kerry report also concluded, "The logic of having drug money pay for the pressing needs of the contras appealed to a number of people who became involved in the covert war. Indeed, senior U.S. policymakers were not immune to the idea that drug money was a perfect solution to the contras' funding problems."[61]

The increased influx of cocaine into the United States had a devastating impact on the Black community. The deleterious effects of drug trafficking and growing substance abuse were compounded by Reagan, Bush, and Clinton's political war on drugs; a war disproportionately aimed at African Americans. The racial politics of the drug war mushroomed into a colossal public debate when it was reported that the CIA and its Contra army were involved in drug trafficking to Los Angeles' Black street gangs.

CIA-CONTRA CRACK CONNECTION

In fall 1996, the politics of global drug trafficking reached banner headlines in the United States when a relatively unknown regional newspaper decided that the lead story on the inauguration of its web site would be the tale of links between Los Angeles' Black street gangs, drug trafficking Central American counter-revolutionaries, and one of the most surreptitious agencies of the United States. Few media stories in recent years have generated as much response from the Black community as the *San Jose Mercury* investigative series charging the CIA-backed Contras' involvement in cocaine trafficking.[62] The Nicaraguan Democratic Force (FDN), popularly known as the "Contras," was a coalition of several groups waging war against the Sandinista government that came to power in Nicaragua in 1970. The FDN was created in mid-1981 by the Reagan administration in its fight against communism.

Written by investigative reporter Gary Webb, the *Mercury* series made several allegations concerning the relationship between drug dealers tied to the Contras and the spread of crack cocaine in the Black community of Los Angeles. Webb asserted that Contras and Contra-supporters imported cocaine into the United States; that the cocaine was sold to at least one major Los Angeles Black drug dealer with ties or membership in the Crips street gang; and that the CIA was aware of the Contra drug activities and choose to either ignore them or to protect the traffickers.

The response to the series was phenomenal and is an instructive lesson in the power of the intersection of race, new technologies, and foreign policy politics. Internet access to the series meant that a rapid and national, indeed global exposure of the stories occurred and spread like wildfire. Reprints of the story were put together and sold on the streets of Harlem, Washington, D.C., and other U.S. cities as well as in Cape Town, Kingston, and Paris. Forums and meetings as well as demonstrations and other protests also took place. Calls for investigative hearings came from Black members of Congress and other Black civil rights and community leaders.

Major broadcast media initially responded to the series by either ignoring its existence or, as in the case of the *Los Angeles Times*, the *New York Times*, and the *Washington Post*, did stories imputing Webb's motives, research skills, and fundamental assertions. The Department of Justice, the CIA, and other U.S. agencies also denied the validity of Webb's allegations, and made promises of internal investigations. The backlash was so strong that even Webb's editors at the *San Jose Mercury* began to speak with some hesitancy in their support for his work and even launched their own investigation of Webb's charges.[63]

The story, however, could not be contained. Available on the Internet, it had a global reach and helped to expose a connection between drugs and politics that many in the Black community long suspected but had little evidence to prove. The *Mercury* stories appeared to many to confirm these suspicions. The Contra drug dealers, according to Webb, "met with CIA agents both before and during the time they were selling the drugs in L.A."[64] More specifically, Webb's investigation states that from 1982 until 1986, L.A. cocaine trafficker Danilo Blandon and his San Francisco–based supplier Norwin Meneses sold hundreds of kilos of cocaine to "Freeway" Rick Ross, a Black twenty-two-year-old street dealer with ties to the Crips street gang.[65] Ross, according to Webb, turned the cocaine he received from Blandon and Meneses into crack. Ross grew to be a major dealer in the Los Angeles area, and had broad influence over the spread of crack. This was partly due to the fact that he was able to receive kilos from Blandon and Meneses at prices well below the normal costs and could undersell other dealers.

The millions in profits made from the drugs sold to Ross, according to court records obtained by the *San Jose Mercury*, were "then used to buy weapons and equipment for a guerrilla army" created by the CIA to overthrow the Sandinista government in Nicaragua.[66] When the *Mercury* allegations appeared, CIA and Contra leaders stated Meneses was not a key player in the Contra war and that they were surprised to find out that he was involved in drug trafficking. Those disclaimers don't ring true, however. Meneses says that, for at least five years, he raised funds for the Contras, visited Contra camps, and sent people to Honduras to work for the Contras.[67] Although Adolfo Calero, the U.S.-based political leader of the FDN, downplayed Meneses' involvement and says he was unaware of his drug trafficking, Meneses and Calero were photographed together at a Contra fundraiser in San Francisco and Calero concedes Meneses visited Contra camps numerous times during the 1980s.[68] Also, Calero's denial of knowledge about Meneses' trafficking activities is not credible. The *San Francisco Examiner*, according to the *Los Angeles Times*, did a detailed story on the linkage between Meneses' drug trafficking and his Contra connections.[69] Not only was Meneses well known in the United States as a large dealer, as the *Mercury* pointed out, he was heralded in Nicaraguan newspapers as "Rey de la Droga" (King of Drugs).[70]

Webb writes that the cocaine sold to Ross and later turned into crack created "the first mass market in America" for the drug with which the Black community is all too familiar.[71] It is generally agreed that the eruption and broad growth of crack in Los Angeles occurred around this time. While Webb perhaps overenthusiastically writes that Ross was "the Johnny Appleseed of crack in California," which led the *Washington Post* to charge in its attack on the articles that Webb claimed that Ross was the key to the crack epidemic, Webb never states that Ross solely was responsible for the spread of crack. The series did not state, as some in the media accused, that the CIA, Blandon, or Ross initiated or invented crack. Webb clearly stated that crack existed before the Blandon-Ross relationship, and, as one of the articles notes, Blandon's entry into cocaine trafficking coincided with when "street-level drug users were figuring out how to make cocaine affordable . . . by changing the pricey White powder into powerful little nuggets that could be smoked—crack."[72] The series also does not say that the CIA as an agency or any identifiable employees of the CIA directly sold drugs in the United States or specifically targeted the Black community. Neither the series nor other reports and studies provide evidence of such high-level authorization and targeting of the Black community. While there are examples of U.S. officials being arrested and convicted of illegal narcotics trafficking, no conspiratorial network of top officials inside of the CIA has ever been identified. This is not to clean the moral or political slate of the CIA, however. First, as noted above, the record shows that high CIA officials did nothing to stop and often protected traffickers. Second, no official sanctions or authorities were necessary for the events being charged to have happened. As noted in the *Los Angeles Times*, "If you ask: In the process of fighting a war against the Sandinistas, did people connected with the U.S. government open channels which allowed drug traffickers to move drugs to the United States, did they know the drug traffickers were doing it, and did they protect them from law enforcement? The answer to all those questions is yes."[73]

On October 23, 1996, at a U.S. Senate hearing, CIA Inspector General Frederick P. Hitz testified that based on their investigation, there is "no credible information" to support the *Mercury* stories.[74] Other government agencies, including the Department of Justice, reached similar conclusions. Despite the closure to the issue sought by the federal government, Black activists and policy-makers remained committed to investigating the story and seeking corroboration from other sources. While financial gain and political interest are at the roots of the international drug traffic, the principal actors in this drama are the global crime enterprises that have grown in power and reach in this period.

GOBAL LINKS OF CRIMINAL ENTERPRISES

The most important role of organized crime in this sector is to provide and invest capital.
—*The World Drug Report*

In the 1990s, criminal organizations have united on a global scale. While the drug trade has always been international in scope, an unprecedented expansion of collaboration has occurred among leading international criminal enterprises. The Colombian cartels, Italian Mafia, Russian gangs, Japanese Yakuza, and the Chinese Triads along with smaller trafficking gangs from Jamaica, Nigeria, Mexico, and elsewhere, have developed networks of economic interests that rival the capacities and drive of the traditional corporate world. Increasingly, these organizations work in alliance with each other as they too take advantage of the new opportunities and new technologies opened up by economic and political globalization.

In writing about the global drug trade, French journalist Roger Faligot noted, "The Colombian cartels produce the cocaine, the Chinese take it in exchange for heroin that can then be smuggled into the U.S. The triads bring cocaine to Japan and distribute it with the help of the Yakuzas. Then the Asian mafiosi launder their drug money in Europe."[75] In 1987, a similar deal was made between the Medellin cartel and the Sicilian Mafia that resulted in Colombian cocaine being distributed in Europe and Asia by the Mafia, and the cartels distributing Mafia heroin in the Americas. In March 1997, in another notable instance, a Russian national, Ludwig Fainberg, was arrested in Miami as he was negotiating the illegal sale of a stolen submarine to two Cubans, Juan Almeida and Nelson Yester, who were frontmen for the Colombian cartels. The submarine was to be used to smuggle drugs from South America. Fainberg had been previously involved in the sale of two Russian helicopters to the cartels in 1992.[76]

According to a report issued by the United Nations Economic and Social Council, in addition to drug trafficking, global organized crime networks are engaged in money laundering, weapons smuggling, selling stolen nuclear weapons, smuggling illegal immigrants, trafficking in body parts, and female and child prostitution. These activities reap billions of dollars in profits and touch nearly every society. Drug trafficking, however, remains the life blood of global organized crime.

African American crime figures and organizations have also been engaged and aligned in international trafficking enterprises. From New York's legendary Ellsworth Raymond "Bumpy" Johnson, Frank Lucas, Frank Matthews, and Leroy "Nicky" Barnes in the 1960s and 1970s to Black street gangs in Los Angeles, Chicago, and elsewhere in the 1980s and 1990s, a vibrant relationship has existed as foreign suppliers have responded to the "Black" takeover of drug trafficking in the Black community. Johnson, for example, had been indicted in 1967 on charges of smuggling drugs from Peru.[77] Some researchers view the Vietnam War as a turning point in the ascension of African Americans as narcotics smugglers. Schatzberg and Kelly contend, "Former African American servicemen accomplished in a few short years what others had been unable to do under nearly two hundred years of White oppression. They broke the bonds that forced them to buy heroin from White importers in the United States—mostly La Cosa Nostra—and started their own smuggling and distribution networks, controlling operations from poppy cultivation to the selling of bags in ghetto streets."[78]

While nationals in source countries remain at the top of the traf-ficking pyramid, and African Americans occupy disproportionately the low end of street retail sales, it would be a mistake to assume Black crime organizations lack the sophistication and resources to operate on an international scale. As long as opportunities in the illegal drug market are vastly superior to the other more limited options faced by those who have been marginalized, crime gangs will continue to pro-liferate. The post–civil rights era has meant integration into *every* aspect of society.

HARM REDUCTION AND THE FUTURE OF DRUG POLICIES

The drug crisis challenge confronting African Americans and the rest of the nation continues despite the tens of billions of dollars that have been invested to address the issue. While it remains critical for communities within the United States to learn from each other and share programs and policies that have demonstrated effectiveness in addressing sub-stance abuse and trafficking, lessons from the global community are also necessary.

Around the world, many nations have taken a "harm reduction" approach to the problem of illegal narcotics. Recognizing that neither full legalization nor an unenforceable prohibition have been successful, drug reformers have attempted to find a common ground between the two extremes and balance law enforcement with a health-oriented approach to assisting addicts. The harm reduction movement stresses limiting the harm on society as a priority in addressing the drug prob-lem rather than punishment of the user as the main focus of drug pol-icy. Along these lines, innovative ideas such as needle exchange, more funds for treatment, and decriminalization are being tried by national governments and activists in both the developed and developing worlds.

A number of countries have experimented with needle exchange as one means of harm reduction. These programs allow health profession-als to provide "clean," that is, unaffected and disposable, needles to addicts without either the providers or users being subject to arrest or criminal charges. The purpose of the programs are to primarily stop the spread of diseases and viruses, such as AIDS or hepatitis, that comes from users sharing dirty needles. Needle exchange programs (NEPs) have been growing around the United States and globally. In 1993, there were 37 NEPs operating in 13 states.[79] By 1997, the number had increased to 115 programs in 29 states plus Puerto Rico and Guam. In the United States, the movement has grown large enough to form a national organization, the North American Syringe Network, and support for needle exchange has come from mainstream organizations such as the American Bar Association, U.S. Conference of Mayors, American Public Health Association, American Academy of Pediatrics, and American Medical Association.[80] In February 1997, a panel of the National Institutes of Health endorsed NEPs. Overall, however, the Clinton White House has rejected support for NEPs despite studies from within the administration that demonstrate the programs' effectiveness. Also, in February 1997, U.S. Secretary of Health and Human Services Donna Shalala took a tepid step forward when she demurred from the administration and wrote "needle exchange programs can be an effective component of a comprehensive strategy to prevent HIV and other blood-borne infectious disease in communities [that] choose to include them."[81] That position was challenged by Gen. Barry McCaffrey, who wrote in a press release, "Federal treatment funds should not be diverted to short term 'harm reduction' efforts like needle exchange programs."[82]

Over the years, study after study has demonstrated that treatment works, or as researcher Peter Reuter notes, it works well enough to be worth the social expense. One older study, the Treatment Outcome Prospective Study (TOPS), examined the impact of treatment on 10,000 addicts in 37 programs in 10 different cities from 1979 to 1981. The study concluded that while 20 percent went back to using drugs regularly, 80 percent stayed clean, most found full-time jobs, and their involvement in crime dropped from one-half to one-third.[83] In the 1990s, studies by the RAND Corporation confirm the notion that treatment is the most cost-effective means of cutting the harm out of drug use. It found that the cost of reducing cocaine consumption by one percent was $783 million a year if spent on source-country control efforts. To achieve that same one percent reduction by spending treatment would only cost $34 million.

RAND also discovered that a reduction in cocaine consumption was best achieved by treatment rather than longer sentences or conventional law enforcement. Longer sentences and conventional law enforcement led to a reduction in use of 13 kilograms and 27 kilograms per million dollars spent respectively. Treatment, on the other hand, led to a use reduction of 104 kilograms.

For African American activists and policy-makers, it is critical to seek alternatives to the present "war on drugs." That means looking beyond our national borders. A global community has emerged representing governments, nongovernmental organizations, and citizen-activists that seeks to collectively address the issues and problems faced by the world's peoples. Hunger, poverty, environmental destruction, and drug trafficking and abuse are global concerns as well as national and local ones. Resolving these issues will require not only efforts at the local and national levels, but increasingly a coordinated and shared global effort involving all those who are committed to eliminating the harm wrought by drug abuse and drug trafficking.

NOTES

1. Apparently, rollers on bank money counting machines have picked up so much microscopic traces of cocaine that those traces are passed on to nearly all U.S. currency. "Cocaine Money," *NewScientist* (UK), October 4, 1997, p. 2.

2. *Keeping Score*, Drug Strategies Inc., Washington, D.C., p. 32.

3. Centers for Disease Control and Prevention, "Advance Report of Final Mortality Statistics, 1994," *Monthly Vital Statistics Report*, September 1996, p. 58.

4. Dawn Day, *Health Emergency 1997: The Spread of Drug-Related AIDS among African Americans and Latinos*, Dogwood Center, Princeton, N.J., 1996, p. 1.

5. Ibid.

6. Ibid., p. 1.

7. Ibid., p. 20.

8. Wilhelmina A. Leigh, "Health of African American Youth," *Joint Center Fact Sheet*, Joint Center for Political and Economic Studies, Washington, D.C., n.d., p. 1.

9. "Minorities and HIV Infection," National Institute of Allergy and Infectious Diseases, National Institutes of Health, May 1997, p. 1.

10. Serge F. Kovaleski, "Poverty, Drug Abuse Fuel Caribbean AIDS Outbreak," Washington Post, January 14, 1998, p. A12.

11. Ibid.

12. Ibid.

13. Robert Pear, "AIDS Numbers Make a Giant Leap," *International Herald Tribune* (London), November 27, 1997, p. 1.

14. Ibid.

15. See Eric R. Lotke, "Hobbling a Generation," National Center on Institutions and Alternatives, Washington, D.C., August 1997, and Cheryl Thompson, "Washington, D.C., Young Blacks Entangled in Legal System," *Washington Post*, D.C., August 26, 1997, p. B1.

16. Lotke, "Hobbling a Generation."

17. Marc Mauer, "The Drug War's Unequal Justice," *The Drug Policy Letter*, Winter 1996, p. 11.

18. Ibid., p. 12.

19. Ibid., p. 11.

20. Lotke, "Hobbling a Generation."

21. "Half of Young Black Men in Nation's Capital In or Being Pursued by Criminal Justice System," *NewsBriefs*, September-October, 1996, p. 7.

22. Anti-Drug Abuse Act of 1988, Public Law No. 100–690.

23. Bureau of Justice Statistics, *Drugs, Crime and the Justice System*, a national report, Department of Justice, December 1992, p. 24.

24. U.S. Sentencing Commission, Monitoring Data Files, April 1–July 1, 1992. This was a representative sampling of all drug cases for FY 1992.

25. Jefferson Morley, "White Gram's Burden," *The Drug Policy Letter*, Winter 1996, p. 17.

26. Steven Holmes, "Black Lawmakers Criticize Clinton over Cocaine Sentencing," *New York Times*, July 24, 1997.

27. Patricia McRae and David Ackerman, "The Illegal Narcotics Trade (INT) as a TNC: Implications for the TNC/Government Interface," paper presented at the American Political Science Association annual conference, Washington, D.C., 1993, p. 1.

28. Alfred McCoy, *The Politics of Heroin: CIA Complicity in the Global Drug Trade* (New York: Lawrence Hill and Co., 1991), p. 2.

29. McRae and Ackerman, "The Illegal Narcotics Trade (INT) as a TNC," p. 1.

30. *The World Drug Report*, United Nations International Drug Control Programme, June 1997, p. 124.

31. Ibid.

32. Ibid., p. 31.

33. Ibid., p. 124.

34. Ibid., p. 123.

35. Dan Weikel, "Mexican Cartels Tied to State's Illicit Groves of Marijuana," *Los Angeles Times* (Washington edition), September 15, 1997, p. B1.

36. Gerri Smith, "Mexico's Drug Problems Are Also NAFTA's," *Business Week*, March 10, 1997.

37. Douglas Farah and Molly Moore, "Mexican Drug Traffickers Eclipse Colombian Cartels; Onetime Underlings Extend Reach into U.S.," *Washington Post*, March 30, 1997.

38. Manuel Castells, *End of Millennium* (Malden, Mass.: Blackwell, 1998), p. 202.

39. Ibid., p. 168.

40. Farah and Moore, op. cit.

41. Juanita Darling, "Nicaragua's Coastal Epidemic; A Deadly Habit is Devastating Miskito Communities on Nation's Remote Eastern Shores, *Los Angeles Times*, February 8, 1997.

42. Clyde H. Farnsworth, "Canada's Justice System Faces Charges of Racism," *New York Times*, January 28, 1996.

43. Ibid.

44. Ibid.

45. Ibid.

46. Brian Freemantle, *The Fix* (New York: Tom Doherty Associates, 1985), p. 32.

47. Henrik Kruger, *The Great Heroin Coup* (Boston: South End Press, 1980), pp. 14, 31.

48. McCoy, *Politics of Heroin*, p. 18.

49. Kruger, *The Great Heroin Coup*, p. 89.

50. McCoy, *Politics of Heroin*, p. 25.

51. Ibid., p. 19.

52. Ibid.

53. Ibid., p. 437.

54. Ibid., p. 438.

55. Ibid., p. 439.

56. Ibid., p. 478.

57. Ibid., p. 483.

58. "Drugs, Law Enforcement, and Foreign Policy," Subcommittee on Terrorism, Narcotics, and International Operations of the Committee on Foreign Relations, U.S. Senate, December 1988, p. 36.

59. In fact, the *Post*'s own ombudsperson criticized the paper's coverage of the CIA-Contra-Crack story. Geneva Overholser wrote, "The *Post* (among others) showed more energy for protecting the CIA from someone else's journalistic excesses." Geneva Overholser, "The CIA, Drugs, and the Press," *Washington Post*, November 10, 1996.

60. Ibid.

61. Ibid.

62. See articles by Gary Webb, *San Jose Mercury*, August 18–20, 1996 at http://www.sjmercury.com/drugs.

63. "CIA Official Sees No Evidence of Crack Role," *New York Times*, October 24, 1994.

64. Gary Webb, "America's 'Crack' Plague Has Roots in Nicaragua War," *San Jose Mercury*, August 18, 1996.

65. It should also be noted that Blandon sold automatic weapons and sophisticated communications equipment to Ross and his partner. At one point, he even tried to sell them a grenade launcher. See Gary Webb, "Testimony Links U.S. to Drugs-Guns Trade," *San Jose Mercury*, August 19, 1996.

66. Webb, "America's 'Crack' Plague Has Roots in Nicaragua War."

67. Douglas Farah, "Drug Dealer Depicted as Contra Fund-Raiser," *Washington Post*, October 6, 1996.

68. Ibid.

69. Doyle McManus, "Examining Charges of CIA Role in Crack Sales," *Los Angeles Times*, October 21, 1996.

70. Gary Webb, "Shadowy Origins of 'Crack' Epidemic," *San Jose Mercury*, August 19, 1996.

71. Ibid.

72. Ibid.

73. McManus, "CIA Role in Crack Sales."

74. "CIA Official Sees No Evidence of Crack Role," *New York Times*, October 24, 1994.

75. Quoted in John F. Kerry, "Organized Crime Goes Global While the U.S. Stays Home," *Washington Post*, May 11, 1997, p. C4.

76. Castells, *End of Millennium*, p. 172, note 13.

77. Rufus Schatzberg and Robert J. Kelly, *African American Organized Crime: A Social History* (New Brunswick, N.J.: Garland Publishing, 1997), p. 109.

78. Ibid., p. 110.

79. *Keeping Score*, Drug Strategies Inc., Washington, D.C., p. 19.

80. Ibid.

81. Ibid.

82. Ibid.

83. Jim Rua, *Treatment Works*, National Association of State Alcohol and Drug Abuse Directors, Washington, D.C., March 1990, pp. vi–vii. Also, see *Methadone Maintenance*, GAO Report to the Chairman, Select Committee on Narcotics Abuse and Control, House of Representatives, 1990.

CHAPTER 4

The International Convention on the Elimination of All Forms of Racial Discrimination: Implications for Challenging Racial Hierarchy

James Jennings

From July 23 to 25, 1900, thirty-two individuals from around the world gathered in London at the behest of Trinidadian barrister Henry Sylvester-Williams. The purpose of this meeting was to bring together delegates to serve under the first Pan-African Congress. At this meeting a Committee on Address to the Nations of the World was appointed with one of the delegates, W. E. B. DuBois, as its chair. In his committee report, shared with "sovereigns in whose realms are subjects of African descent," DuBois proposed the following:

> In the metropolis of the modern world, in this the closing year of the nineteenth century, there has been assembled a congress of men and women of African blood, to deliberate solemnly upon the present situation and outlook of the darker races of mankind. The problem of the twentieth century is the problem of the color line, the question as to how far differences of race—which show themselves chiefly in the color of the skin and the texture of the hair—will hereafter be made the basis of denying to over half the world the right of sharing to their utmost ability the opportunities and privileges of modern civilization.[1]

DuBois was touching on an issue that was not simply a problem of ignorance and misunderstanding, but more fundamentally one of power utilized to maintain colonialism and racial world order. DuBois' report is important for two reasons. First, it identifies the fact that the "color line" is significant. Second, it suggests that the nature of this division is not simply one of attitudes, or individual prejudices between groups of people, but, instead, a reflection of power and inequitable distributions of social, economic, and cultural resources. In a slightly different way, Richard Falk describes the enduring impact of issues related to race and ethnicity in the international arena, both in the current century and very likely the next one: "One of the great current problems of world order [is] . . . the condition and status of national minorities within sovereign states that have either historically subjugated these groups, or continue to force them to accommodate to a collective identity defined by the state's most powerful interests."[2] A quick survey of racial and ethnic tensions today, as well as a review of the plight of national minorities as suggested by Falk, illustrates that the next century will open with the same problem described by DuBois. In fact, it seems that U.S. problems associated with racial and ethnic divisions and consequent racial discrimination continue with frequency and intensity in many societies, as suggested in a recent study published by the Human Rights Watch: "The manipulation of ethnicity to further political ends [in 1996] was an ever-present factor" in Africa, Asia, Latin America, and Europe.[3] Thus, although initially adopted by the General Assembly of the United Nations on December 21, 1965, the International Convention on the Elimination of All Forms of Racial Discrimination continues to be relevant and to serve as a useful mechanism for understanding how to reduce or eradicate invidious racial and ethnic divisions as the twenty-first century unfolds.[4]

The convention was considered a major development in advancing human rights in the international arena. Despite this, the United States resisted its adoption and ratification for many years. There are several factors that explain this resistance. When the convention was first adopted by the United Nations, the United States was in the midst of the Cold War with the Soviet Union. The issue of human rights was treated at times as a political football between the two superpowers. Another factor underlying the United States' slow pace in ratifying the convention is the federalist structure of the U.S. government. Federalism may actually work to inhibit an aggressive posture toward human rights on the part of national administrations. Some treaties and agreements between the executive branch and international bodies had to be approved by the U.S. Senate, introducing another level of negotiations. Yet another factor molding the U.S. posture toward human rights is the relative political weakness of the Black community in this country— still a relevant explanation today. It was not until the passage of the Voting Rights Act of 1965, the same year that the convention was passed by the United Nations, that Blacks enjoyed the legal enforcement of their right to register and vote in elections. A politically stronger Black community would have possibly served to put pressure on government representatives to ratify the convention earlier than was the case.

Despite the fact that Blacks have the right to vote, however, the U.S. resistance to the strengthening and expansion of human rights continues in the current period. According to the Human Rights Watch, in 1996 "politically popular proposals made by Congress and the White House contributed to the accelerated erosion of basic due process and human rights protections in the United States. Despite his public proclamations in support of civil and human rights, President Bill Clinton displayed a startling lack of will to preserve rights under attack, and in some cases took the lead in eliminating human rights protections."[5]

Added to the factors above is the traditional U.S. posture that its own domestic arena is off limits to international bodies. As was observed some time ago by Dana Fisher, "Objections to accepting international human rights obligations via treaty have ranged from frivolous to reasonable concerns about conflicts with United States law. . . . There have been fears that the treaties would authorize what the Constitution prohibits even though the Supreme Court has always upheld the Constitution when there was a conflict."[6] Fisher continues: "Problems with the concept of economic and social rights will be formidable. The Constitution is silent on economic and social rights. In the American tradition the right to life has meant the right to the protection of a policeman, not to the services of a physician."[7] The differentiation of social and economic rights from political rights explains the limitations of U.S. approaches to the problem of racial discrimination.

Although the United States has realized much racial progress and has enunciated its stand, through legislation, court decisions, and amendments to its Constitution, that racial discrimination is no longer permissible, the state of race relations is in some ways similar to that described by the Kerner Commission report almost three decades ago—that is, that U.S. society is characterized by a deeply entrenched racial division.[8] In light of such continuing divisions, it is interesting that a cursory view of race relations in the United States today indicates that, at least compared to thirty years ago, certain racial conditions have vastly improved. And certainly, albeit to a limited degree, attitudes have changed toward wide support for values related to racial equality in the United States.[9] Regardless of this finding, a comprehensive assessment of race relations shows that racial divisions provide systemic advantages to Whites, at the expense of people of color, but especially Blacks. The distribution of economic, social, and cultural benefits in this nation reflects a well-ingrained hierarchy based on race. The existence of racial hierarchy, as well as its implicit approval and exploitation by representatives of White power structures, greatly limits the aim, reach, and ultimately the effectiveness of the convention.

Surveys showing a decline in the level of White prejudice toward Blacks in the United States are strikingly juxtaposed with the fact that the number of hate groups and incidents of racial harassment and violence is increasing. Further examples of concomitant support for the rhetoric but growing resistance to the implementation and actualization of racial equality include the approximately 2,900 incidents of racial harassment and violence reported across the United States between 1980 and 1986, including 121 murders, 138 bombings, and 302 assaults.[10] A 1989 report from the Southern Poverty Law Center states that hate violence based on race in the United States has reached a crisis stage. The report indicates that there are 230 known organized hate groups, and that more than half of all hate crimes in the past decade occurred during the last two years of the 1980s.[11]

While Black and White Americans seem to be interacting more in the workplace, residential segregation continues to be a major problem among racial and ethnic groups. A major work by Douglas Massey and Nancy Denton, appropriately titled *American Apartheid*, documents the fact that Black residential segregation is greater today than in previous periods, leading these two authors to use the term hypersegregation to describe this situation.[12] These authors state that "despite the optimism of the early 1970s, a comprehensive look at trends and patterns of racial segregation within large metropolitan areas in the ensuing decade provides little evidence that the residential color line has diminished in importance."[13] Thus, in spite of the extent and nature of racial progress realized in this country, "among the metropolitan areas where a large share of African Americans live, segregation persists at extremely high levels that far surpass the experience of other racial and ethnic minorities. In sixteen metropolitan areas that house one-third of the nation's Black population, racial separation is so intense that it can only be described as hypersegregation."[14] The authors conclude that hypersegregation of Blacks has become accepted by most Whites as a natural feature of this society.

In addition to residential segregation, there exists growing job segregation as pointed out by urbanist Edward J. Blakely and others.[15] Blakely describes a primary job market composed of the most desirable jobs and higher wages that is predominantly occupied by Whites, and a secondary job market of low-level service jobs where Blacks and Latinos appear in concentrated numbers. In particular, he notes, Black women are especially dominant in the lower-wage service sectors:

Workers in these [segregated] areas of the city are vulnerable to job shifts as economic cycles and lower-waged world labor markets produce volatile job movements. Furthermore, technological innovation might eliminate these jobs entirely. This form of employment segregation covers many occupational categories ranging from manufacturing to clerical areas. Individuals in this type of employment seldom have any job security and enjoy few benefits from their employers. Typical wages in these occupations average around $4.25 per hour, only marginally above the poverty line. As a consequence, individuals and/or families in most urban areas are forced to send more members of the family to work, including working-age children.[16]

It should be noted, again reflecting a racially divided society, that Blacks and Whites also hold different political attitudes regarding the extent of racial discrimination and the appropriate government responses to such discrimination.[17]

The apparent inconsistency between racial progress and continuing racial divisions, including major differences in the political attitudes of Blacks and Whites, can be explained by the concept of racial hierarchy, or what others have referred to as racial stratification or subordination. Racial hierarchy is the social fact that Blacks continually and consistently occupy positions lower in status than Whites, regardless of certain social, political, or economic advances that have been made by Blacks either as individuals or as a group. Racial hierarchy is manifested economically, educationally, culturally, and politically in all facets of life in the United States. Even when class factors are controlled, there is strong evidence of racial hierarchy in the United States. This means that even poor Whites in a context of racial hierarchy are much better off than poor Blacks; working-class Whites as well as middle-class Whites are much better off and enjoy a higher status than their Black counterparts. Other illustrations of racial hierarchy include the fact that female-headed White families are significantly better off than female-headed Black families; the poverty rate for Black families headed by a married couple is usually twice the rate of that for White families headed by a married couple; and unemployment rates for Blacks are generally higher than those of Whites with comparable levels of education.[18]

The consideration of the existence of racial hierarchy is key to understanding and ultimately eliminating racial discrimination. While legal responses to racial discrimination and bigotry might be effective at one level of social interaction, it is not enough to erase racial hierarchy. There are important differences between bigotry, discrimination, and racial hierarchy. Bigotry and discrimination involve attitudes felt by one group about another, or individual acts of harassment or violence that are directed at one group or exchanged between groups. Racial hierarchy involves a pervasive system of caste based on race. While bigotry and discrimination typically feature "horizontal" racial relations; racial hierarchy reflects a "vertical" order of domination. The differentiation of these concepts helps to illustrate why a legal apparatus that enforces antiracial discrimination does not solely guarantee the actualization of racial equality or social justice. Legality is far more effective in resolving horizontal relations that reflect bigotry and discrimination. But unless it is linked to human rights, legality is often ineffective in resolving vertical structures of domination based on race.

While the International Convention on the Elimination of All Forms of Racial Discrimination is limited insofar as it focuses on racial discrimination, it can serve as a mechanism or bridge to move this society from simple, legal responses to the problem to more comprehensive approaches of abolishing racial hierarchy. It can serve this purpose because it places the issue of racial discrimination within the context of the international arena and encourages nations to consider the basic rights that should be available to all people regardless of national boundaries. The focus on rights as they cross national boundaries also means that there is less intellectual and legal emphasis on the cultural, institutional, or political factors used to explain or justify the failure of societies in guaranteeing these rights. The focus is, rather, on human rights that should be enjoyed by all people, and thus all the obstacles to the existence of such a state, including racial hierarchy, must be examined and challenged. Furthermore, the convention, by making a strong linkage between human rights and racial discrimination, discourages a simplistic or purely legalistic definition of the latter concept. Thus, racial discrimination will exist as long as human rights are not directly addressed.

A review and analysis of the Convention by the International Human Rights Law Group states that "the Convention represents a milestone in the world's search for an end to discrimination on the basis of race, color, decent, and national or ethnic origin."[19] The definition of racial discrimination utilized by the convention is "any distinction, exclusion, restriction or preference based on race, colour, descent or national or ethnic origin which has the purpose or effect of nullifying or impairing the recognition, enjoyment or exercise on an equal footing, of human rights and fundamental freedom in the political, economic, social, cultural or any other field of public life."[20] This definition represents a broader conceptualization of racial discrimination than has been traditionally identified in the United States.

This last point is explained further by Y. N. Kly, who writes that "the concept of non-discrimination has traditionally been understood within the context of the right of individuals to equality before the law.

However, the right to non-discrimination in the human rights context includes the dimension of individual and collective affirmative action."[21] Effective responses to racial discrimination, therefore, have to incorporate the concept and social existence of national minorities and their own group interests in order to eliminate the basis and manifestations of racial discrimination. This approach is not inconsistent with but certainly greater than a focus on individual remedies to problems of racial discrimination. According to Kly, the definition of racial discrimination within a human rights context is supported by a range of legal instruments established internationally that are aimed at expanding human rights. Such support is reflected specifically in the "notion of 'effective remedy' . . . included in ART. 2.(3a) of the International Covenant on Civil and Political Rights and in ART. 6 of the Declaration on the Elimination of All Forms of Racial Discrimination."[22] Elevating the issue of racial discrimination to the arena of human rights leads one to approach racial hierarchy as a fundamental cause for continuing tensions between racial and ethnic groups.

Although frequently overlooked in public and scholarly dialogues in the United States, the relationship between racial discrimination and human rights is fundamental, as suggested by many observers including the late Supreme Court Associate Justice Thurgood Marshall.[23] He argued that civil rights aimed at preventing racial discrimination are strongly linked to the fate of human rights in a society. Justice Marshall observed that the fact that "the fates of equal rights and liberty rights are inexorably intertwined was never more apparent" than in the current period.[24] The weakening of the civil rights of minorities, he explained, actually facilitates challenges to the actualization and maintenance of human rights for other groups: "The Court's decisions last term put at risk not only the civil rights of minorities, but of all citizens. History teaches that when the Supreme Court has been willing to shortchange the equality rights of minority groups, other basic personal civil liberties like the right to free speech and to personal security against unreasonable searches and seizures are also threatened."[25] Thus, the link between eliminating racial discrimination and expanding traditional understandings of what encompasses human rights should not be overlooked.

This linkage is reviewed by political scientist Winston Langley in a research report, "Human Rights, Women and Third World Development," as it specifically applies to the human rights of women.[26] He summarizes some of the conventions of the United Nations and shows that increasingly the intersection of racial and gender discrimination is approached within a global framework of human rights. Urban affairs specialist Walter Stafford also notes the connection between racial discrimination and human rights when he observes that in "a period in which affirmative action laws are being weakened in the United States, it is important to assess how these policies and practices resonate with broader conceptions of racial discrimination and human rights."[27] Examination of this question is significant because placing racial discrimination and bigotry within a context of human rights represents a critical step in achieving fully the goals of the convention. This step includes exploring effective responses to problems like racial hierarchy in the United States and in the international arena. The proposition that combating overt racial discrimination through legal mechanisms is necessary though limited in advancing democracy and racial justice was expressed by President Lyndon B. Johnson on June 4, 1965, at the commencement ceremonies of Howard University in Washington, D.C. President Johnson suggested that legal solutions declaring racial discrimination illegal are not effective alone in expanding U.S. democracy and social justice:

> Freedom is not enough. You do not wipe away the scars of centuries by saying: Now you are free to go where you want, and do as you desire, and choose the leaders you please. You do not take a person who, for years, has been hobbled by chains and liberate him, bring him up to the starting line of a race and then say, "you are free to compete with all the others," and still justly believe that you have been completely fair. Thus it is not enough just to open the gate of opportunity. All our citizens must have the ability to walk through those gates. This is the next and the more profound stage of the battle for civil rights. We seek not just freedom but opportunity. We seek not just legal equity but human ability, not just equality as a right and a theory but equality as a fact and equality as a result. . . . To this end equal opportunity is essential, but not enough, not enough.[28]

The president proceeded to explain that for the great majority of Blacks who are poverty-stricken or continuously unemployed, "court orders and laws" and "legislative victories" are not adequate responses to their inequality.[29]

President Johnson's admonition was delivered almost a decade after the famous *Brown v. Board of Education of Topeka, Kansas* decision, which declared segregation unconstitutional. Johnson's call for a focus on substantive racial equality in areas like housing, health, economic development, and education, rather than stopping at the mere opening of the gate of opportunity, reflected the reasoning underlying the *Brown* decision. Donald E. Lively observes:

> A fundamental tenet of Brown was that desegregation was essential for equal educational opportunity and thus was a means rather than a mere end in itself. The Court thus characterized education as "the most

important function of state and local governments . . . success in life . . . [and] a right which must be made available to all on equal terms." Post-Brown jurisprudence largely has foreclosed the possibility of equal educational opportunity as a function of constitutional imperative. By concluding that education is not a fundamental right, wealth classifications are not suspect and racially disproportionate impact by itself is insufficient to establish constitutional responsibility, the Court has more than repudiated Brown's potential.[30]

President Johnson was proposing, in effect, that legal redress to the problem of racial discrimination is but a first step toward the realization of substantive racial equality. Such a state cannot be achieved by outlawing racial discrimination while at the same time ignoring and permitting the existence of racial hierarchy.

The Convention on the Elimination of All Forms of Racial Discrimination serves as a framework for identifying, first, racial discrimination as a major cause of social, political, and economic tensions throughout the world, and second, effective legal strategies for eliminating this problem across nations. Despite the urgency of these particular goals, the problem of racial hierarchy must be resolved in order to reduce the possibility of violence and tension and to implement the convention fully. In addition to its use as a legal and constitutional tool for eradicating racial discrimination in the United States and abroad, the convention and similar instruments can be effective in challenging the existence of social, economic, and cultural hierarchies that are also racialized. Such arrangements encourage and facilitate racial and ethnic discrimination and tension. Ignoring racial hierarchy limits the reach of the convention as a tool for eliminating racial discrimination.

In a review of earlier UN conventions and activities directed at the problem of discrimination against women, Langley cautions that

> if one defines concrete action in terms of ratification of or accession to the instruments in question, the states have done well, although not spectacularly. In the case of the most important convention, that on the Elimination of All Forms of Discrimination Against Women [CEDAW], over 85 nation-states have ratified or acceded to it. Indeed, at the beginning of 1985, some 74 states were parties to it; but, in honor of the end of the U.N. Decade for Women, some 30 or more states took the necessary steps to become parties thereto. However, ratification or accession, as important as they are, do not by themselves, mean much if nothing else is done. . . . One of these states that has ratified CEDAW is Egypt; yet, in 1985, as seen before, many of the rights enjoyed by women under a 1979 law were eliminated by a court decision. China also ratified the above-cited convention, but it has not foregone its traditional preference for zones. . . . And Zimbabwe, which is supposed to be one of the more progressive of Sub-Sahara African

states, has a constitution that bans discrimination on the basis of race, tribe, geography of origin, political opinion, or religious persuasion but omits sex on the basis that to do otherwise would be to offend traditional culture.[31]

This reminder is not intended to minimize or deny the significance of the work reflected in the convention, nor of much racial progress that has been realized in the United States as stated earlier.

As observed by Dr. Martin Luther King Jr., at the same time that the United States has achieved significant racial progress, in large part due to the legal reforms borne out of the civil rights movement, an entrenched hierarchy of race is a fact of life in this country. He wrote in his last major work, A Testament of Hope:

> The largest portion of White America is still poisoned by racism, which is as native to our soil as pine trees, sagebrush and buffalo grass. Equally native to us is the concept that gross exploitation of the Negro is acceptable, if not commendable. Many Whites who concede that Negroes should have equal access to public facilities and the untrammeled right to vote cannot understand that we do not intend to remain in the basement of the economic structure. . . . This incomprehension is a heavy burden in our efforts to win White allies for the long struggle.[32]

Similar to the sentiment described by King is the major conclusion of a national study involving numerous scholars focusing on race in the United States: that is, legal mechanisms may be established forbidding racial discrimination and calling for equality at the same time that racial stratification is strengthened. Referring to this study, E. Yvonne Moss and Wornie L. Reed note:

> Scholars in this study have sought to evaluate developments in race relations, particularly since 1940, by examining racial stratification, subordination, and change in various aspects of American life. Our general conclusion is that despite improvements in various aspects of American life, racial stratification has not changed in any fundamental sense. In addition to the structural mechanisms that perpetuate differential status, researchers point to social factors—attitudes, values, ideology, and racial violence—that reinforce racial domination. Legal doctrines and the courts have always provided justification and legality for whatever structural form the system of racial stratification has taken. Historically, the U.S. Constitution has been one of the primary supports for White supremacy.[33]

Moss and Reed continue that "the established image of 'equality' has meant that African Americans can possess all manner of civil rights in the abstract, but little property. Wealth remains in White hands so that even under this so-called equality the social results are the same. The equality doctrine both makes and justifies the prevailing inequalities. Mechanisms other than color distinction are employed to subjugate Black citizens. Growing disparities between Black and White Americans coincide with the legal expansion of equal rights."[34]

The issue of whether racial hierarchy is intentionally constructed and maintained is not as important as its very existence because the question of intent does not diminish the impact of such a hierarchy on the social conditions of Blacks. The existence of racial hierarchy and the evidence that it is indeed becoming more rigid suggest that racism is still a major problem for American society. Even if acts of bigotry could be somehow erased or eliminated today, we still could not assert that racism is no longer a problem. As long as Blacks systemically occupy social positions lower than Whites—that is, as long as racial hierarchy exists in this society—racism remains a significant problem. Racial hierarchy is fundamentally a social, economic, and cultural reality for Americans. Racism and racial discrimination emerge from and are facilitated by the existence of racial hierarchy, and legally preventing racial discrimination does not necessarily alter racial hierarchy.

While bigotry in the United States is still a significant concern in terms of race relations, it is not the critical problem that has to be resolved; rather, it is but a manifestation of a more fundamental issue. Bigotry is defined by sociologist Ellis Cashmore as any learned beliefs and values that lead an individual or group of individuals to be biased for or against members of a particular group. Technically, then, there is positive and negative prejudice, though, in race and ethnic relations, the term usually refers to the negative aspect where a group inherits or generates hostile views about a distinguishable group based on generalizations.[35]

Thus bigotry is any act of racially, ethnically, or religiously based prejudgment, harassment, or violence. As such, bigotry is not synonymous with racial hierarchy, although it is certainly a form of racial discrimination. Racism, in contrast, is the existence and institutional maintenance of a racial hierarchy in American society. This definition is similar to the definition of institutional racism utilized by the National Conference of Christians and Jews in 1972: "Any policy or practice of an institution which benefits one race at the expense of another. It is not the motivation of the institution or its members that counts. It is what results from the policy or practice that counts and determines whether that institution is racist."[36]

Bigotry, racism, and racial hierarchy are often treated similarly, which leads to faulty analysis of the state of race relations and thereby incomplete responses to racial discrimination. But it is a mistake to approach racism as insignificant based solely on the absence of signs of bigotry. As a result of this error, an interesting situation arises in which well-meaning people fight bigotry at the same time that they ignore— and therefore strengthen—racial hierarchy, which in turn gives rise to racism. This confusion is frequently reflected even among Whites who consider themselves liberal or progressive. Journalist Mimi Rosenburg, for example, writes that

> even while the White left participates in demonstrations against spe-
> cific acts of brutality, it has not taken on an organizational character
> to develop a systematic and long-range approach to racism. The White
> left has devoted little time to developing a theoretical perspective on
> the circumstances and state of consciousness of White people that per-
> mit White supremacist ideology to take hold. Even less effort has been
> spent evaluating how the White left's fundamental Euro-centric orien-
> tation has impeded our understanding of world affairs and constricted
> our vision of the process of social change. . . . We must identify racist
> ideas and then direct ourselves to the cultural apparatus that gives
> expression to them. The media, religious organizations and the school
> system are the dominant vehicles for the delivery of ideas.[37]

Generally, the dominant vehicles identified by Rosenburg reflect the existence of racial hierarchy.

We can reiterate this argument by using the metaphor that historian Peter Steinfels develops in his book *The Neo-Conservatives*: that many Whites approach racism in the United States as if it were merely graffiti on a solid brick wall of social justice and equality; but, in fact, it is big- otry that represents graffiti on a wall containing a major racial fault.[38] The absence of bigotry in a particular setting is not a guarantee of the absence of racism or racial hierarchy. An existing racial hierarchy is socially, economically, and culturally beneficial to Whites as a group. Racial hierarchy, as suggested earlier, is treated as a "natural" feature of society and therefore not considered in much of the analysis, or treat- ment, of racial discrimination. Donald Lively's point cited earlier regarding desegregation is resonant here: like desegregation, the out- lawing of racial discrimination has become an end rather than a means to a more just society.[39]

Sociologist Robert Blauner proposed that White Americans enjoy the benefits of a racial order even if they consciously abhor prejudice and racism: "It cannot be avoided, even by those who consciously reject the society and its privileges."[40] Psychologists W. H. Grier and P. M. Cobbs have argued similarly that racism has become prominent, almost natural, even among well-intentioned Whites: "The hatred of blacks has been so deeply bound up with being an American that it has been one of the first things new Americans learn and one of the last things old Americans forget. Such feelings have been elevated to a position of national character. . . . The nation has incorporated this oppression into itself in the form of folkways and storied traditions."[41] And in their book *The Bakke Case: The Politics of Inequality*, Joel Dreyfuss and Charles Lawrence state that the continuing rigidity of this "new racism is a major problem in overcoming the gap between the two American societies." They go on to state that the "greatest danger that the New Racism poses to minority efforts at equality is its assumptions that racism no longer exists, that Whites have finally overcome several hundred years of cultural reinforcement, and that they can make objective judgments about the ability and performance of minority-group individuals."[42]

The existence of racial hierarchy gives rise to certain ways of thinking about people of color generally, and Blacks in particular, which make it difficult for society to eliminate racial discrimination simply on the basis of legal instruments, without considering more comprehensive policy tools that go beyond legal redress as well. Eliminating racial hierarchy in the United States would require the elevation of Black life and community in the psyche of Whites and others in this society. This involves educational strategies that celebrate the nation's multiracialism. It involves political practices that seek to ensure the full participation of Blacks and other people of color in the electoral process. It means that governmental appointees would reflect the nation's racial diversity. And it means that Black communities could be places that do not overwhelmingly carry the burden of dilapidated housing, unemployed workers, or poverty-stricken individuals and families. Such widespread changes call for an expansion of social welfare policies as well as greater investment in the urban areas where most Blacks reside.

Incidents of racial bigotry occur frequently because Whites have been socialized to think of Blacks as somehow lower than or not as important as Whites. This socialization takes place because U.S. citizens constantly see and experience racial hierarchy and because they learn values within a framework of this hierarchy. The suggestion that a particular social and economic order leads to a way of racialized thinking calls to mind a recent observation by Adele D. Terrell, program director for the National Institute against Prejudice and Violence:

> My point is that the crossburnings and harassment which occur when an African-American family moves into a traditionally White neighborhood, or the name calling which occurs when an African-American student walks across an Ivy-League campus, or the racist cartoons that appear on the desk of the newly promoted African-American supervisor are all to some extent manifestations of the same thought process . . . [that includes] long-held beliefs that some groups of people are different and can be treated by different standards.[43]

Despite such caveats, many nations have responded to the problem of racial discrimination merely by relying on legal regulations prohibiting discrimination. Establishing such regulations without reference to the history of racial oppression or ongoing racial stratification in a particular society is not enough to wipe out racial discrimination. Ironically, as social scientist Paula Rothenberg argues, color-blind social policies that ignore racial differentiation and its impact in this society but that are nonetheless developed within a historical context of racism may actually perpetuate racial discrimination rather than eradicate it because racial hierarchy remains a fact of life.[44] In a similar vein, Lively writes that when the "presence and implications [of race] are pervasive and selectively unattended to, jurisprudence seriously confounds even the limited aims of the Fourteenth Amendment. The Court actually may impede progress toward real color blindness insofar as premature insistence on neutrality may deter morally inspired initiatives intended to remedy the consequences of past policy and practice."[45] If racial hierarchy is instead openly acknowledged, then public dialogue can move from the debate about the resolution of racial discrimination to a focus on what social justice and racial equality might look like in the United States.

Effective responses to racial hierarchy have to be more comprehensive in nature than merely legal solutions are. Bigotry on the campus or on the street, for example, may be lessened or eventually eliminated through legal action or even through an educational process that raises the level of awareness and respect for cultural and racial diversity. While the eradication of bigotry is an important social goal for all Americans, the demise of racial hierarchy, which facilitates both bigotry and racism, will take place only when Blacks and others have the political power to challenge and change both public and private institutional arrangements and practices that maintain racial hierarchy.

Overall, responses to racial discrimination in the United States reflect a strong commitment to the idea of pluralism, an ideology that posits that any group in society can organize freely in order to influence political decision making to get a response to its interests. And while some groups may win some favorable decisions, they may lose at other times, and, therefore, keeping the political system open and available for bargaining between groups is fundamental to any democratic society.[46] In part, this ideology of pluralism has discouraged U.S. leadership from treating the problem of racial discrimination as one of human rights. This occurs because it is presupposed that society is free and just, and that any deviation from such a state can be rectified by a person acting on his or her injured interests. But the suggestion that all people, including Blacks, simply can act effectively based on injured interests can be challenged in terms of U.S. history as well as the plethora of legal cases raised under the umbrella of discriminatory practices.

Again, noting the observations of Walter Stafford, "historically, the United States had refrained from ratifying the Covenants and the Convention because they went beyond the American concept of rights. The American conception of rights grew out of a commitment to government for limited purposes. This concept of negative rights . . . has emphasized civil and political rights that government activities must not violate."[47] But a review of the history of pluralism regarding race shows that this ideology has major limitations in its utility for eliminating racial discrimination or for advancing the social interests of masses of Blacks. A major finding of this critical literature is that social and legal analysis based on the presumption that the United States is a pluralist society by nature either overlooks issues related to race and class or simply negates the significance of race and class.[48] The ideology of pluralism permits this conceptual oversight because it does not consider the existence of racial hierarchy. Abstract appeals to the value of color blindness are utilized by pluralist apologists to justify this stance.

It is assumed by the leadership of some countries, including the United States, that racial discrimination is simply a problem of legality, and thus, once discrimination is outlawed and neutral, and once color-blind government regulations are applied equally to all citizens, society will have completed its task regarding racial and ethnic divisions. Such divisions may exist, it has been argued, but they are no longer the province of government. This was the stance of the United States in refusing to ratify the above convention over a long period of time unless its proposed changes were adopted. Despite a focus on legal technicalities, and even on what Justice Marshall referred to as "hypertechnical language games," recent U.S. history of racial discrimination reflects some ambivalence about a purely legal approach to eliminating racial discrimination.[49]

Affirmative action in the United States is an example of this ambivalence of the American public regarding effective responses to racial equality. Affirmative action, and other policies aimed at equipping Blacks, Latinos, and other communities of color as well as women with resources to make them more competitive and effective in the labor market, has significant political support. But at the same time, many others support the popular and electorally exploited notion that enough has been done about the problem of racial discrimination and that additional responses are unnecessary, as is suggested in the United States' responses to the convention. As Kly observes, "Thus far, however, the U.S. has not seen fit to give a fuller and more serious content to its affirmative action programs. In fact, it appears that the notion of affirmative action as introduced into the heavily social Darwinist–oriented American society (as a form of reverse job and education discrimination) has been predictably rejected."[50] Until the concept of racial hierarchy is considered, the validity of affirmative action as a tool remains confined by the issue of whether or not racial discrimination exists. Yet we now know that racial discrimination can be legally eliminated even in the presence and impact of racial hierarchy.

Although the United States has realized substantial legal advances aimed at ensuring racial equality, several recent Supreme Court decisions illustrate the tenuous status of laws and court decisions, considered critical by some, for moving American society toward social and racial equality. A shift has occurred in U.S. jurisprudence from the pursuit of substantive racial equality as reflected in the Warren Court, and particularly reflected in the *Brown* decision, to a response to racial discrimination by merely requiring the use of legal language that is color-blind. For instance, the decision in *Wards Cove Packing Company v. Antonio* shifts the burden of proof of invidious racial discrimination to the alleged victim of racial discrimination. The *Martin v. Wilks* decision gave White male employees of the Birmingham Fire Department the right to challenge a 1974 consent decree to hire qualified minorities, although these same White firemen were not employed at the time of the decree. The *Richmond v. Croson* decision outlawed a requirement that 30 percent of construction contracts be minority set-asides in the city of Richmond, Virginia. The program was established as a result of the finding that over a period of several decades Blacks comprising 30 percent of Richmond's population by 1990 had received less than 1 percent of all construction contracts from the city. And the *Runyon v. McCrary* decision made it more difficult for an alleged victim of discrimination to sue under one of the oldest civil rights laws in the United States—section 1981 of the 1877 Civil Rights Act.[51] Thus, while in some ways the country has initiated movement toward the idea of racial equality, it has also retarded this development significantly by insisting on a singular focus on racial discrimination.

One recent decision of the U.S. Supreme Court is useful in illustrating the limitations of approaching racial discrimination as simply an issue of rectifying legal aberrations in a fundamentally color-blind society. In the *Shaw v. Reno* decision, which dealt with the redrawing of voter districts in North Carolina and was submitted in the summer of 1993, the Supreme Court ruled that redistricting congressional boundaries resulting in Black representation is unconstitutional, even if the expressed purpose is to increase Black representation in regions with a history of Blacks lacking representation.[52] Writing for the 5-to-4 majority, Associate Justice Sandra Day O'Connor reasoned in part that racial "gerrymandering, even for remedial purposes, may balkanize us into competing racial factions." This presupposes that society has eliminated the racial balkanization described in the Kerner Commission report in 1968 and the continuing racial divisions documented in numerous studies since the 1960s. Associate Justice O'Connor argued further that redrawn districts that reflect racial considerations will encourage racial stereotyping and continue patterns of racial bloc voting. Her rationale seems to have been based on a profound faith in the notion that color blindness has been a value practiced in all arenas of social and economic life in this country.

Some of the conceptual and legal reasoning underlying the majority opinion is certainly not new. In fact, as suggested earlier, the argument that all should strive for a color-blind society has been used throughout U.S. history to defend the racial status quo with its hierarchy of Whites at the top and Blacks at the bottom. The social reality, as described by the eminent historian John Hope Franklin, is that the "color line is alive, well, and flourishing in the final decade of the twentieth century. It thrives because we have been desensitized to its significance over two centuries, and it permeates our thinking and our actions on matters as far apart figuratively as New York's Harlem and New York's Upper East Side, or an African American mayor of Los Angeles and the video-taped beating of Rodney King by four members of the Los Angeles Police Department."[53] Once again, the color line is not a recent occurrence but has strong historical roots in the United States.

In *The Black Laws in the Old Northwest* historian Stephen Middleton explains that under the Ordinance of 1787, the Northwest Territory of the United States was ordained to be a land free of slavery where Blacks were entitled to citizenship.[54] Yet despite the legal affirmation of racial equality, "clever White residents found ingenious ways to violate America's antislavery and civil rights document."[55] Middleton shows how states like Ohio passed "racially neutral" or "color-blind" legislation with the knowledge that Whites could easily continue subjugating Blacks economically and politically and thus maintain racial hierarchy, even though overt racial discrimination had been outlawed. In the 1990s, Justice O'Connor's reasoning regarding the existence of racial hierarchy has not progressed far from the position of powerful Whites trying to keep Blacks "in their place" in the 1790s. The position that racial discrimination is merely a matter of legality and, therefore, that the United States as a color-blind society has resolved the problem of race has encouraged some interests to challenge the very laws and legal interpretations that were passed to eliminate racial discrimination. This society is still at a stage where the constitutional propriety of its legal apparatus aimed at eradicating racial discrimination is debated. As suggested here, the Supreme Court of the United States has taken a lead role in encouraging this kind of debate. The United States and other nations will not resolve the problem of racial discrimination in the remaining years of this century, or in the next, without considering how this problem is intricately related to—and perpetuated by—racial hierarchy. While the convention is an important first step, it will flounder if the international community does not consider it as but a first step in building a more hopeful vision of life and society. Acknowledging the existence of racial hierarchy, and how it is maintained, is critical to understanding race relations and the deteriorating living conditions of Black people in the United States. As an idea, racial hierarchy can be used as a conceptual bridge by which to transform the issue of racial discrimination into a broader concern for human rights.

NOTES

1. Cited in Philip S. Foner, *W. E. B. DuBois Speaks: Speeches and Addresses, 1890–1919*, p. 125 (1977).

2. Richard Falk, "The Struggle of Indigenous Peoples and the Promise of National Political Communities," in *The Rights of Indigenous Peoples in International Law*, ed. Ruth Thompson, 1987.

3. Human Rights Watch, *Human Rights Watch World Report 1997*, p. 7 (1996).

4. International Convention on the Elimination of All Forms of Racial Discrimination, United Nations, General Assembly, December 21, 1965.

5. Human Rights Watch, *World Report*, p. 315, note 3.

6. Dana D. Fisher, "The International Protection of Human Rights," in *The Changing United Nations: Options for the United States*, ed. David A. Kay (1977), p. 51.

7. Ibid., p. 52.

8. See Kerner Commission; for a description and analysis of racial and economic divisions in the current period, see Judith W.Wegner (ed.), "Symposium, The Urban Crisis: The Kerner Commission Report Revisited," *North Carolina Law Review*, vol. 76 (1993).

9. For an overview and changes of racial attitudes in the United States since the Second World War, see Howard Schuman, Charlotte Steeh, and Lawrence Bobo, *Racial Attitudes in America* (1985). Sociologist A. Wade Smith shows that despite greater consensus among Whites in support of the values of social equality, White attitudes and Black attitudes have grown increasingly apart; see A. Wade Smith, "Racial Insularity at the Core: Contemporary American Racial Attitudes," *Trotter Review*, vol. 10 (Summer 1989). Professor of Politics and Public Affairs Jennifer L. Hochschild also discusses major attitudinal differences between Blacks and Whites in her book *Facing Up to the American Dream* (1995).

10. J. Guess, "Race: The Challenge of the 90s," *Crisis*, November 1989, p. 28.

11. Report, "White Supremacy and National Violence: A Decade of Review 1980–1990," Southern Poverty Law Center, Atlanta (December 1989).

12. Douglas S. Massey and Nancy A. Denton, *American Apartheid* (1992).

13. Ibid., p. 81.

14. Ibid.

15. Edward J. Blakely, *Planning Local Economic Development* (1994).

16. Ibid., p. 15.

17. See Schuman et al., *Racial Attitudes*; see also Smith, "Racial Insularity"; see also Hochschild, *Facing Up to the American Dream*.

18. For an overview of poverty and racial characteristics, see James Jennings, *Understanding the Nature of Poverty in Urban America* (1994).

19. Report, "U.S. Ratification of the International Convention on the Elimination of the Forces of Racial Discrimination: An Overview of United States Law," International Human Rights Law Group, Washington, D.C. (1994), p. 1. It should be noted that several observers have noted and discussed the limitations of legal restrictions against racial discrimination in completely eliminating this problem. See Committee on the Elimination of Racial Discrimination, *Human Rights Law Journal*, vol. 14 (1993), p. 249.

20. Ibid., p. 15.

21. Y. N. Kly, "Human Rights, American National Minorities, and Affirmative Action," *Black Scholar* 25 (Fall 1995), p. 25.

22. Ibid., p. 66.

23. Thurgood Marshall, Remarks Made at the Second Circuit Judicial Conference, September 8, 1989, *Trotter Review*, vol. 4 (Fall 1990).

24. Ibid., p. 4.

25. Ibid.

26. Winston E. Langley, "Human Rights, Women, and Third World Development," Research Report no. 7, Trotter Institute (1988).

27. Walter Stafford, "Human Rights and Racial Discrimination in the United States" (June 1996), p. 1.

28. Lyndon B. Johnson, "To Fulfill These Rights: Commencement Address at Howard University," June 4, 1965, in *Public Papers of the Presidents of the United States: Lyndon B. Johnson, 1965*, book 2 (1966), p. 636.

29. Ibid., p. 637.

30. Donald E. Lively, *The Constitution and Race*, p. 174 (1992). Lively makes reference to the following cases in this citation: *Brown v. Board of Education*, 347 U.S. 483, 493 (1954), and *San Antonio Independent School District v. Rodriguez*, 411 U.S. 1, 36 (1973).

31. Langley, "Human Rights, Women, and Third World Development," p. 40.

32. Martin Luther King Jr., "A Testament of Hope," in *A Testament of Hope: The Essential Writings of Martin Luther King*, ed. James M. Washington (1986), p. 316.

33. E. Yvonne Moss and Wornie L. Reed, "Stratification and Subordination: Change and Continuity in Race Relations," *Trotter Review*, vol. 4 (Summer 1990), p. 3.

34. Ibid., p. 4.

35. Ellis Cashmore, Dictionary of Race and Ethnic Relations (1994), p. 257.

36. This quote appears in Robert Blauner, *Racial Oppression in America* (1972).

37. Mimi Rosenburg, *The Guardian*, September 27, 1989.

38. Peter Steinfels, *The Neo-Conservatives* (1979).

39. Lively, *The Constitution and Race*.

40. Blauner, *Racial Oppression*, p. 23.

41. W. H. Grier and P. M. Cobbs, *Black Rage* (1968).

42. Joel Dreyfuss and Charles Lawrence, *The Bakke Case: The Politics of Inequality* (1979), p. 160.

43. Adele D. Terrell, Forum, National Institute against Prejudice and Violence, Baltimore, Md., September 1989.

44. Paula Rothenberg, "The Hand That Pushes the Rock," *Trotter Review*, vol. 3 (Summer 1989), p. 5.

45. Lively, *The Constitution and Race*, p. 178.

46. The literature describing and analyzing the political theory of this idea is enormous. A starting point, however, would be *The Federalist Papers* (Mentor Books, 1961) published in 1787 and 1788 by Alexander Hamilton, James Madison, and John Jay under the name of "Publius." Of the eighty-five essays in this work, essays 51 and 10 are particularly helpful in explaining the connection between "security for civil rights" and the maintenance of "multiplicity of interests" in society.

47. Stafford, "Human Rights," p. 2.

48. For a review and summary of major racial critiques of pluralism, see Herman George Jr., "Black America, the Underclass, and the Subordination Process," *Black Scholar*, vol. 19 (May/June 1988).

49. Marshall, "Remarks," p. 4.

50. Kly, "Human Rights," p. 67.

51. See *Wards Cove Packing Company v. Antonio*, 109 S.CT. 2115 (1989); *Martin v. Wilks*, 109 S.CT. 2180 (1989); *Richmond v. Croson*, 109 S.CT. 706 (1989); and *Runyon v. McCrary*, 427 U.S. 160 (1976).

52. See *Shaw v. Reno*, 113 S.CT. 2816, 125 L.Ed.2d 511 (1993).

53. John Hope Franklin, *The Color Line: Legacy for the Twenty-First Century*, p. 72 (1993).

54. Stephen Middleton, *The Black Laws in the Old Northwest: A Documentary History* (1993).

55. Ibid., p. xv, cited in Foner, *W. E. B. DuBois Speaks*.

CHAPTER 5

United States Human Rights Petitions before the UN

Charles P. Henry
and
Tunua Thrash

INTRODUCTION

On October 24, 1955, United States Representative Charles C. Diggs, one of three African Americans in Congress, wrote to United Nations Under-Secretary Ralph Bunche for assistance in "submitting the race question in America to the proper agency within the United Nations." Diggs added that he was essentially interested "in assuring political rights to all people—the right to vote to every United States citizen."[1] The Detroit congressman had recently traveled to Mississippi to attend the Emmett Till trial and professed a particular knowledge of intimidation in that state. Diggs had recently read a UN commission report on Africa and saw his objective as "the same as that of the British in submitting the problem of the race situation in Africa."[2]

Ironically, Diggs seemed unaware of previous attempts by Black Americans to lay their grievances before the international body including the first U.S. petition on human rights drafted in the congressman's hometown of Detroit at the National Negro Congress convention and submitted in 1946. Nor did he seem aware of the fact that Bunche, a fellow Detroiter and a co-founder of the National Negro Congress, had escorted W. E. B. DuBois to the UN Human Rights Commission in 1947 to present a much more extensive petition on behalf of the NAACP. Still Digg's interest in the UN machinery as a source of pressure for promoting domestic human rights compares favorably to the virtual absence of such interest in today's Congressional Black Caucus and domestic nongovernmental organizations (NGOs) concerned with racial issues.

RACE AND THE UNITED NATIONS

Race and the UN has a long and ignoble history. The pattern was cast by the UN's precursor, the League of Nations. At the Paris Peace Conference following World War I, Japan made strenuous efforts to insert a simple racial equality clause in the Convenant of the League. The attempt to secure "equal and just treatment in every respect, making no distinction either in law or in fact, on account of race or nationality"[3] attracted intense hostility. While the effort attracted worldwide attention it failed at the hands of President Woodrow Wilson. Shortly thereafter, the British Foreign Office issued a prophetic confidential memorandum that warned the issue was "highly combustible" and had "no cure." It stated that the "racial equality" question in its present stage,

> primarily concerns the following countries: Japan, China, British India, United States of America (especially California and the Pacific States), Canada, Australia, New Zealand, South Africa. The first three countries demand the right of free immigration and freedom from discriminatory disabilities for their nationals in the territories of the last five countries. The question can be regarded from an economic or from a political point of view, but in its essence it is a racial one.[4]

The memorandum noted that the races cannot and will not amalgamate and where immigration threatens the White race must remain dominant. "Only one of the aggrieved coloured races has acquired sufficient material strength to demand a hearing," stated the memorandum, "and that is Japan." The impact of Japan on the domestic situation of Japanese Americans had not gone unnoticed by Marcus Garvey, who drafted his own "UNIA Declaration of Rights" in 1920.[5]

With the rise of Adolph Hitler and World War II, the doctrine of racial superiority, which had been largely ignored by the League of Nations took center stage. Franklin Roosevelt gave early expression to the issue of human rights in his message to Congress in January 1941 and with the Atlantic Charter the foundations of a new international order were laid. As the UN began to take shape at the Dumbarton Oaks Conference in 1944, China, well aware of the Japanese efforts in Paris, again raised the issue of racial equality. China officially proposed two fundamental principles:

1. The International Organization shall be universal in character, to include eventually all states.
2. The principle of equality of all states and all races shall be upheld.[6]

Despite their fears that opposition to the principle of racial equality would seem to place them in sympathy with Nazi philosophy, the United States, Great Britain, and the Soviet Union successfully rejected the Chinese proposal. While the Chinese, as the only nation of color to participate in the preliminary talks, sought to "do something to give a moral tone to the character of the new organization," the only reference to human rights to emerge in the draft document was buried deep in a section dealing with economic and social cooperation.

That the issue was not buried at the organizing conference in San Francisco owed much to the participation of nations not represented at Dumbarton Oaks and pressure from NGOs. In the opening speeches to the conference, representatives of India, Haiti, and Uruguay promoted the ideals for which so many had suffered and died during the war, particularly the "repudiation of doctrines of racial division and discrimination."[7] Iraq argued that racial discrimination was a "Nazi philosophy" that had to be "discarded forever" in international relations while General Carlos Romulo of the Philippines reminded the delegates that many different races had fought in the Second World War together.

Three weeks into the conference, Edward R. Stettinius Jr., Secretary of State and head of the American delegation, admitted that the United States had moved to a more progressive stand on human rights and trusteeship due to public opinion and pressure from domestic groups. The Americans now supported amendments to the Dumbarton Oaks proposals that would guarantee freedom from discrimination on account of "race, language, religion, or sex." In addition, the United States agreed to support a trusteeship system but only for areas with League of Nations mandates, territories taken from the enemy in the war, or mandates and protectorates that nations might voluntarily surrender to the international organization.[8]

Although the trusteeship provisions fell short of an outright promise of independence to colonial peoples, the new U.S. position was a significant accomplishment for domestic NGOs. Three years earlier, NAACP leader Walter White, among others, had warned Roosevelt that peoples around the world would immediately see the Atlantic Charter and Declaration of the United Nations as confining human rights only to those of a particular race. The Committee on Africa, the War, and Peace Aims, organized by philanthropist Anson Phelps Stokes in 1941, produced a detailed study on *The Atlantic Charter and Africa from an American Standpoint* written by Stokes, Ralph Bunche, Charles S. Johnson,

Thomas Jesse Jones, Emory Ross, and Channing Tobias. The study declared the old colonialism had to go and suggested a gradual transition under international supervision to self-government for African countries. Other organizations adding their voice to the colonial question included the National Council of Negro Women who secured a special meeting with Assistant Secretary of State Archibald MacLeish. The NAACP through its board of directors on September 11, 1944, asked President Roosevelt to state clearly that the United States would not support the continuation of colonial exploitation. In two pamphlets, "What Does San Francisco Mean for the Negro" and "The San Francisco Conference and the Colonial Issue," the Council on African Affairs highlighted the importance of an effective international organization to questions of racial equality and colonialism.

Prior to the conference, DuBois and the NAACP sponsored a colonial conference at the 135th Street branch of the New York Public Library that attracted forty-nine representatives from the Caribbean, India, Southeast Asia, and Africa. On the eve of the San Francisco conference, a large Harlem rally sponsored by the Council on African Affairs, NAACP, West Indian National Council, and the Ethiopian World Federation emphasized the end of colonialism and imperialism as prerequisites for world peace and security. Although the NAACP, represented by Walter White, Mary McLeod Bethune, and DuBois, was the only Black organization among the forty-two American organizations that were official consultants to the United States delegation, other African American organizations sent observers. Moreover, Ralph Bunche was technical expert to the United States delegation and played a leading role in drafting the trusteeship language of the charter.[9]

Following the conference, Bethune organized a National Conference of Negro Leaders on June 23, 1945, in Washington, attended by fifty persons representing some thirty groups with a combined membership of more than eight million African Americans. The conference approved the UN charter with the understanding that under article 87, the Trusteeship Council could hear oral petitions from colonized peoples. The Council on African Affairs encouraged ratification of the charter even though it did not guarantee the advancement of colonial peoples. Similarly, DuBois endorsed the charter while questioning the absence of colonial representation on the Trusteeship Council and the right of oral petition without the consent of the specific colonial power. All agreed that the Trusteeship Council was an advance over the League of Nations mandates and a positive first step.[10]

At the beginning of the new charter article 1 listed among the major purposes that of achieving human rights and fundamental freedoms "for all without distinction as to race, sex, language, or religion." Article 13 repeated the same basic provision when discussing the activities of the General Assembly. Similarly, article 55 spoke of respect "for the principle of equal rights and self-determination of peoples" and the promotion of human rights without discrimination. Articles 62 and 68 reiterated these objectives in terms of the programs of the Economic and Social Council. Finally, articles 73 and 76, referring to the United Nations trusteeship system, stated that administration of these territories should be regarded as "a sacred trust" where there would be "just treatment" for individuals, "protection against abuses," and respect "for human rights and fundamental freedoms for all without distinction as to race, sex, language, or religion."[11]

Of course, endorsement of these high ideals by governments came at the equally high price of the supremacy of domestic jurisdiction. Few states, and certainly not the major powers, were willing to sacrifice elements of their sovereignty for the sake of human rights by authorizing the international community to intervene in their own internal affairs. When John Foster Dulles raised his concern that the human rights and nondiscrimination provisions might not create difficulties for "the Negro problem in the South," his American colleagues assured him that the inclusion of a domestic jurisdiction provision (article 2, paragraph 7) would preclude this possibility. In the words of Senator Tom Connally of the United States delegation, this article "was sufficient to overpower all other considerations."[12]

THE PETITIONS

Almost immediately, domestic NGOs utilized the new international organization to attack U.S. racism. At the Tenth Anniversary Convention of the National Negro Congress (NNC), the delegates voted to address a "Petition to the Economic and Social Council of the United Nations," and to append thereto the accompanying digest of "The Facts" on "The Oppression of the American Negro." The document was prepared by Marxist historian Herbert Aptheker and presented to representatives of the UN meeting at Hunter College in New York on June 6, 1946, by NNC President Max Yergan and Executive Secretary Revels Cayton. The petition was to be supported by a drive to obtain five million signatures endorsing the document. In addition, supplementary testimony on discrimination was to be collected at an "American People's Tribunal." The NNC placed a great deal of hope in the Soviet Union and small powers to advance the petition.[13]

The petition itself cited the relevant sections of the UN Charter pertaining to equal rights and the responsibilities of the Economic and

Social Council (ECOSOC) and its yet to be organized Human Rights Commission to protect minorities from racial oppression. Using statistics supplied by U.S. government documents, the petition summarized the gaps between Black and White Americans in terms of family income, occupations, housing, health, education, and other public services. It pointed out the restrictions on Black voting and civil liberties and noted the violence directed toward African Americans. The petitioners asked on behalf of 13 million Negro citizens that the UN:

1. Make such studies as it may deem necessary . . .
2. Make such recommendations and take such actions as it may deem proper . . .
3. Take such other and further steps as may seem just and proper to the end that the oppression of the American negro be brought to an end.[14]

While the NNC petition did not generate any formal action by the UN it did attract a good deal of international attention. As such it represented a last gasp of a dying organization. The National Negro Congress emerged from a conference in May 1935 at Howard University on the economic status of the Negro. Sponsored jointly by the Social Science Division of the University represented by Ralph Bunche and the Joint Committee on National Recovery directed by John P. Davis, the conference heard from a wide range of speakers including government officials, Communist leaders, domestic workers, laborers, agricultural workers, and civil rights leaders as well as academics. Following the conference, a select group of Black leaders met at Bunche's home—which was on the campus—to consider calling together a National Negro Congress. After a considerable promotion effort involving the distribution of 50,000 pamphlets, over 817 delegates representing some 585 organizations with an estimated 1.2 million members met in Chicago on February 14, 1936 for the first convention. Crowds of more than five thousand members of the public jammed the sessions as a broad array of groups ranging from Republican and Democrats to Garveyites and Communists debated the issues. Bunche thought the range of interests represented—which included Whites—was too broad to produce a coherent agenda. He had argued with Davis for an organization more focused on labor and lost. Therefore, Bunche played only a minor role in Chicago and was out of the country for much of the next two years. During his absence the Congress established active local councils across the country. Gunnar Myrdal commented that the NNC chapters were the most important Negro organizations in some cities. By 1940, however, Communists had come to dominate the proceedings and A. Philip Randolph was replaced as president by Max Yergan.[15] By 1946, the organization was a shell of its former self with little domestic credibility. Thus while the first UN General Assembly acted on a variety of other human rights items without waiting for recommendations from its yet to be convened human rights commission, it did not act on the NNC petition.

The attention the NNC petition attracted was not lost on W. E. B. DuBois who had been brought back to the NAACP in 1944 primarily to work on colonial and international issues. DuBois suggested to NAACP Executive Secretary Walter White that the organization consider submitting a more exhaustive petition to the UN noting "that other groups of people, notably the Indians of south Africa, the Jews of Palestine, the Indonesians and others are making similar petitions."[16] The NAACP had grown dramatically during World War II with 1,400 branches now enrolling over 452,000 members. With its new clout, the NAACP might force the U.S. government to live up to the ideals it reluctantly agreed to accept in San Francisco although mass pressure was a departure from the organization's usual strategy.

In a sense, the NAACP was returning to its original agenda, which linked it with the struggle of people of color and the colonized worldwide. The reference to "colored peoples" in the organization's name reflects this solidarity and the NAACP's first President (from 1910 to 1920) Moorfield Storey was also president of the American Anti-Imperialist League (1905 to 1920). Of course, DuBois the only Black executive officer of the original NAACP, was at the Paris Peace Conference to urge the end of colonialism. The NAACP gave him official leave of absence and a modest appropriation of funds to assist in the organizing of four Pan African Congresses beginning in Paris in 1919.[17]

Ralph Bunche escorted DuBois to the Commission on Human Rights to present the ninety-four-page NAACP petition, *An Appeal to the World*, to the commission's director, John Humphrey. It was divided into six sections with each section having an individual author. DuBois wrote the introduction; Earl B. Dickersen, an assistant attorney general of Illinois and president of the National Bar Association, wrote section II—"The Denial of Legal Rights of American Negroes: 1787–1914," Cornell Professor Milton R. Konvitz prepared the third section entitled "The Legal Status of Americans of Negro Descent since World War I"; section IV was prepared by Chicago attorney William K. Ming Jr. and dealt with "The Present Legal and Social Status of the American Negro"; "Patterns of Discrimination in Fundamental Human Rights" was written by an attorney and former social worker, Leslie A. Perry; the final section on "The Charter of the United Nations and Its Provisions for Human Rights and the Rights of Minorities and Decisions Already Taken under This Charter" was written by Howard University historian Rayford W. Logan. The heavily legalistic and scholarly tone of the petition may be contrasted to the much shorter presentation of economic and sociological indicators in the NNC petition and the more militant tone of the Civil Rights Congress petition in 1951.

Hundreds of African American organizations endorsed the petitions including the NNC, the Council on African Affairs, the National Baptist Convention, the National Fraternal Council of Negro Churches, the Urban League, the National Association of Colored Women, the Congress of Industrial Organizations (the American Federation of Labor [AFL] agreed to help), the National Medical Association, the Negro Newspaper Publishers Association, the National Bar Association, the Southern Negro Youth Congress, Black fraternities and sororities, Adam Clayton Powell, Senator Arthur Capper, and Mary McLeod Bethune. International support came from the Trades Union Congress of Jamaica, Jomo Kenyatta, the Caribbean Labor Congress, the Kenyan African Union, Nnamdi Azikiwe and the National Council of Nigeria and the Cameroons, Kwame Nkrumah of the West African National Secretariat, the Nyasland African Congress and Liberia. News of the petition was widely reported in the colonial press and socialist press.

Apparently this attention was the primary goal of the petition since the action requested by the petitioners was very vague. After demonstrating that the discrimination practiced in the United States also infringed upon the rights of visitors to the United States as well as the ideals of the UN, DuBois asked that "the organization in the proper way take cognizance of a situation which deprives this group of their rights as men and citizens, and by doing so makes the functioning of the United Nations more difficult, if not in many cases impossible." [18]

Madame Pandit of the Indian delegation vowed to place it before the Assembly or the Economic and Social Council and support came from Pakistan, Poland, Egypt, Ethiopia, Belgium, Haiti, Mexico, Norway, China, the Soviet Union, and the Dominican Republic. The Soviet Union played a leading role in promoting the petition, which drew the ire of U.S. officials. Nonetheless, the "humiliation" of the U.S. government led to an enlarged and strengthed Civil Rights Division of the Justice Department.

Unfortunately, the petition itself faired no better than the NNC petition. The opposition was led by Eleanor Roosevelt, a U.S. delegate to the commission and an NAACP board member. She believed it would be an embarrassment to the United States to have its racial practices discussed in an international forum and added that it was an affront for any other country to sponsor the petition. Mrs. Roosevelt and commission director Humphrey also believed the petition might negatively influence passage of the International Bill of Rights being drafted by the commission. DuBois responded that Roosevelt and Humphrey "have buried complaints and drowned themselves in a flood of generalities by seeking to re-write in verbal platitudes of tens of thousands of words, those statements on human rights which the American Declaration of Independence and the French Declaration of the Rights of Man set down a century and a half ago in imperishable phrase which no man can better today."[19] Humphrey suggested the petition be sent to the Subcommission in the Prevention of Discrimination and Protection of Minorities.[20] At the subcommission, despite intense lobbying by DuBois, the petition was voted down four to one with seven abstentions. The United States voted no.

On December 9, 1948, the General Assembly of the UN adopted the Genocide Convention, which defines genocide as any killings on the basis of race, or, in its specific words, as "killing members of the group." When the convention entered into force in 1951 with twenty states ratifying it—the United States signed it but did not ratify the convention until 1988—the Civil Rights Congress submitted a petition under this treaty charging genocide against Black people in the United States by interpretation of article II of the convention. According to article II of the Genocide Convention the crime of genocide carries the following meaning:

> Any of the following acts committed with intent to destroy, in whole or in part, a national ethnical, racial or religious group as such:
>
> (a) Killing members of the group
> (b) Causing serious bodily or mental harm to the members of the group
> (c) Deliberately inflicting on the group conditions of life calculated to bring about its physical destruction in whole or in part
> (d) Imposing measures intended to prevent births within the group
> (e) Forcibly transferring children of the group to another group.[21]

The petitioners of the Civil Rights Congress (CRC) set out to prove that the majority of these criteria applied to the plight of Black Americans in the United States.

> Under Article II of the Convention it provides that the following acts shall be punishable:
>
> (a) Genocide
> (b) Conspiracy to commit genocide
> (c) Direct and public incitement to commit genocide
> (d) Attempt to commit genocide
> (e) Complicity in genocide

Through the use of citing incidents reported by individuals, newspapers, and research institutions the CRC charges genocide citing the president of the United States, the United States Congress, the United States Supreme Court, and the United States Department of Justice of being guilty with complicity of genocide.

The Civil Rights Congress existed for a decade, from 1946 to 1956, with the dual goals of fighting racism and anticommunism. Consisting of former members of the National Negro Congress, the International Labor Defense, and the National Federation for Constitutional Liberties, its attorneys won a number of civil liberties rulings that expanded the rights of all in the United States. These rulings included cases involving extradition, standing, excessive bail, the right to be silent before a grand jury and others. Long before it became fashionable, the CRC fought for and won an affirmative action or quotas case involving Black supermarket employees in California. The fact that Communist Party USA members were strongly tied to the CRC meant that the latter was a target for red-baiting. Thus, the Cold War had the ironic effect of precipitating the persecution of radical leaders by government officials and at the same time advancing civil rights for Blacks to avoid international embarrassment of these same officials.[22]

Protecting the rights of minorities is a theme that runs throughout the three petitions as a means to maintaining peace around the world. The threat of war was one of the compelling reasons behind the establishment of the Genocide Convention, "Genocide became an international crime because it was an international danger . . . it must be of world concern when that treatment includes a war breeding genocide that may engulf the world."[23] Genocide in this case against any group, including the Negro is a threat to all people. "We plead for all mankind," the CRC reminds the UN.[24] Calling on the UN to follow through with its obligations to maintain peace and international security, all three petitioning bodies agreed that the United States' racist tendencies could have a negative impact on the rest of the world.

The CRC, led by Black attorney William Patterson, asked the UN to find the United States guilty of genocide against the Negro people of the United States. It asked for a condemnation of the United States for failure to implement and observe its international obligations and it requested UN action under the charter for the prevention and suppression of acts of genocide. Like the earlier petitions, the United States was able to prevent any formal consideration of their requests.

However, unlike the immediate postwar period of optimism in which the earlier petitions were submitted, the United States was now engaged fully in the Cold War. In August, 1950, the U.S. government revoked the passport of Paul Robeson for eight years. The following year, DuBois—now a leader of the anti–atomic bomb movement—was indicted for allegedly serving as an agent of a foreign power.[25] The Civil Rights Congress itself was the target of government repression and its Executive Secretary, Patterson, had his passport seized by the State Department. The submission of the CRC's petition played a role in the introduction of a constitutional amendment by fifty-five U.S. senators to bar the constitution from being overridden by treaties and executive agreements such as the Genocide Convention. Senator John Bricker of Ohio led these isolationist efforts and "Brickerism" was only stopped when President Eisenhower agreed not to sign or pursue ratification of any international treaties.[26] Ironically, the United States, which had forced the commission to issue a nonbinding declaration first and divide the Human Rights Covenant into two separate documents now withdrew totally and work on the convenants was de-emphasized until 1966.

It would be grossly misleading to state that the early petitions to the UN were counterproductive. For example, in 1947 the President's Committee on Civil Rights cited our domestic civil rights shortcomings as a serious obstacle undermining U.S. influence in foreign policy. Citing the then Acting Secretary of State Dean Acheson to the effect that "it is quite obvious . . . that the existence of discriminations against minority groups in the United States is a handicap in our relations with other countries,"[27] the committee called for a significant strengthening of the machinery for protecting civil rights. In a 1948 decision, four justices of the U.S. Supreme Court noted the importance of the charter's nondiscrimination provisions in *Oyama v. California*. The Court found that a California statute that excluded Japanese from certain categories of land ownership violated the Fourteenth Amendment. In a concurring opinion Associate Justice Murphy described the law as "designed to effectuate a purely racial discrimination." Justices Black, Douglas, and Rutledge joined Murphy in maintaining that as a matter of national policy the United States should honor its pledge to respect the UN Charter's human rights provisions.[28] Shortly after this decision, the Supreme Court struck down racially restrictive private real estate covenants in the famous *Shelley v. Kraemer* case. Throughout the proceedings, the petitioners as well as many briefs filed as *amici curiae* cited the human rights and nondiscrimination provisions of the UN Charter. The attorney general and solicitor general noted that the United States has been embarrassed in the conduct of foreign relations by acts of discrimination taking place in this country.[29] And of course the most famous civil rights case of the twentieth century, the *Brown* case, has been frequently cited as an example of the influence of foreign opinion on domestic race relations. While the UN Charter was not specifically cited by the plaintiffs in *Brown*, it was cited in the companion case *Bolling v. Sharpe*.[30]

THE PETITION PROCESS

The United Nations is first and foremost an organization of govern-ments. Its primary concern was and is state-to-state relations. The peti-tion process undermined governmental control of the international agenda by opening up the system for issues presented by ordinary citi-zens and NGOs. Therefore, the petition process is regarded with suspi-cion by most governments and given little support.

Most of the UN bodies that receive petitions or individuals operate in the areas of decolonization and racial discrimination. The split between "activist" and "passivist" states in regard to human rights peti-tions became evident at the second meeting of the Commission on Human Rights. The secretariat, not the delegates, made the decision not to present all communications to the commission but to prepare a list of received communications with names withheld to protect the petitioners from possible repercussions. At the third session, General Romulo of the Philippines expressed the view that after the International Declaration on Human Rights was adopted, he expected the commission to serve as a kind of Supreme Court of Appeal for plaintiffs all over the world. Mr. Ebeid of Egypt questioned what means were available to the commis-sion to remedy any problems reported to it. At this point, Mrs. Roo-sevelt said that, for the moment, the commission had no power to con-duct an inquiry or to put its recommendations into force but only to submit them to the Economic and Social Council.[31]

Those members of the commission who were opposed to an activist role for the UN in the area of communications were the United King-dom, Australia, and the USSR. Apparently their influence was decisive when the commission took the unusual step of recognizing in its report to ECOSOC "that it ha[d] no power to take any action in regard to any complaints concerning human rights."[32] Two attempts to soften this gap between rhetoric and action by Rene Cassin of France and by Mrs. Roo-sevelt were voted down by the commission with the opposition led by the Australian delegation.

The Economic and Social Council quickly endorsed the commis-sion's statement that it had no power to act on human rights complaints prompting an unprecedented move by the Secretary-General. Stating that the commission's position, though technically correct, undermined the status of the UN as an organization, he invited the commission to reconsider its stand on the issue of petitions. The commission ignored the invitation.

Major changes in the petition process did not occur until 1970 and they were the result of the decolonization process. In 1960, when sev-enteen new African states joined the UN, the General Assembly adopted the Declaration on the Granting of Independence to Colonial Countries and Peoples. The Special Committee created on implementation of the declaration was directed by the assembly to both receive written petitions and hear petitioners. As a direct result of the Special Committee's work ECOSOC invited the Commission on Human Rights (in 1966) to examine violations of human rights and fundamental freedoms in all countries. This more activist commission was faced with the task of creating more effective procedures including the petition process. What eventually emerged from the new machinery in 1970 was ECOSOC Resolution 1503. This resolution set out a detailed procedure for dealing with complaints about violations of human rights that began with a working group appointed by the subcommission that received a confidential list of communications containing complaints about human rights violations and any government responses on a monthly basis. The full subcommission decided whether to refer particular situations involving a "consistent pattern of gross and reliably attested violations of human rights" to the commission. Once a situation had been referred to the commission it could either study the situation itself and report with recommendations to ECOSOC or it could set up an ad hoc committee to investigate the situation.[33]

Under the 1503 procedure, the United States is regularly charged with fundamental human rights violations. In recent years, the commission has received seventy to eighty petitions a year regarding human rights violations in the United States. The overwhelming majority of these petitions concern three areas—prison conditions, Indian land claims, and the incarceration of political prisoners (Puerto Rican nationalists and members of the Black Panther Party). Each year the U.S. State Department coordinates a response to each petition and submits it to the commission that has never formally acted on such a petition.

COVENANTS AND CONVENTIONS

While the primary vehicle for bringing human rights complaints to the United Nations has been the petition process, other avenues of redress are also available. As seen in the Civil Rights Congress petition on genocide, UN covenants and conventions are also vehicles of expression. There are currently approximately thirty such covenants, conventions, and declarations. The most far-reaching of these international instruments have monitoring bodies that oversee their implementation and require ratifying states to report on the status of specific rights in that country.

As we have seen, the Cold War and domestic appeals to the UN caused conservatives in this country to withdraw from any commitments to these international instruments. However, with the end of the Cold War the United States has slowly moved to ratify some of the less controversial treaties. After forty years of consideration, the United States ratified the Genocide Convention at the end of the Reagan administration in 1988. In October 1990, the Senate gave its advice and consent to ratification of the Convention Against Torture and Other Cruel, Inhuman and Degrading Treatment or Punishment. The necessary implementing legislation for that treaty was not enacted until the Clinton administration and the instrument of ratification was deposited with the UN.

In 1992, the United States ratified the ILO Forced Labor Convention (No. 150) as well as the International Covenant on Civil and Political Rights. This covenant along with the International Covenant on Economic, Social and Cultural Rights, the Convention on the Elimination of All Forms of Racial Discrimination, and the American Convention on Human Rights were all signed by President Jimmy Carter in 1978 and sent to the Senate for consideration. The Senate Foreign Relation Committee held hearings on all four in November 1979 but took no further action.

Ratification of the International Covenant on Civil and Political Rights (ICCPR) commits the United States to such basic rights as the right to vote and to participate in government, freedom of peaceful assembly, equal protection of the law, the right to liberty and security, and freedom of opinion and expression. The United States made several reservations in ratifying the treaty—some to prevent conflict with our own Bill of Rights and others to prohibit any expansion of rights in areas not already covered by domestic law. The most important reservation, which the United States has required of every treaty, is that it is non–self-executing. That is, provisions of the convention cannot become basis for legal action without reference to comparable national law.

Despite these very significant reservations, the ICCPR has already become a source of domestic activism and controversy. Under provisions of the covenant the United States is required to disseminate the covenant and report on a regular basis to the treaty's monitoring body, the Human Rights Committee. In the fall of 1994, the United States filed its report on political and civil rights in the United States with the Human Rights Committee. This was the first report ever by the U.S. government to an international body on civil and political rights in the United States. While the 200-plus-page report is largely an examination of federal laws and their compliance with provisions of the ICCPR, the brief introduction by Assistant Secretary of State John Shattuck, which acknowledged the gross human rights violations against African Americans, Native Americans, and women, came under intense fire by conservatives. Shattuck and other federal officials from the Justice Department, the Bureau of Indian Affairs, and the Department of Education were called on to defend the report and answer questions from Human Rights Committee members in March 1995 at the UN headquarters in New York. In his remarks at this public session, Shattuck stated that the United States "was equally committed to the principle of equal protection and non-discrimination which underly the racial, ethnic and religious diversity of our democratic society."[34] Several committee experts posed questions concerning prison conditions, the death penalty, the voting status of Washington, D.C. residents, "English only" rules, voter registration and participation, immigration practices, and Indian self-government. The report and the U.S. responses to the Human Rights Committee went virtually unreported in Black-oriented media, and domestic NGOs like the NAACP and Urban League were invisible at the committee sessions. Other NGOs such as Amnesty International, Human Rights Watch, and the American Civil Liberties Union were present. In fact, a joint Human Rights Watch and American Civil Liberties Union report entitled *Human Rights Violations in the United States* provided an important critique of U.S. compliance with the ICCPR that the U.S. government was forced to address.

The Clinton administration gave first priority to ratification of the Convention on the Elimination of All Forms of Racial Discrimination, which had been adopted by the UN in 1965 and signed by the United States in 1966. In May 1994 the Senate Foreign Relations Committee unanimously approved the administration's proposed package of reservations, understandings, and declarations and the full Senate consented to ratification shortly thereafter. Along with the declaration that the treaty is not self-executing, the reservations prohibit any restriction of free speech (the "hate" speech issue), deny any obligation to enact legislation dealing with "private conduct," and demand the consent of the U.S. government before any case can be brought to the International Court of Justice. There is also an understanding that makes a distinction between federal and state implementation.

The United States pursued a course of silence during consideration of the Race Convention and consequently few persons outside the government and human rights organizations are aware that it is in force. Wade Henderson, director of the Washington office of the NAACP, testified at the Senate hearings on the treaty, but the NAACP declined an offer from the State Department to discuss the convention at the organization's 1995 annual meeting. There is a general lack of interest in the convention among domestic civil rights groups despite the fact that the treaty deals with such current issues as affirmative action and that a report on U.S. compliance under the treaty is due this year.

OTHER MECHANISMS

The UN and the commission on Human Rights also have at their disposal a variety of special programs and special rapporteurs that deal with important international issues. As a part of the UN's Programme of Action for the Second Decade to Combat Racism and Racial Discrimination, the Commission of Human Rights asked the special rapporteur on contemporary forms of racism, racial discrimination, xenophobia, and related forms of intolerance to undertake missions to specific countries and report his findings to the commission. In October 1994, the special rapporteur, Maurice Glele-Ahanhanzo of Benin, undertook a mission to the United States. He adopted the following eleven focal points for his investigation: health, education, housing, employment, political participation, criminal justice and the application of the death penalty, police violence, incitement to racial hatred, anti-Semitism, migrant workers, and asylum seekers. Together with an official from the UN Centre for Human Rights, the special rapporteur visited Washington, D.C., New York, Los Angeles, and Atlanta. He met with a number of federal and local officials and representatives from a variety of NGOs including the African American, Mexican American, Asian American, Arab American, Indian American, and Jewish communities. He even met with Mexican governmental officials in the United States on the problems of migrant workers and Mexican immigrants.

His forty-plus-page report along with its twelve sweeping recommendations proved intensely interesting to delegates from "developing" countries attending the 1995 session of the commission in Geneva. In its written response to the report, the United States said the following:

> While there is much to commend in your report, the emphasis tends to be on economic, cultural and social rights. Recognizing that such rights are co-equal in status with civil and political rights, the report tends to downplay the remarkable progress made by minorities in civil and political rights during the last 50 years.[35]

In a statement to the Commission on Human Rights, the U.S. representative stated that "no country had gone as far as the United States in implementing so comprehensive an array of legal measures against racial and ethnic discrimination in voting rights, housing, employment and access to public services."[36] The government noted that it was paying particular attention to your recommendations but added that "conduct by private actors and social and economic forces (are) not readily subject to government action."[37]

The special rapporteurs report was complimented by the World Council of Churches Tribunal on Racism in the United States, which after yearlong hearings in the United States culminated in a forum at the commission meeting in Geneva. The tribunal supported many of the findings made by the special rapporteur and was attended by representatives of the U.S. government. In an oral intervention under Item 16 of the commission's agenda, the World Council raised its concern and made several recommendations to combat racism and racial discrimination in the United States. Its International Eminent Persons Team that participated in the hearings in the United States heard a great deal of testimony on the Crime Bill being considered by Congress in 1994. They expressed their dismay that the Racial Discrimination Clause was excluded from the Violent Crime Control and Law Enforcement Act of 1994 and that over fifty new crimes are now punishable by death. The World Council's intervention also cited the publication of the book *The Bell Curve* and stated "that there seems to be a disturbing alliance between these eugenics scholars and the new conservative right in the United States; much of Mr. Newt Gingrich's Contract with America parallels the policy proposals in *The Bell Curve*." Finally, the World Council concluded that for the first time U.S. citizens were now seeing these violations as human rights violations with international avenues of recourse rather than civil rights violations with only domestic remedies.[38] Unfortunately, as this work has attempted to demonstrate, domestic awareness of international mechanisms that address racial discrimination seem to be at an all-time low rather than on the rise.

Although the commission report and the tribunal marked one of the most thorough discussion ever of U.S. racial practices in an international governmental forum, the events and their findings were largely ignored by the media. If anything, the events in Geneva were more widely reported among opponents of "internationalization of the issue" rather than its supporters. For example, the *Washington Times* quoted Howard University Professor Russell Adams as saying, "the problem with hearings and executive reports . . . is that they can miss the subtle process of social progress." He added that "this is the weakness of traveling shows . . . they are absolutist. We have gone from A to C and they want us at Z."[39]

CONCLUSION

The post–Cold War world offers the best opportunity since the 1940s to build an international society promoting peace and resting on equal justice. As Malcolm pointed out in the 1960s, a purely nationalist attitude is limiting in scope and promotes minority thinking. It was only with the end of the Cold War that the United States began to ratify some of the major international human rights instruments that it had helped give birth to. Even with reservations these treaties can expand domestic human rights laws. For example, the Convention of the Elimination of All Forms of Discrimination Against Women and the Convention of the Rights of the Child have both been signed by President Clinton and contain important guarantees affecting Black women and children. They also provide excellent opportunities to form coalitions with other groups interested in expanding human rights and fundamental freedoms. Yet there is little pressure on the Senate to hold hearings and consent to ratification.

Even less promising are the prospects for ratification of the International Covenant on Economic, Social and Cultural Rights. This covenant is cited by many as one of the two most important international human rights documents along with the International Covenant on Civil and Political Rights. In his address to the World Conference on Human Rights in Vienna in 1993, Secretary of State Warren Christopher promised that the Clinton administration would make ratification of the Covenant a top priority. Certainly, such Black leaders as Martin Luther King Jr. and Malcolm X recognized that the Civil Rights Movement had shifted to a focus on economic rights. Yet the prospects for action are even dimmer than those of the more specific coventions dealing with women and children.[40]

Currently 130 countries have ratified the covenant. Not only has the United States not ratified the covenant but it has hindered the convenant's implementation. The United States insisted on two separate convenants and then worked to ensure that the economic covenant's language was "softer" than its political twin. While the latter resounded with legal vigor and enforceable rights including an Optional Protocol that invited individual and state complaints, the former only expects states "to take steps . . . to the maximum of its available resources" to achieve the rights proclaimed in the covenant. Moreover, in 1985 when the UN's Economic and Social Council established an expert Committee on Economic, Social and Cultural Rights, the United States was the only member state to cast a negative vote. Of course, until recently the United States government has been quite open in stating its preference for political and civil rights. It is not alone in that the vast majority of nongovernmental organizations in the United States emphasize political and civil rights almost exclusively.

The early human rights petitions discussed in this chapter met with virtually no success in a formal sense. However, the publicity surrounding their submission performed a valuable public education function that eventually resulted in concrete pressures for change. Moreover, the coalition of domestic groups brought together by these human rights petitions stands in stark contrast to the "world tours" taken by some Black leaders today as well as the international conferences on business development among Africans and the diaspora.

Two factors have fundamentally changed the UN environment that confronted the NNC, NAACP, and the CRC. By 1960, the entrance of a substantial number of former colonial states into the UN and the development of the nonaligned movement enhanced the role of the General Assembly and challenged the dominance of the major powers. One result, for example, was the development of a whole new area of rights now labeled "solidarity rights."

A second fundamental shift was the proliferation of nongovernmental organizations. At the international level this development is best symbolized by the awarding of the Nobel Peace Prize to Amnesty International in 1977. These NGOs, which now number in the thousands, have permanently altered what had been state-to-state relationships. Most of the conventions, declarations, reporting requirements, and theme mechanisms are the direct result of pressure from these organizations.

The fact that the vast majority of such groups and certainly those with the most resources are based in the West and focus on "traditional" civil and political rights issues has had some very negative consequences. As a result, a North-South split has developed in the UN and at the commission on a number of key issues. There is an excellent opportunity for human rights groups in this country concerned about issues of racial discrimination to build bridges with the "Third World" that are impossible for either White Americans or Africans in the diaspora to construct alone.

NOTES

1. Charles C. Diggs Jr. to Ralph J. Bunche, October 24, 1955, Ralph Bunche Papers, UCLA, box 15, folder D.

2. In his lengthy reply Bunche explained the petition process including the issue of domestic jurisdiction. He recommended that Diggs take note of the Subcommission on the Prevention of Discrimination and the Protection of Minorities, which was engaged in a series of studies on discrimination in education that included the United States and a similar study on employment and occupation being conducted by the International Labor Organization. See ibid.

3. Paul Gordon Lauren, "First Principles of Racial Equality: History and the Politics and Diplomacy of Human Rights Provisions in the United Nations Charter," *Human Rights Quarterly*, vol. 5, no. 1 (February 1983), p. 2.

4. Ibid., p. 2.

5. See the UNIA Declaration in Robert A. Hill (ed.), *The Marcus Garvey and UNIA Papers*, vol. 2 (Berkeley: University of California Press, 1983), pp. 571–77.

6. Lauren, "First Principles," p. 10.

7. Ibid., p. 15.

8. Robert Harris, "Ralph Bunche and Afro-American Participation in Decolonization," in Robert A. Hill, *Pan-African Biography* (Los Angeles: UCLA and Crossroads Press/African Studies Association, 1987), p. 130.

9. See Charles P. Henry, *Ralph Bunche: Model Negro or American Other?* (New York: New York University Press, 1999).

10. Ibid., p. 197.

11. Lauren, "First Principles," pp. 17–18.

12. Ibid., p. 19.

13. See the December 14, 1946 issue of the NNC paper, *Peoples Voice*, p. 16.

14. National Negro Congress, *A Petition to the United Nations on behalf of 13 million Oppressed Negro Citizens of the United States of America*, June 6, 1946, p. 7.

15. Lawrence S. Wittner, "The National Negro Congress: A Reassessment," *American Quarterly*, Winter 1970.

16. Gerald Horne, *Black and Red* (Albany: State University Press of New York, 1986), p. 76.

17. Herbert Aptheker, *Afro-American History* (Secaucus, N.J.: Citadel Press, 1973), pp. 273–74. Aptheker also notes that Storey later became president of the American Bar Association.

18. NAACP, *An Appeal to the World!* (New York: NAACP, 1947), p. 13.

19. W. E. B. DuBois, *Against Racism*, ed. Herbert Aptheker (Amherst: University of Massachusetts Press, 1985), p. 264. In 1949, DuBois submitted another petition to the Human Rights Commission concerning the death sentence a Black sharecropper, Rosa Lee Ingram, and her two sons received at the hands of an all-White Georgia jury. The petition itself was presented by Mary Church Terrell and as a result of the worldwide attention directed to the case, the Ingrams were eventually paroled and finally their sentences were commuted. See pp. 261–65.

20. On the handling of the petition see Gerald Horne, *Black and Red*, pp. 75–76, and Kenneth Janken, *Rayford Logan* (Amherst: University of Massachusetts Press, 1993).

21. Civil Rights Congress, *We Charge Genocide* (New York: Civil Rights Congress, 1951), p. 32.

22. Gerald Horne, "The Case of the Civil Rights Congress," in Judith Joel and Gerald M. Erickson (eds.), *Anti-Communism: The Politics of Manipulation* (Minneapolis: MEP Publications, 1987), p. 120.

23. Civil Rights Congress, *We Charge Genocide*, p. 32.

24. Ibid., p. 196.

25. Patterson asked DuBois to present the CRC petition to the UN; however, DuBois, suffering from the toll taken by his indictment, declined. See Horne, "The Case of the Civil Rights Congress."

26. Bricker proposed an amendment to the Constitution that would not only prevent treaties from becoming the supreme law of the land but would also prevent the president from concluding any executive agreements with interna-

tional organizations or foreign powers without some type of formal approval by Congress. See Francis A. Boyle, "The Hypocrisy and Racism behind the Formulation of U.S. Human Rights Foreign Policy: In Honor of Clyde Ferguson," *Social Justice*, vol. 16, no. 1, pp. 71–93.

27. The President's Committee on Civil Rights, *To Secure These Rights* (Washington, D.C.: U.S. Government Printing Press, 1947), p. 59.

28. Lauren, "First Principles," p. 24.

29. Ibid., p. 25.

30. See Richard Kluger, *Simple Justice* (New York: Knopf, 1976) for a discussion of the politics surrounding *Brown*. See Bert B. Lockwood Jr., "The United Nations Charter and United States Civil Rights Litigation: 1946–1955," *Iowa Law Review*, vol. 69 (1984): 901–56, for an examination of the use of the Charter in domestic civil rights cases.

31. Ton J. M. Zuijdwijk, *Petitioning the United Nations* (New York: St. Martin's Press, 1982), p. 3.

32. Ibid., p. 4.

33. Ibid., pp. 14–27.

34. John Shattuck, Statement before the Human Rights Committee on U.S. Implementation of the ICCPR, UN Headquarters, March 29, 1995, p. 1.

35. State Department, internal document, Draft Response to Mr. Maurice Glele-Ahanhanzo.

36. "Elimination of Racism and Racial Discrimination," UN General Assembly, A/50/476, September 25, 1995, p. 13.

37. Ibid., p. 14.

38. World Council of Churches, "Oral Intervention," Item 16: Implementation of the Programme of Action for the Third Decade to Combat Racism and Racial Discrimination, UN Commission on Human Rights, 51st Session, February 1995.

39. Larry Wisham, "Human Rights in U.S. Face Review by U.N. Commission," *Washington Times*, February 1, 1995.

40. See Audrey R. Chapman, "A 'Violations Approach' for Monitoring the International Covenant on Economic, Social and Cultural Rights," *Human Rights Quarterly*, vol. 18 (1996), pp. 23–66, for an excellent discussion of the problems in implementing the covenant.

PART II

Country and Regional Issues

CHAPTER 6

Sanctions, Black America, and Apartheid: Vindicating the Promise of Peaceful Change

Winston P. Nagan

Economic sanctions are one of the most important instruments of U.S. foreign policy. In 1997, approximately thirty-five countries were the target of some form of American economic, political, or military sanctions. The United States deploys not simply deprivations relating to the economic instrument to express its disapproval, concern, or message of disagreement; it also uses military and political assets as instruments of strategic conditioning and deprivation in the national interest. The "sanctions" regime is often a contextually defined response to a serious foreign-relations issue or problem. As a consequence, no two sanction responses are essentially the "same." This itself generates complexity for both the investigator of governmental policy as well as those who prescribe and apply policy, and may be of especial concern to those whose interests are directly impacted by targeted sanctions. For example, the target-state may not understand *why* it is singled out and *what* it must do to terminate the sanctions regime. U.S. interests may similarly be impacted, and those interests may not know whether they are indeed within the technical reach of the sanction's prescriptions and how exactly their conduct must be modified to both conform to the law and minimize their potential losses.

Consider for a moment the substantive range of practical matters that, in the past, have been the target of U.S. sanctions policy: "weapons of mass destruction and ballistic missiles, promote human rights, end support for terrorism, thwart drug trafficking, discourage armed aggression, protect the environment, and oust governments."[1] Sanctions specifically target economic arenas (foreign assistance; export/import policy; freezing foreign assets; import/export quotas; most-favored-nation status; trade relations; investment limitations, disincentives, or outright proscription; air and communications linkages; financing credit; selective purchasing laws (state/local); limits on public agencies doing business or investing abroad (disinvestment, divestment; state/local). Sanctions that target the military arena include arms embargoes as well as nuanced reductions in security assistance. Sanctions that target the diplomatic arena include phased processes of derecognition, which implicitly carries the stigma of delegitimation in the political sense; this "delegitimation" includes bilateral withdrawal or reductions in diplomatic status, the use of visa policy as an instrument of coercion, the politics of power and influence in international political, economic, and security organizations. Sanctions are also frequently employed in arenas of crisis or perceived crisis. They provide a flexible response that purchases "time" and "flexibility," meaning that foreign relations specialists can increase the level of sanctions or decrease or retreat from them and avoid the inflexibility of a no-retreat invocation of a violent level of intervention via the military instrument.

According to the Haass study, sanctions by the United States cost U.S. companies some $15 to $19 billion and "affected some 200,000 workers." In addition, "secondary sanctions" that target our trade partners who may not wish to sanction a state being sanctioned by the United States increases the problems of more collaborative trade relations with our allies or trade partners. In short, the problem of sanctions poses the following problems:

1. National interest versus private or special interests (capital and labor)
2. National interests versus international interests
3. The economic cost of sanctions versus some other level of intervention versus the overall efficacy of sanctions to achieve its ostensible objectives.

These are, of course, interrelated points, but they all, in some degree, intrude on any legal, political, or economic assessment of the policies and practices of U.S. sanctions. One of the deep and critical concerns about the nature, scope, and efficacy of sanctions is this: Sanction considerations are tied to conceptions of national interest. In the context of the Cold War, those interests were often of a strategic character and were conditioned less by altruistic considerations than by superpower competition. During the Cold War period, the structure of world order was conditioned more by superpower spheres of influence and superpower security doctrines, understandings, and interests. These interests were not always coextensive with the purposes and objectives of the UN Charter. In short, the special interests of the superpowers were not necessarily congruent with the larger common interests of the international community. This meant that sanctions could often be more influenced by Cold War considerations, which were often collapsed into national security interests and which could invariably reflect parochial, self-serving concerns. In short, some dictators might be given tolerant or preferred standing and others be the subject of targeted sanctions and more.

We are now in the post–Cold War period. There is no talk of a "bipolar" world order. If the term "polar" appears, it is prefixed by the term "uni." The key unipolar power is the United States. In the absence of a Cold War enemy, how is the United States to formulate the strategic and tactical elements of its foreign relations policy and its security concerns? U.S. interventions now seemingly rely more on some form of sanctions rather than techniques of covert, and sometimes overt, unilateral military interventions. However, the cost of sanctions shifts the burden from the military and political establishment to the "private sector." In the main, this means American business, and to some extent, American labor; hence, Haass' point that the cost of sanctions to American business runs into billions of dollars. Business interests are doubtless concerned about an expanding burden that they must assume to advance the foreign relations interests of the United States. Still, a further indirect tack that supports these concerns is the belief that now that the U.S.S.R. is no more, and Russia is no serious threat to the United States, U.S. policy should become more inward-looking, more "parochial," and correspondingly radically diminish foreign entanglements.

How the national conversation about the principles, strategies, and tactics of foreign policy evolved to this point is a complex, and indeed, large undertaking. One of the key parts of that analysis and description *must*, however, account for U.S. policy in South Africa, a policy that culminated in a remarkable piece of legislation, the Comprehensive Anti-Apartheid Act of 1987 (U.S. sanctions) (*Comprehensive Anti-Apartheid Act of 1986*, Pub. L. No. 99–440, 100 Stat. 1086 [1986]). The bill was not supported by the Reagan administration. Congress, in fact, was able to overcome a Reagan veto and enact the bill into law. American sanctions were, in many ways, the coup de grace for White supremacy in South Africa. It also represented a high-water mark in the influence of Black America on the content and character of U.S. foreign policy. Briefly, the interesting question is how did this "improbable" thing happen?

Our brief odessy begins with the United Nations. South African discrimination appeared on the agenda of the General Assembly in 1946, and in expanded form, remained on the agenda until 1960. In 1960, the Sharpville massacre occurred. The event triggered international attention and condemnation. In 1961, the General Assembly switched its focus on South Africa to emphasize concrete strategies to change the headlong march of apartheid. In Resolution 1761, it recommended sanctions in the diplomatic area, transport (closing ports), boycotting South African goods (including arms), and landing rights of aircraft.

By 1969, the situation had so deteriorated in South Africa that UNGA Resolution 2506 provided a much more precise framework for economic sanctions. The General Assembly also called the attention of the Security Council to South Africa as a situation likely to endanger international peace and security. The Security Council responded by prescribing an arms embargo against South Africa. This resolution was later strengthened and broadened to include the suspension of foreign investment, guaranteed export loans, and more.[2] In sum, the UN sought to establish a military and economic sanctions regime to change the apartheid regime in South Africa.

In the United States, the initial issue was the corporate stake in South Africa. The moral/political issue was that U.S. corporations were investing in an economy of racial dominance and deriving economic benefits from it. Indeed, during the 1960s it was seen in surveys that American corporate executives were pro–South African (apartheid) and that there was a "further hardening of pro–South African feelings." In this period, there were over six thousand Americans living in South Africa, and according to surveys quoted above "[f]ew newly arrived Americans have difficulty getting settled; . . . the climate is excellent, Black servants are cheap . . . virtually all consumer goods sold in America are available here." It was said that the typical American executive lived in a fashionable suburb; one such suburb was reported to have "more swimming pools than any place outside of Southern California." An American normally had two to five Black servants, including cook, garden boy, and nanny for their small children. There were no "Yankee go home" signs displayed or permitted. The general attitude regarding agitation against apartheid in the United States simply amounted to gratuitous comment when the situation in the United States was in a mess. During the late 1960s and early 1970s, vast loan/credit packages were arranged for the South African government by American financial interests.

In the United States, left-oriented groups, inspired by a growing South African exile community, began to raise concerns about the moral and political foundations of the economy of apartheid and about the

U.S. role in it. U.S. policy for much of the 1960s had been to neither encourage nor discourage doing business with the apartheid regime. The rise of the Nixon administration represented a radical shift from this position as indicated in the notorious National Security Study Memorandum 39, which suggested that White control would hold for the indefinite future in South Africa, and U.S. policy should come to terms with this reality. By "coming to terms" was meant that the United States should slowly, but purposefully, become more of an ally to the White regime of South Africa. In short, Option 2 of this document recommended continued "public opposition to racial repression but relax[ed] political isolation and economic restrictions on White states."

The Carter administration, coming under the influence of Black Americans like Andrew Young, revised the policy of the Nixon-Kissinger regime and itself improved the position of the United States in the anti-apartheid context. However, the most important change in the U.S. policy, and one that was to have a galvanizing effect on Black American perspectives, was the Reagan policy of constructive engagement with the apartheid regime in the 1980s. There can be no question but that the escalating pressures inside South Africa, led by the African National Congress, the UDF, COSATU, and the Mass Democratic Movement, in addition to the defection of many Afrikaner Whites from the dogmas and depredations of militaristic apartheid, provided a radical contrast to the Reagan policy of constructively engaging the increasingly fragile apartheid regime. As levels of state repression increased and were broadcast instantaneously to all parts of the world, public opinion, led by Black Americans in the United States, coalesced around concrete strategies to undo the Reagan policy of blanket support for White supremacy and international racism. These efforts culminated in the comprehensive sanctions bill known as the Comprehensive Anti-Apartheid Act of 1986.

How did the conscious levels of Black mobilization occur to achieve this outcome? First, it must not be thought that the changes in U.S. policy were exclusively a matter of ethnic politics. The issues of the corporate involvement in the economy of apartheid caught the attention and concerns of labor interests, as in the Polaroid situation where they generated a widespread movement on campuses in the United States, calling for corporate and university divestment or disinvestment for South Africa. Additionally, church groups and NGOs, as well as charitable foundations, all played a crucial role in the evolution of the policy of economic sanctions against South Africa. For example, the Gary Declaration of 1972 was a high-water mark in a growing concern of Black Americans that Black interests on the domestic scene could not be effectively addressed if Black interests on the international scene were not also part of the framework of political identification, political claim, and political expectation. The Gary Declaration stipulated the following:

> Traditionally the over-riding considerations of hunger, poverty, the necessity to survive and struggle for our very existence has given Black people a vision of their priorities which is confined to domestic issues. This has been true with the exception of one great stream of history which involved comparably few in the Pan Africa and "Back to Africa" movements we know so well. We have just begun to witness, however, the increasing awareness of some Black people about the degree to which their domestic freedom is tied to what America does overseas in terms of its energy and resources. These international commitments, then, must become important to us as a people, for they not only bear a direct relationship to our immediate survival in America as a people. They bear a direct relationship to our immediate survival in America not only through the fact that we are involved in a two-way death struggle (oppression and nuclear) but that our kin in the African world are also similarly threatened by what we do or fail to do with regard to international issues.

This orientation was further supplemented by the Black political agenda that listed the following as its prime foreign policy goals, "progress of the revolutionary movements especially in . . . South Africa, Namibia, Mozambique, Angola, Zimbabwe . . . Guinea-Bissau and armistice to African countries in their movement towards independence." Later in 1972 the African Liberation Day March on Washington generated a crowd of twenty thousand participants. Foreign affairs, Black American concerns, and mass mobilization were getting a grassroots focus.

The pathway traversed by Black America was not a linear one. Efforts were consistently made to buy off Black leadership or to redirect energies away from "foreign concerns" when Black leaders who sought to blunt the edge of radical action were coopted. The role of the Reverend Leon Sullivan and the moderation of labor exploitation in South Africa rather than the confrontation of apartheid with the sharp edge of sanctions is an illustration of this trend.

The activities of such NGOs as the American Committee on Africa, Trans-Africa, the Lawyers Committee for Civil Rights under Law, as well as the Congressional Black Caucus, the National Black Conventions, and many more groups were able to capture the attention of the media and political leaders in Congress. It is hard to imagine a greater turnaround in the U.S. foreign policy than the repudiation of constructive engagement and the imposition, in its place, of a comprehensive sanctions program to combat racial domination. Although P. W. Botha remained defiant, the writing was on the wall. The sanctions bill had actually provided a script of the directions that change had to assume in order to secure a lifting of the sanctions regime.

The sanctions regime codified in the Anti-Apartheid Act was important for a number of reasons. From an international point of view, the key superpower had put its weight and influence squarely behind the United Nations efforts to secure a relatively peaceful resolution of the South African problem. Additionally, it put that superpower squarely on the side of those opposed to international racial dominance as evidenced in the apartheid situation. In the context of South Africa the policy was in radical contrast to the Reagan administration's effort to legitimate the apartheid regime through the policies of "constructive engagement." The message sent to the White South African establishment was far from Botha's "adapt or die" formula for his neo-apartheid solution. On the contrary, the new policy was *change* or confront an economic and political catastrophe. The Anti-Apartheid Act provided a critical stimulus for the forces committed to change in South Africa to emerge as the key players in the process of transition to democratic rule. In the context of domestic American politics the Anti-Apartheid Act was a kind of coming of age of the efforts of the Black political caucus and their allies in internationalizing the Black American *political* perspective. The victory in South Africa was also a victory for Black identity, for Black historical identification with Africa and in the aftermath of South African transformation, a powerful identification with Africa's first Black industrial and nuclear power state. Moreover, the persona of Nelson Mandela is as much a symbol of redemption, sacrifice, faith, courage, and stature for all South Africans as it is for Black Americans.

However, the Anti-Apartheid Act should not be construed as just another sanctions bill designed to punish some delinquent state (as the United States sees it). On the contrary, the sanctions bill was extremely complex, covering both incentives and discentives for change. The bill also suggested the licit or acceptable objectives of transformation, indicating key initial conditions and processes to secure change. As a conceptual matter, the sanctions bill required a reconceptualization of the very idea of sanctions itself. Sanctions are not simply the invocation of a coercive economic strategy for intervention and change. Sanctions would turn out to be much more comprehensive. Thus the comprehensive view of a rational sanctions policy will seek to integrate and coordinate several interrelated strategies of action.

The major purpose of the Anti-Apartheid Act was to present a "comprehensive and complete framework to guide the efforts of the United States in helping to bring an end to apartheid in South Africa and lend to the establishment of a nonracial, democratic form of government." The Anti-Apartheid Act effectually enacted a program of comprehensive positive and negative sanctions to secure these ends. The positive sanctions sought to signal a policy of economic and social reconstruction concerns. Thus the act earmarked millions of dollars for scholarships for Black students, funding for legal assistance to political detainees and political prisoners and their relatives. The act also funded further development of Black business enterprise and the training of trade unionists. Moreover, the act also sought to codify adherence to the Sullivan principles.

Regarding the political ends of the act, the act prescribed a four-point plan as follows:

1. An end to the state of emergency and the release of the political prisoners, including Nelson Mandela
2. The unbanning of the African National Congress, the Pan African Congress, the Black Consciousness Movement, and other groups willing to suspend terrorism and participate in negotiations and a democratic process
3. A revocation of the Group Areas Act and the Population Registration Act and the granting of universal citizenship to all South Africans, including homeland residents
4. The use of the international offices of a third party as an intermediary to bring about negotiations, with the object of the establishment of power-sharing with the Black majority.

The negative sanctions part of the act established a regime of economic sanctions against South Africa and contained provisions to ensure that other states not opportunistically take advantage of U.S. sanctions. The act specifically directed the executive branch to "seek international cooperative agreements . . . to bring about the complete dismantling of apartheid." When a resolution was put before the United Nations Security Council including the operative language of the Anti-Apartheid Act, the Reagan administration in flat violation of the act used its veto in the Security Council. It was a veto that represented the last pathetic public act to salvage a lost policy, namely, that of constructive engagement. The role of U.S. sanctions should not be seen to detract from the courage, tenacity, and steadfast faith of the anti-apartheid forces in South Africa, especially the ANC and its leaders, or indeed the sacrifices experienced by the Southern African frontline states in their support for the forces of liberation. Still Black American groups were a critical strategic factor in not simply neutralizing U.S. covert support for South Africa, but actually bringing the power and influence of the United States more squarely behind the forces of progress in South Africa. The timing of sanctions coincided with two critical facts about fundamental change or transformation. First, the ruling White group clearly had lost confidence in apartheid and neo-apartheid formulas. Second, Black South Africans knew they could win. Interestingly, a 1985 poll in South Africa showed that 63 percent of Whites believed apartheid would not exist in ten years. For Blacks polled the figure was 59 percent.

Taking the case of the Senate one needs only to look at the predecessor proposed Anti-Apartheid Act of 1985 to see the powerful senatorial forces bent on blocking the legislation. For example, Senator Helms led a filibuster to block the bill and garnered support from conservative Republicans like Denton, East, Garn, Hatch, Hecht, Humphrey, Laxalt, McClure, Symms, Thurmond, and Wallop. This bill died in the Senate.

CONCLUSION

The role of Black America in South Africa has of course triggered a larger concern of how Black America identifies with Africa as a whole. For the first time since the postwar period a vast strategic change has occurred in sub-Saharan Africa. South Africa is no longer a destabilizing threat for the region. It is in fact a force for security, economic and political collaboration, and integration. The consummation of the Ugandan Constitution and free and fair elections, the victory of the Rawandan Patriotic Front (RPF) in Rwanda and the African initiative to get rid of Mobutu, one of the most corrupt and retrograde forces in all of central Africa, have generated immense prospects for peace, and the prospect of building, upon the peace, progressive structures of governance and enterprise. Black Americans have been indirectly involved in some of these changes and have an even greater role to play in ensuring that the policies of the last hegemon are ones that enhance African interests rather than undermine them. The victory in South Africa is a coming of age and the symbol of a coming together of a progressive South Africa and a progressive Black America, a dynamic bridging of the diaspora. More than that as Africa contemplates the birth of a new African renaissance, Black America will feed off the success of this vision and will experience the restorative value of an inclusive identification with her African heritage.

POSTSCRIPT

In 1991 Inter Press Service carried a story indicating that U.S. prosecutors were preparing criminal charges against the South African arms

producer Armscor for smuggling sensitive U.S. military technology to
Pretoria (October 31, 1991). Implicated in Armscor's deals was the
Pennsylvania arms dealer, James Guerin. According to the report Guerin
was part of a secret U.S. plan to have South Africa share intelligence
information with Washington. Guerin maintained he was regularly
debriefed by the CIA during the Reagan era on matters relating to the
South African armed forces. The report further suggests that the
National Security Council (NSC) and the Central Intelligence Agency
(CIA) under Reagan apparently cooperated in "sending spare parts for
fighter planes and missile systems to South Africa via Central America
and the Caribbean." If these allegations are true, then the scope of Reagan's commitment to apartheid South Africa apparently extended to
violations of both U.S. law and international law.

The 1991 indictment of Armscor and others carried all sort of innu-
endo related to the conduct of Reagan's CIA director, William Casey.
These included efforts to have the South Africans supply Sadam Hussein
with arms because of problems with the war against Iran. Casey himself
had strong ties with the South African intelligence community. However, the full scope of these activities will not be known because of
Casey's untimely death.

When the government of national reconciliation was elected in
1994, Nelson Mandela became the first democratically elected president
of nonracial South Africa. Since the arms embargo no longer applied to
South Africa, the issue emerged about whether the indictment against
Armscor (a state company) would be aborted. Armscor was now an
instrument of the new, nonracial postapartheid democratic regime. In
the new climate of international reconciliation with South Africa, Armscor became an important element of South Africa's effort at economic
reconstruction in the postapartheid era. In furtherance of this objective,
Armscor secured a contract to supply the United Kingdom with $6 bil-
lion worth of helicopters. In order for these helicopters to function
within NATO's defense system, certain communications parts were
required from the United States. The U.S. response to Armscor competition was to reinvigorate the prosecution of Armscor for violations of
U.S. law and international law during the apartheid era. The argument
seemed to be that the anti-apartheid regime of Mandela was to be
responsible in a criminal proceeding for the acts of the apartheid regime.
It is an utter irony why these indictments were not aborted and why the
Mandela regime should have to be answerable for the acts of a regime
that sought to destroy him and his political party, the African National
Congress (ANC). Indeed, the invidiousness of the Mandela regime having to defend itself in a criminal proceeding in a foreign country, defending the apartheid regime's conduct that it had sought to change, is

indeed an odd way to reward the struggle against apartheid. Moreover, such an indignity would in its essence insult the sovereign dignity of the first democratic regime in South African history. Perhaps the answer to this mystery lies in the intense levels of competition that still pervade the sale of armaments on the world market. In fact, as a result of the U.S. embargo on selling the relevant parts to South Africa, South Africa (Armscor) lost the contract. This is a very unusual posture to assume, for the United States, unless one assumes that special interests have prevailed over the national interests of the U.S. in this regard. It is unclear whether a Black industrial country with and arms industry of sophistication is tolerable in a context in which Black states are consumers rather than producers and distributors of military hardware, especially to first world states. The affair was finally settled with a low key no contest plea. The entire episode is still an affront to Africa's leading democracy. In short, to the extent that "race" is a muted factor in these matters, Black Americans still have a vitally important role to play to ensure that African interests are not disparaged by short-sighted U.S. policies and that freedom, equality, and fairness at home are fed and nurtured by freedom, fairness, and equality abroad.

NOTES

1. Richard N. Haass, "Sanctioning Madness," *Foreign Affairs*, November–December 1997.

2. See generally Nagan, "Economic Sanctions, U.S. Foreign Policy, International Law and the Anti-Apartheid Act of 1986," *Florida Journal of International Law*, vol. 4, no. 1, pp. 85–229.

CHAPTER 7

United States Foreign Policy, Democratization, and Challenges of Nation-State Rebuilding in Post-Conflict Liberia

Keith Jennings
and
Celena Slade

INTRODUCTION

In the post–Cold War era the United States has emerged as the country most identified with providing democracy assistance to other members of the international community. Under the Clinton administration, democracy promotion became one of the core elements of U.S. foreign policy. In fact, efforts to support democratic transitions and to address human rights disasters and democratic reversals are seen as being central to advancing U.S. strategic interests. According to the Clinton administration,

> A world of democratic nations provides a more stable and secure global arena in which to advance U.S. objectives. Advancing U.S. interest in the post–cold war world will often require efforts to support democratic transitions as well as to address human rights disasters and democratic reversals. Promotion of democracy and human rights, including the rights of women and minorities, reflect fundamental values of the American people.[1]

The State Department's 1998 International Affairs Strategic Plan suggests that the purpose of democracy promotion is to increase foreign governments adherence to democratic practices and respect for human rights. Such a goal is arrived at on the basis of the view held by most policy-makers that democratic countries do not go to war with each other, and therefore, a world full of democratic states would be a more peaceful and stable world. The U.S. government's strategies for supporting democratic development include:

> Support democratic transitions, especially in regions and countries of importance to the United States; build, strengthen, and employ international forums to secure democratic transitions, prevent conflict, promote human rights, including labor rights, and support multilateral sanctions. Promote development of national and multilateral institutions for the promotion of human rights and the rule of law; support respect for human rights globally and intervene in selected human rights cases; support democratic transitions through bilateral and multilateral assistance and exchanges, broadcast, and informational programs to establish and consolidate [the following]: competitive political processes, including free and fair elections, politically active civil societies, enhanced women's political participation, free media, representative labor movements, and other pluralistic organizations, transparent and accountable government institutions, the rule of law including neutral and professional law enforcement.[2]

Three key assumptions undergird the strategies. They are as follows:

1. The international environment will increasingly favor democracy, leading governments to profess democratic principles, but democratic practices will vary, depending in particular on the will and intentions of leaders.
2. The transition and consolidation of democracy varies from state to state, but international influence can be crucial to the outcome.
3. U.S. pursuit of democratic transitions in certain countries and circumstances will be subject to countervailing influences and interests.[3]

The Africa region is one where democracy promotion by the U.S. government and U.S. supported institutions has increased most significantly, moving dramatically from $5.3 million in 1990 to over $119 million by 1994 and totaling over $1 billion dollars between FY 90 and FY 97.[4] Such a pivotal increase in funding and attention, signified even by the appointment of U.S. civil rights leader, the Rev. Jesse Jackson, as a Special Ambassador for Human Rights and Democracy Promotion in Africa by the Clinton administration,[5] further attests to the importance of African Americans being keenly aware and knowledgeable of the core principles of U.S. foreign policy, the key actors and players, and how this particular aspect of U.S. foreign policy is implemented generally but especially on the African continent.

The democratization debate in Africa, has been one of the most vigorous in the 1990s.[6] Democratic advances in Benin, Mali, Mozambique, Namibia, and South Africa have been matched and at times overshadowed by democratic setbacks in countries such as Angola, Central African Republic, the Gambia, Kenya, Sierra Leone, and Zambia. Collectively however, these transitions have produced a struggle for new leadership, a new body of relevant literature and at times some of the same old false conceptions and perceptions of what the democratic process is. Recently several critics of U.S. democratic-assistance efforts have suggested that African conditions might not be appropriate for western-style liberal democracy and that other factors should be promoted first such as economic development.[7]

Liberia is one country where the disparate issues of economics, politics, culture, civil war, ethnic mobilization, historical circumstances, and U.S. foreign policy all come together and make for a useful examination of the possibilities and challenges for the transition to and consolidation of the democratic process in Africa.

Following seven years of civil war and almost ten years of autocratic rule before that, 75 percent of the registered Liberian electorate voted on July 19, 1997, for Charles Taylor as the country's president.[8] Taylor was often identified as the main "warlord," the chief human rights violator, the initiator of the seven-year civil war, and his rebel force was known as an internal occupation army. Moreover, the fact that Liberia was a "collapsed state" with at least one faction openly receiving material assistance from "external rogue states" and the only place where a regional peacekeeping operation had succeeded anywhere in the world, makes the Liberian case worthy of scholarly investigation.

In order to make a contribution to the debate on democratization in Africa and motivate greater interest and involvement of African Americans in U.S./Africa foreign policy the following essay reviews the developments that led to and occurred during the seven-year civil war in Liberia, the recent elections of July 1997 and their implications for democratic consolidation or peace-building, the role that the United States played in the Republic of Liberia immediately prior to and during the seven-year crisis, illuminates some of the challenges that currently exist in Liberia and offers recommendations regarding the possible role the United States or African Americans could play in the process of nation-state rebuilding in postconflict Liberia.

The essay is divided into four interrelated sections. The first section reviews historical linkages and the "special relationship" between Liberia and the United States. The second section reviews the civil war, the various factions, and the collapse of the Liberian state under the weight of a seven-year civil war. The third section outlines and considers U.S. foreign policy aims in Liberia and democracy assistance, including support for the Economic Community of West African States regional peacekeeping force known as ECOMOG. Finally, the fourth section outlines several contemporary and future challenges of democratization in Liberia and attempts to explore possible policy options open to African Americans for the promotion of democratic consolidation in Liberia.

DEMOCRATIZATION: THE ISSUES AND THE DEBATE

The democratization debate has intensified over the past decade following the collapse of communism and the fall of numerous autocratic one-party states across the international community.[9] Also throughout the international community today, movements for democracy and democratic reforms are increasing. In Africa, Asia, Europe, and Latin America, the movement for democratic reform has been likened to a "sea change," especially since the end of the Cold War. The waves of popular movements against political repression, autocratic rule, and human rights violations have continued to wash away undemocratic systems and usher in new directions in the flow of political development.

One of the key issues central to the democratization debate is whether the high correlation between levels of democracy and levels of economic development in western societies will be the same in nonwestern societies and to what extent does economic liberalization fuel the democratization process.[10] For example, one may ask whether China, Chile, and Singapore are the models to be watched, that is, countries where authoritarian rule has produced exceptionally high rates of growth or are Russia and South Africa more relevant examples where political liberalization has run ahead of economic growth but those countries would not be seen as emerging markets with tremendous growth potential if it were not for the political liberalization that has taken place.[11]

The African continent is one region of the world where the movement toward democracy has been most evident and contradictory. Although major civil conflicts, ethnic tensions, underdevelopment, and human suffering continue to plague the region, it is significant that between 1990 and 1999 more than thirty countries have had popular pro-democracy movements that resulted in democratic elections or some form of political liberalization. The "winds of change" have not blown in such powerful gusts since the 1960s independence movements. In fact, during the years of 1999 and 2000 there are at least eighteen countries that are scheduled to hold multiparty elections.

The impact of globalization on the consolidation process of democratic transitions has not been researched in any great detail, although several authors have reviewed the impact of economic reform on democratization efforts, but many times the international economic context within which the reform is occurring is neglected.[12] Therefore, the question of whether democracy will achieve a state of consolidation in countries where it has recently emerged is also an important aspect of the democratization debate. This is especially true for the African continent where over 80 percent of the countries have adopted and implemented some form of International Monetary Fund (IMF)– or World Bank–inspired Structural Adjustment Program.[13]

The late renowned Nigerian writer Claude Ake argued in his book *Democracy and Development in Africa* that

> Sub-Saharan Africa is mired in one of the deepest and most protracted crisis of modern history. This crisis has been phenomenally harsh, tragic and demoralizing. . . . Not many people view the development of Africa as a viable proposition. This is not surprising. The world has been mesmerized by the dismal statistics of declining productivity and growth rates, escalating indebtedness, and chronic malnutrition, famine and disease. The high incidence of political instability and violent conflict in some parts of Africa, such as Burundi, Rwanda, Liberia, Somalia, Sudan and Sierra Leone has not helped matters.[14]

Samuel Huntington, author of *The Third Wave*,[15] has argued that modern democracy is a product of western civilization and that its roots lie in social pluralism, the class system, the civil society, the belief in the rule of law, the experience with representative bodies, the separation of spiritual and temporal authority, and the commitment to individualism that began to develop in Western Europe a millennium ago. Therefore, according to Huntington, the question of consolidation is best answered by the two factors of economic development and the receptivity to democracy of nonwestern cultures.[16] Huntington further argues that,

> Democracy is incompatible with total economic equality, which can be achieved only by a coercive dictatorship, but it also is incompatible with gross inequalities in wealth and income. Economic growth eventually reduces these inequalities and hence facilitates the emergence of democracy.[17]

Whether Huntington is correct or just Eurocentric in his perspective on the preconditions necessary for democracy to take root and grow, his view is typical of the dominant perspective in democracy studies. Conversely, radical African theorist Issac Shivji has argued that there are three identifiable perspectives that underlie the debate on democratization in Africa. They are the liberal, the statist, and the popular perspectives.

According to Shivji, the liberal perspective "draws its inspiration from western liberalism centered around notions of limited government, individual rights, parliamentary and party institutions, the centrality of the economic and political entrepreneur of the market place, etc."[18] In addition, the liberal perspective disagrees with anything that "smacks of a collective right."

The statist perspective focuses "on developmentalist concerns best summed up in the rhetoric, 'what use is free speech to a starving peasant.'" It does not reject democracy per se and its present-day African versions even argue that development is not possible without democracy (i.e., it has moved from the position state as an instrument of development). He also suggest that the statist position often dismisses the true right to self-determination by raising the specter of a further balkanized continent that would eventually drop off into tiny pieces.[19]

The popular perspective, according to Shivji, remains the most undefined of the views. Nevertheless, it "opposes both the statist and liberal in their typically top-down orientation by emphasizing popular struggles and mass movements from below. It challenges the universality of liberal values and authoritarianism of the statist positions. But in the present debate . . . it remains fuzzy and confused precisely because of the triumph of the liberal. That which would clearly distinguish the popular perspective—position on imperialism, state, class, class struggle etc.—remains unsaid by its intellectual proponents for fear of being condemned as old fashioned or even demagogic." The popular perspective, "while recognizing the right to self-determination as an important democratic principle, agonizes over its contradictory character: the relation or interface between national liberation, embodied in the right to self-determination . . . and social emancipation projected by popular class struggles."[20]

Most pro-democracy activist in African context tend to promote a more substantive approach to democratic construction. In other words, they not only believe that multipartyism, periodic elections, governmental succession by constitutional and electoral procedures guaranteed under the rule of law have to exist, but also a more explicit commitment to norms such as redistributive socioeconomic reforms, equality, broad popular participation, and human rights. The debate on the definition and content of democracy is critically important to understanding the contemporary Liberian political realities.

U.S.-LIBERIAN RELATIONS IN HISTORICAL PERSPECTIVE

Liberia is, perhaps only second to South Africa, the country in Africa where there has been the strongest historic Pan-African connection between African Americans and Africa in the twentieth century. However, today most African Americans are not knowledgeable of what has taken place over the past two decades in Liberia beyond the rare thirty-second sensational media coverage of atrocities committed by child soldiers during the seven-year crisis.[21] Thus, in an effort to grasp the current realities of U.S.-Liberian relations it is first necessary to briefly outline what the relations have been historically.

Liberia was founded in 1822 by former enslaved Africans who returned to the continent from the United States. These African Americans were assisted by the American Colonization Society (ACS), a private organization whose purpose was to promote the voluntary return of freed slaves back to Africa.[22] The Republic of Liberia became a sovereign state in 1847 under a constitutional and governmental arrangement modeled after that of the United States. The capital city of Monrovia was named after U.S. president James Monroe. The returnees became known as Americo-Liberians after resettlement in Liberia. The U.S.-Liberian relationship has often been described as a "special relationship" based on the aforementioned historical events that led to its founding.

By 1860, Americo-Liberians numbered more than eleven thousand. This group and their descendants dominated government in Liberia for more than 130 years and established a form of settler colonialism somewhat similar to what Europeans had done in Kenya, Zambia, Zimbabwe, or South Africa. The relationship between the settler class and the "country people" although not as pronounced as it was before the 1980 coup, still remains today. While the political preeminence of Americo-Liberians and their support by the United States ensured stability and some economic development in the country, it also increased resentment by indigenous groups who far outnumbered them.

Shadrach Tubman served as Liberia's nineteenth president. He remained in office for an unprecedented twenty-seven years, from 1944 to 1971, a period that also coincided with the upsurge of the anticolonial struggle in Africa, Asia and Latin America."[23] Tubman was elected four times to four-year terms, twice to eight-year terms, and died in office before his inauguration to a sixth term. Tubman was a popular leader who led the country in a unification campaign and increased foreign investment in the country. Although Tubman viewed Liberia as a model of development for the rest of Africa by the West, many of Liberia's African neighbors did not hold the country in as high a regard but rather viewed it as another African nation ruled by "settlers." It appeared as though the Americo-Liberians were psychologically isolated from African elite groups in the rest of Africa. They did not share an interest in concepts or movements such as the "African personality," or "negritude," nor did the settler mentality, so prevalent among them, find much value in defining Liberia's African heritage. In fact, during the 1960s the more radical African political leaders were known as the "Casablanca group," while the more conservative African leaders were popularly referred to as the "Monrovia group."[24]

On July 23, 1971, Tubman died at the age of seventy-four. William Tolbert emerged as president after serving as Tubman's vice-president for twenty years. Initially, he served a six-month interim term as "provisional president" and in January 1972 was sworn in as president after enactment of special legislation that enabled him to begin a four-year term in his own right instead of completing the unexpired term he had initially filled.[25]

Under Tolbert's administration from 1971 to 1980, the contradictions between the settler class and the indigenous population increased. For example, 4 percent of the population controlled over 60 percent of the country's wealth. Moreover, problems of development began to manifest themselves more clearly. Rural economic stagnation drove many to the capital city of Monrovia. Much of the population remained unemployed and impoverished during the 1970s. Additionally, Liberians were burdened by an increasingly high rate of inflation. It was during this period that young radicals such as Baccus Matthews, began pushing for changes in the governance structures of the country. The agitation led to what became popularly known as the "rice riots."[26] Rice is the main staple food for Liberians. In the international sphere however, the Tubman regime did begin to show a little more independence from U.S. foreign policy perspectives in Africa, especially on the question of apartheid and liberation in southern Africa but was also critical of Tanzania's invasion of Uganda to overthrown the Amin regime. However, internally, the long-standing resentment and disproportionate distribution of wealth between the Americo-Liberians and the indigenous Liberians, contributed to the tensions that erupted in an armed revolt in April 1980. The Tolbert regime was overthrown in a bloody coup led by Samuel Doe, a master sergeant in the Liberian Army and a descendant of one of the indigenous ethnic groups known as the Krahn.[27]

Doe suspended the constitution, banned political parties, released political prisoners from jail, and suspended the Senate and the House of Representatives, and many of the other nominally democratic institutions were abolished. Doe justified the popularly supported coup by citing political oppression practiced by the Tolbert regime as well as the corruption, unemployment, and the high cost of living that burdened the poor.[28] Tolbert and a good number of his associates were humiliated, paraded in the streets naked, and publicly executed by the new governing authorities. Under Samuel Doe, many of the other indigenous ethnic tribes such as the Kpelle, Bassa, Gio, Kru, and Vai were subjected to Krahn domination. Many that rose to power under Doe's regime were members of the Krahn ethnic group. The Krahn had long-held positions within the lower ranks of the army. Doe's rulership became increasingly autocratic leading to appeals from groups within Liberia for the United States to withhold economic assistance to the country until new elections were held within the country.[29]

However, because of U.S. strategic interest in Liberia, for much of the 1980s the Reagan and Bush administrations preferred not to publicly speak out against the Doe regime's systematic human rights abuses, corrupt practices, and institutionally destructive behavior. It was clear even during the early 1980s that U.S. assistance was not going toward the furtherance of democratic practices in Liberia. Yet the United States continued to support the Doe regime. Why was this the case?

At the height of the Cold War, Liberia was one of the main outpost for U.S. policy implementation in Africa. During the Cold War, the principle aim of U.S. foreign policy toward Africa was to contain Soviet influence and to eliminate communist and radical nationalist governments and movements throughout the continent.[30] Specific African nations had strategic importance to the superpower blocs. Many countries in Africa were used as tools of manipulation and exploitation and tyrannical leaders were supported by the Western and Eastern blocs as symbols of a greater alliance based on capitalist or socialist ideals.[31] However after the East-Central European communist regimes collapsed in 1989, calls for democratization crystallized into a worldwide movement.[32]

Liberia was the United States' closest and oldest ally in Africa. As such, Liberia received on a per capita basis, the highest amounts of U.S. assistance in any country in sub-Saharan Africa.[33] The United States could always count on Liberia, similar to Israel, during United Nations votes but more importantly U.S. interest in Liberia played an enormously influential role in determining U.S. policy toward the Doe regime. Over five thousand U.S. citizens worked in the country. This included diplomats, businessmen, missionaries, two hundred members of the Peace Corps, and U.S. military advisers who trained Liberia's Army. Moreover, Liberia hosted the U.S. Central Intelligence Agency's (CIA) station for West Africa. Liberia was also the only nation in West Africa to permit U.S. military planes to refuel on twenty-four hours notice. In addition, Liberia was the headquarters for the Voice of America transmitter for all of sub-Saharan Africa and the Omega navigational tracking station used to track all shipping in the eastern Atlantic.[34] Liberia is also the home of the American-founded Firestone rubber plantation, the largest rubber plantation in the world.

By the mid-1980s, the "special relationship," as interpreted by the Reagan Administration, had resulted in the United States providing Liberia with approximately one-third of its national budget and although human rights violations were increasing systematically, the administration only engaged in mild criticism through private diplomacy.[35] Doe was even received at the White House by Reagan, who referred to him as "Sergeant Moe." The mistake was widely believed to be a Freudian slip because most U.S. observers related Moe to the leader of the hilarious U.S. "slapstick" television clowns known as "the Three Stooges."

After coming to power in the coup, Doe like all military leaders, promised that fresh elections would be held. In 1984, after being urged by the Reagan administration, he temporarily gained some popular support when he lifted his government's four-year-old ban on any form of political activity. This did not last long however. As early as August 1984 key opposition leaders were thrown into prison. Doe's troops invaded the University of Liberia and shot and killed an undetermined number of students, wounded many more, raped women, and stripped professors naked. The Doe government refused to investigate the incident and subsequent to it the country's two largest parties were banned from political activity, more opposition leaders were arrested, and military decrees began to supersede the normal judicial system.[36] In fact, Decree 88 A made it a crime to spread "rumors, lies and disinformation" about the government. Freedom of the press was completely repressed. It was during this period that even a sportswriter was thrown into prison.[37]

International attention and U.S. congressional concerns began to mount and created an embarrassing situation for the Reagan administration. Moreover, the Doe regime began to denounce foreign interference in Liberia's affairs and to further hint at more independence. It was during this same period that the then Liberian foreign minister, clearly under instructions from Doe, announced that he would travel to Libya to discuss the possibility of closer relations between their two countries. Obviously the United States did not greet such news with open arms.

The 1985 election, held on October 15, perhaps marked the beginning of the end for the Doe regime, whose only concern seemed to have been self-perpetuation. According to independent observers, voter turnout was large and orderly, but the voting was marked by widespread reports of fraud. The existence of stuffed ballot boxes and the destruction of voting materials was well documented. In fact, there was a near unanimous opinion among observers and foreign correspondents that the election had been won by Liberian Action Party (LAP) candidate Jackson Doe. However, when the votes were counted by the Doe-appointed commission, Doe was declared the winner with 50.9 percent of the vote.[38]

On November 12, 1985, less than one month after the election a coup attempt took place that initially appeared to be successful and popularly supported. However, after a few days, troops supporting Doe managed to regain control and eventually went on what the Lawyers Committee for Human Rights called a "bloody rampage," targeting innocent civilians.[39] The government's heavy-handed tactics included the somewhat secret detention of at least a hundred people it considered to be a threat to its continued existence, including well-known political leaders such as Jackson Doe and Ellen Johnson-Sirleaf. On December 10, 1985 (Human Rights Day), the then assistant secretary of state, Chester Crocker, was called to testify before the U.S. Senate Subcommittee on Africa. Crocker conceded that there had been "shortcomings" with the Liberian elections of October 1985 but he also made it clear that the Reagan administration was standing behind Doe. Crocker also said that the shortcomings should not obscure the "noteworthy, positive aspects" of the election.[40] Crocker sited as noteworthy activities, the large and orderly turnout, the participation of four political parties and the press's ability to report on opposition activities. Crocker concluded,

> there is now the beginning, however imperfect, of a democratic experience that Liberia and its friends can use as a benchmark for future elections one on which they want to build . . . election day was a remarkable achievement . . . to walk away [from Liberia] would be irresponsible and clearly viewed as such elsewhere in Africa, where we are seen as having a unique responsibility for assisting Liberia.[41]

The U.S. Senate unanimously passed a resolution finding the 1985 Liberian election to be fraudulent and called on the Reagan administration to suspend military aid to Liberia until all political prisoners were released and free elections held. Nevertheless, Samuel Doe was inaugurated president of the Republic of Liberia on January 6, 1986. Even after the adoption of a popularly approved Constitution in that same month, the Doe government began what would eventually lead to the collapse of the Liberian state. Opposition parties were banned from holding public rallies often at gunpoint. Some of the party leaders were arrested and publicly whipped. The independent newspapers were harassed and threatened into silence, including personal death threats from Doe, and the judiciary was cowed into subservience, self-censorship, and simply proved to be unable to rule against the authorities in politically sensitive cases, thereby compromising the rule of law in Liberia. Rampant corruption within the Doe regime led to seventeen financial experts being sent out by the United States in November 1987, however, by November 1988 the team was withdrawn, after commenting that they had failed to curb extrabudgetary operations.[42] For the Reagan administration, from its Cold War perspective it was still business as usual in Liberia.

Despite growing internal and external appeals for Doe to relinquish power in Liberia, he was once heard stating within the Executive Mansion that the only way he would leave the presidency was if his enemies killed him and if he was going down then he would take the country with him.[43] These comments became prophetic as he was brutally assassinated (a videotape of his being tortured and dismembered was later circulated in Liberia) in 1990 following the outbreak of the devastating civil war in 1989, which began as an effort to unseat him and terminate his regime.

WAR, FACTIONS, AND THE COLLAPSE OF THE LIBERIAN STATE

The history of the civil war in Liberia is a catalogue of brutal abuses, the full extent of which may never be known. The war has resulted in the death of an estimated 200,000 Liberians and caused over 600,000 more to flee the country. In early 1997, more than 400,000 Liberian refugees were in Guinea, over 300,000 in Cote d'Ivoire, about 5,000 in Sierra Leone and thousands more in Ghana and Nigeria. At least one million people were internally displaced within Liberia itself. The bare statistics hide countless human tragedies.[44]

In late December 1989, a group of armed militants formed a popularly supported guerilla organization known as the National Patriotic Front of Liberia (NPFL). The NPFL had crossed into Liberia from neighboring Cote d'Ivoire to attack government targets in northeastern Liberia's Nimba County. Eventually the NPFL's activities led to what became known as the "Christmas coup of 1989," which unseated President Samuel Doe.

The NPFL was led by a young charismatic leader, Charles Taylor, who had been a member of Doe's government prior to fleeing the country amidst allegations of embezzlement and corruption.[45] Taylor was arrested in the United States and incarcerated in the Massachusetts prison system but somehow managed to escape and flee the United

States. Taylor and the NPFL initially received popular support from many of Liberia's veteran political leaders as the "Saviors" that had a mission to abolish the oppressive Doe regime. In the initial phases of what became a seven-year civil war, Taylor stated that he was not interested in power but rather was only interested in removing Samuel Doe and his "tyrannical government." Once this was accomplished he would have fulfilled his mission.

On September 9, 1990, moving from the headquarters of the Economic Community of West African states (ECOWAS), a third group led by Prince Yormie Johnson launched a massive attack that led to the capture, torture, and assassination of Samuel Doe.[46] However, as opposed to ending the conflict, Doe's assassination proved to be only another step toward the beginning of one of the bloodiest civil wars in African history.

According to Amnesty International and other human rights international organizations, the conflict in Liberia was marked by a blatant disregard for international human rights and humanitarian standards by all parties.

> The warring factions have terrorized the local population. Fighters have mutilated captives, using their victims's intestines to cordon off areas newly controlled by the victorious group. They have cut up human bodies and scattered them around villages. Many have passed under the control of successive warring factions and Liberia has effectively become a series of competing fiefdoms ruled by factional leaders.[47]

There were between eight and eleven factions fighting in Liberia at any one time. Among the most significant groups were the following: the Armed Forces of Liberia (AFL), the national army often acting as an armed group independent of government control; the Liberian Peace Council (LPC) led by George Boley; the National Patriotic Front of Liberia (NPFL) led by Charles Taylor, which at times controlled more than half the country; the Independent National Patriotic Front of Liberia, which splintered from the NPFL and was led by Prince Yormie Johnson; and the United Liberation Movement for Democracy in Liberia (ULIMO), which split along ethnic lines and was led by Roosevelt Johnson (ULIMO-J) and Alhaji Kromah (ULIMO-K).[48]

In fact, the deliberate incitement of hostility between different ethnic groups was a major part in the war in Liberia. Atrocities were regularly committed against civilians on the basis of their ethnic origins. Civilians were arbitrarily denounced for spying for one faction or another and faced a range of penalties, from harassment and detention to extrajudicial execution. With the collapse of numerous state institutions, including those responsible for maintaining law and order, civilians had little or no recourse against any of the combatants. Moreover, as Liberian citizens fled their villages and communities in search of peace it was not uncommon to be stopped at checkpoints where one would be asked which ethnic group they belonged to only to be killed if the answer was different from the one posing the question. Even among the same ethnic groups, all of one's belongings were likely to be stolen at these "checkpoints." One Liberian survivor of the war, relayed a story in which a man in front of him came to a checkpoint and was faced by rebels who admired his ring and decided to whittle down his finger with a machete rather than simply cut off the finger as a method of torture in an effort to remove the ring. This demonic act left the man without skin or flesh completely down to his bone as he screamed for mercy and now lives with the memory of this event.[49]

During the war, all the main factions received support from various West African states and some from North African states as well.

> The major players in the Liberian conflict have each received support from other West African countries. Nigeria, which dominates the regional peacekeeping force ECOMOG, has supported armed factions opposed to the NPFL, especially during the early years of the conflict. The governments of Burkina Faso and Cote d'Ivoire have at times openly support the NPFL. Guinean security forces have offered tacit support to the ULIMO-K faction. . . . ULIMO-K in Guinea has been allowed to operate with the support of local government officials and members of the Guinean security forces of the same ethnic origin. Guinean authorities have arrested Liberian refugees suspected of supporting factions opposed to ULIMO-K.[50]

In late 1992, armed conflict intensified. Only the capital city of Monrovia remained in the hands of the Interim Government of National Unity (IGNU) led by Dr. Amos Sawyer. The city was protected by the peacekeeping troops from the Economic Community of West African States (ECOWAS). Most of the rest of the country was controlled by the National Patriotic Reconstruction Assembly Government (NPRAG), a rival administration set up in 1990 by Taylor's rebel force.[51]

The bloodbath that was occurring between the main warring groups in the country; the AFL, the NPFL, and the other factions, led to mammoth appeals for the United States to intervene militarily to resolve the conflict based on the "special relationship" of the two countries.

However, despite massive criticism within Liberia and among numerous Liberian-Americans, the United States only deployed Marines to Liberia to evacuate U.S. citizens living within the country. The U.S. policy toward Liberia became one of encouraging a regional solution to an emerging regional crisis. According to Human Rights Watch it was at the height of the war in 1990 when the United States withdrew from its formerly close engagement with Liberia. Human Rights Watch argued that the new direction was through the United Nations and for support of the Economic Community of West African States (ECOWAS),

> the U.S. maintained a policy of neutrality and sought ties with all factions while remaining the leading donor to the victims of the war. Toward the end of 1993, when it became clear that the latest peace plan required substantial U.S. assistance if it was to succeed, the Clinton administration, with congressional support, made Liberia a higher priority. The main tenets of stated U.S. policy toward Liberia are to support conflict resolution efforts by ECOWAS and the U.N., to withhold recognition of any of the governments that have been created since the war began, and to promote ECOWAS and its peace plan. By the end of 1993, the conflict resolution efforts had gained new momentum: on September 30, the U.S. obligated $19.83 million ($13 million in Economic Support Funds and the rest in Foreign Military Financing) to the U.N. Trust Fund for peacekeeping in Liberia. The money is to be used by ECOMOG and the OAU to help finance the deployment of the expanded ECOMOG troops—not for assistance with lethal weapons, but for transportation, food, and non-lethal equipment for the troops. On December 20, 1993, the U.S. allocated an additional $11 million in support for the U.N. monitored African peacekeeping operation in Liberia.[52]

The lack of direct action in U.S./Liberia policy was also heavily influenced by the Gulf War and the "Somalia Syndrome" that resulted following the failure of "Operation Restore Hope," the United States' 1991 "humanitarian intervention" there. The graphic display of a dead White American solider's body being dragged down the streets of Mogadishu was too much for U.S. policy-makers to stomach or explain to their constituents.

Liberian author Bill Enoanyi observed regarding that period,

> Many Liberians felt betrayed by the United States. They felt that the United States should have intervened militarily to prevent the atrocities committed against civilians. They rejected the United States position that it could not interfere in Liberia's internal affairs, arguing not only that the United States has always done just that—and for much less noble causes than preventing civilian deaths—but also that the United States had intervened in other situations where civilians were less at risk. . . . A member of the Interim Government of Liberia stated, "Where was our oldest friend when we were going through this nightmare? Many people flocked to Monrovia thinking that the Marines (which the US had stationed off the coast of Monrovia to protect US citizens if necessary) would land and stop the massacre," or at least create a safety zone in which civilians could seek refuge. "Despite appeal upon appeal upon appeal," he said, that did not happen.[53]

After seven years of fighting and thirteen peace accords, Liberians as well as the international community assumed that peace had come to the war-torn country following the signing of the Abuja Accords in August 1995, the most comprehensive of the thirteen accords. However, the nation was shocked by bitter fighting that broke out April 1996 in Monrovia. The massive offensive occurred when police, believed to be allied with the NPFL, attempted to arrest Roosevelt Johnson, leader of the rival ULIMO-J faction. The initial protagonists were the NPFL and ULIMO-J, but all the other armed groups later became involved in the fighting. The AFL, the LPC, and ULIMO-J fought together against the NPFL and its former rival ULIMO-K.[54]

The April 6 fighting, left the civilian population terrorized as mortars and gunfire filled the air. Armed faction members roamed the streets, looting, maiming, and killing. The mutilated bodies of those killed were openly displayed and piled high on the beautiful white beaches of Monrovia. The fighting centered around the Barclay Training military barracks in central Monrovia. Rival armed groups cordoned off the city into different zones as they pounded on one another and destroyed the remaining infrastructure in the country's once attractive capital city.

Months later the violence and chaos that gripped the capital was quelled by the massive intervention of ECOMOG, under new leadership, and through renewed diplomatic efforts and another round of peace talks that resulted in the signing of a Supplementary Agreement to the Abuja Peace Accord of 1996, which called for massive disarmament, demobilization, and a schedule for presidential and legislative elections in 1997.[55]

In February 1997, a sense of calm and security began to blanket the country following the reported disarmament of over 80 percent of the former combatants and the presence of over 10,000 West African peace-keeping troops, the overwhelming majority of whom were Nigerians. Several former faction leaders transformed themselves into presidential candidates and their factions into political parties. Additionally, an ad hoc election commission was formed to organize Liberia's first elections in twelve years.

In recognition of Liberian efforts toward peace and stability, the international community began actively supporting the electoral exercise. The European Union began massive humanitarian assistance, which included providing drinking water for the entire country. The ECOWAS states increased and diversified their peacekeeping manpower with new troops arriving from Mali, Benin, and Ghana. The United Nations increased its military observer presence in the country and intensified their civic education efforts.

The 1997 July Liberian Special Elections:
A Referendum on Peace?

Following the signing of the Supplemental Agreement to the Abuja Peace Accords, a number of benchmarks set out in the accords began to be met including: large-scale disarmament and demobilization of the armed combatants; significant numbers of externally and internally displaced refugees began to return to the country; government officials interested in contesting the elections resigned from office in compliance with a February 28 deadline and an independent election commission was inducted to administer the elections. In anticipation of the elections, a number of political parties that existed prior to the civil war resurfaced and began organizing themselves in preparation for the legislative and presidential elections then scheduled for May 30, 1997.[56]

By mid-April 1997, the Special Election legislation governing the election had not been released in preparation for the then scheduled May 30 general elections. As a result of the lack of an electoral framework, and weak provisions for voter registration and education among other factors, Catholic Archbishop Michael Francis, called for a postponement of the election date. Thereafter, all the major political parties and nongovernmental organizations, with the exception of Taylor's National Patriotic Party (NPP), echoed that demand. Following appeals from civil society, political parties, and religious leaders, the Election Commission petitioned ECOWAS at its annual summit, which was chaired by Nigerian dictator General Sini Abacha, and the date of the election was postponed to July 19, 1997, to allow for sufficient preparations.

Thirteen political parties or coalitions were accredited by IECOM and participated in the elections.[57] Political parties could legally begin to actively campaign throughout the country on June 16 and had to end their activities by July 17 so that there could be a one-day cooling off period. Citizens could register to vote from June 24 to July 3, 1997. July 4 to July 11 was set aside to allow for a "claims and objection" period where verification and review of the voters list by citizens and political parties could occur. The IECOM voter education effort was one of the main weaknesses of the entire process. For example, IECOM continued to expand the different types of marks that would be acceptable in marking the ballots, making it more difficult to explain clearly to citizens how to mark the ballot. In addition, the number of polling sites continued to change until the day before the elections. IECOM decided at the last minute that it would circulate a sample ballot that had been drawn up by the main domestic monitoring organization, the Liberian Elections Observers Network (LEON). Therefore, the LEON activists who had planned to use the sample ballots as teaching tools were not able to do so.[58]

In what undoubtably will be recorded as one of the most amazing electoral results in modern African politics, Charles Taylor, considered by some as a notorious warlord, emerged victorious. The Taylor landslide victory has been interpreted in many different ways and given the complex political situation in Liberia and West Africa, it will certainly continue to be interpreted from many angles. Several international media agencies portrayed the elections as an opportunity for Liberians to vote for democracy.[59] However, Liberian political observers and activists involved in the process before, during and after the elections, believed that the more appropriate interpretation of the results was that the Liberian people were voting for peace not democracy, and only saw the elections as a stepping stone to democracy. In other words, the vote was really a referendum on peace.[60] The brutality of the warring factions, millions of shattered lives, endless days of doing nothing for seven years, the destroyed dreams, senseless deaths, and stolen childhoods oriented most Liberian thinking as they stood in line for hours and as they entered the polling stations to cast their vote for the first time since October 1985. Most Liberians evidently believed that if Taylor was not elected the war would continue.

The electoral results were nothing short of astonishing considering that some Taylor supporters used the slogan, in the local pigeon English, "You killed my ma, but I will vote for you. You killed my pa but I will vote for you."[61] Over 80 percent of the Liberians who registered under the circumstances described above exercised their franchise leading to the overwhelming victory by the former faction leader Charles Taylor. The NPP won at least 75 percent of the vote and its next closest competitor, Ellen Johnson Sirleaf of the Unity Party received a little less than 10 percent of the total vote. Most international political observers, as well as a good number of domestic political commentators, had believed that a run-off between Taylor and former Liberian finance minister, Johnson-Sirleaf, would be the more likely outcome because of the size of the perceived "antifaction" vote based in Monrovia.[62] As pointed out above, there was a relatively high voter turnout across the country. However, this must be seen in the context of a lower than expected voter registration and turnout in Montserrado County, the most populated county in Liberia where the capital city, Monrovia, is located. Additionally, and perhaps more importantly, because of the lack of adequate data it is probable that a majority of Liberians, who at the time of the vote were refugees located in camps in the neighboring countries, were not allowed to vote. The elections commission was unable to make adequate provisions for them to vote.[63]

The newly elected members of the Liberian Congress were sworn into office on August 2, 1997. Five parties won enough votes to be represented in the House of Representatives: the National Patriotic Party (NPP), the Unity Party (UP), the All Liberian Coalition Party (ALCOP), the Alliance (APP), and the Liberian People's Party (LPP). Taylor's NPP won 21 of 26 or 86 percent of the Liberian Senate seats and 49 of 64 or 77 percent of the seats in the Liberian House of Representatives.[64]

The Liberian special elections were significant to the West African region for a number of reasons. Many observers believed that the possibility of a resolution to the conflict in Sierra Leone existed because of the results in Liberia.[65] A second important reason that the peaceful elections were seen as being significant internationally had to do with the regional peacekeeping role played by ECOWAS, through its ECOMOG forces under the command of Nigerian General Victor Malu. The presence of over fifteen thousand military personnel at polling sites (often inside the polling station), backed up by police in most settings would cause many promoters of democratic development to say that there is no way the elections could have been free and fair. Moreover, the observation by domestic and international monitors of the often overzealous involvement of ECOMOG soldiers in the voting process in several areas would further confirm such an opinion.

However, the special elections were "special." Most Liberians believed that the elections were legitimate and acceptable, and certainly would not have been peaceful were it not for the presence of ECOMOG. In fact, the most popular slogan in the country at the time of the elections was, "Thank God for ECOMOG." Secondly, on election day many of the IECOM registrars were unprepared to assist large numbers of illiterate voters. Thus, the opportunity for ECOMOG involvement, to some extent, was generated out of necessity. However, the victory by the person most associated with wartime atrocities, presented a number of institutions with perplexing prospects for continued work in Liberia. Was there a level playing field in Liberia? One could say that election day itself was one of the most peaceful days in Liberia's recent history. However, only reflecting on election day, as most international observation delegations tend to do, would be a tragic mistake in the Liberian situation especially if one were asked to determine or evaluate the fairness of the entire process. The pre-electoral period, the campaign period and the immediate postelection period, were all marred by serious administrative problems and well-known acts of intimidation by several former faction leaders. In fact, access for some presidential candidates was rather restricted to selected parts of the country. Additionally, the vast majority of the population residing outside of the capital had no source of information other than short-wave radio controlled by Taylor or through the Kiss FM radio, the radio station confiscated by Taylor during the civil war.[66]

The new head of the Elections Commission, Paul Guah, claims that there was not one complaint of intimidation or threats. This is not true. Not only were there open attempts to intimidate but several confrontations occurred. According to the LEON observers and the Friends of Liberia reports, acts of intimidation were reported by the Unity Party and ALCOP to the Elections Commission. More importantly, the Election Commission itself was threatened by the NPP leader. Then candidate Taylor warned that "all the angels in heaven" could not protect IECOM Chairman Henry Andrews if the commission changed the elections date. George Boley, leader of the Liberia Peace Council (LPC), released a statement of response to Taylor's threat saying, "The angels are already here." Taylor explained that he was misunderstood. He had to do this because technically any candidate threatening the commission was automatically disqualified.[67] Everyone knew that the commission would not disqualify Taylor but nevertheless the appearance of being in control of the process had to be maintained. Therefore, the commission issued a strongly worded statement that it would not be intimidated by anyone. It is obvious that the new commission chair has either forgotten about this or did not include the commission itself as a target of intimidating activity he was asked about.

The United States' democracy-assistance package totaled $7.5 million and was focused on two main areas. The first area was providing financial and logistical support to the ECOMOG peacekeeping forces and their effort. Secondly, the United States, in consultation with other western donors, provided the bulk of direct support to the Election Commission and its activities to organize the special elections.[68] The U.S.-based nongovernmental organization, the International Foundation for Electoral Systems (IFES), coordinated that effort. The overall United States effort was coordinated through the U.S. embassy because the USAID mission there had been looted and closed years earlier. Activities by U.S.-based nongovernmental organizations such as the National Democratic Institute (NDI), the Carter Center, and a group of former Peace Corps workers called the Friends of Liberia centered mainly around the formation of a domestic election monitoring organization (NDI) and the organizing and deployment of an international election observers delegation (Carter Center).

The role played by Jimmy Carter both during and after the civil war was seen as being critical but quite controversial by many Liberians who believed that the former U.S. president was too close to Taylor and therefore not completely objective in his views. Before the elections, the

United States was by far the largest donor to the Liberian relief effort. The United States mainly provided humanitarian assistance, since other assistance was prohibited by the Brooke amendment, which suspended aid to countries that have failed to repay their loans to the United States.[69]

U.S. democracy assistance was built on a strategy of supporting activities that would foster favorable conditions for good governance, including the establishment of a legal basis for a decentralized public sector and a viable local government with the ability to tax and incur debt in the future. The U.S. government's postelection assistance programs therefore, under the auspices of the U.S. Agency for International Development (USAID), involved enhancing democracy in both the private and public sectors and included civic education programs, capacity building programs for human rights groups and civic organizations that promote political participation, radio programming, and training for the newly elected legislators. USAID's assistance also included training Liberian police and members of the judiciary.

In the immediate postelection period several key components of the U.S. democracy assistance program were conducted by two U.S.-based nongovernmental organizations that were involved during the elections, that is, NDI and IFES.[70] According to USAID, NDI has continued its work to strengthen civil society that it began in the pre-election period. NDI provided orientation and training programs for newly elected Liberian legislators on the role and function of a legislature in a democracy. NDI sponsored, through its civic education program, a Civic Forum, small group discussions throughout Liberia on a variety of democracy-related topics designed to promote constitutional education at the grassroots level. NDI also provided grants to several domestic civic organizations so that Liberians could conduct civic education programs themselves.

IFES continued its work with the Elections Commission to strengthen the electoral infrastructure established during the elections. IFES also attempted to create a nongovernmental resource center to provide civil society groups, newly elected officials, government institutions, and the media with information on a range of topics. The resource center was to organize regular forums on topics of national interest. Additionally, IFES conducted with the assistance of Liberian civic groups, public opinion research to assess public attitudes in order to assist civic groups to build constituencies and develop targeted civic education programs. Through subgrants of USAID funding from IFES, several U.S. and international organizations will support a variety of democracy-related activities in Liberia. These include Search for Common Ground and the Carter Center.

Search for Common Ground's independent radio studio, Talking Drum, is currently supplying programming to numerous Liberian radio stations. Programs focus on news and social issues, with an orientation towards promoting "common ground" between differing sides of issues, and emphasize themes of reconciliation, democratization, and civil society. These programs are produced as social dramas, news magazines, short spots, and round table discussions, and all are in English or local Liberian languages. The Swiss NGO Foundation Hirondelle will continue operating Star Radio, an independent radio station established in Liberia in July to provide impartial and factual information to Liberians living in-country and in neighboring regions, with broadcasts in English, French, and 14 local languages.[71]

The Carter Center's program focuses on monitoring human rights developments and organizing a series of consultations on the structure and function of the planned Liberian Human Rights Commission. The Carter Center is also working with the Ministry of Education to incorporate human rights and democratic citizenship education into school curriculums.[72]

In addition to different USAID-supported activities, the Department of Justice's International Development Assistance Training Assistance Program provided election related programs for Liberian police and members of the judiciary. The U.S.-trained five hundred policemen under this program prior to the July special elections on how to provide a secure environment for the elections, and additional civil police training activities are planned. Training was also provided to judges on how to arbitrate disputes related to the elections. Future activities are designed to focus on training and staffing members of the courts in order to strengthen the rule of law.[73]

According to *African Voices*, USAID's newsletter on democracy and governance in Africa, the U.S. embassy in Monrovia requested support for several possible projects under the joint Department of State and USAID Democracy and Human Rights Fund (DHRF), which supports activities to promote civil and political rights. Possible DHRF activities include workshops on issues related to women's and children's rights and the development of curriculum materials on conflict resolution.[74]

The U.S. Information Service (USIS) has also undertaken several training programs and consultative visits by human rights activists and legal experts from the United States, and implemented exchange programs focusing on the rule of law, human rights, and civic education.[75] What the impact of all the aforementioned programs has been remains to be seen. In fact, most of the programs were temporarily interrupted because of the shoot-out at the American embassy in September 1998 between Liberian security forces and former faction leaders Roosevelt Johnson discussed below.

Although many people took a wait and see attitude toward the Taylor government some initial moves by the new regime did send signals that it was prepared to move on and rebuild Liberia. In the months immediately following Charles Taylor's election victory several very noteworthy developments occurred on the reconciliation front. The curfew between 12 midnight and 6 a.m., which had been in place for years was lifted and a number of the roadblocks throughout the capital were removed. The positive psychological impact of those action are hard to describe. A good number of opposition political leaders were granted posts in the new government. Alhaji Kromah, one of the main faction leaders, was appointed head of a special government commission, the National Reconciliation and Reunification Commission. Several ministries were headed by opposition party leaders. Roosevelt Johnson was offered the post of minister of rural development and later the post as ambassador to India. A strong and independent-minded woman, Gloria Scott, was named chief justice of the Liberian Supreme Court and instantly revived faith among large sectors of the population that some semblance of the rule of law could possibly return to the country and its judicial system. The two interim heads of state, Amos Sawyer and Ruth Perry, were given the status of Eminent Persons. Additionally, a promised government-supported Human Rights Commission was established.[76]

However, there were also some ominous signs of things to come. Alhaji Kromah turned down his appointment as Chairman of the National Reconciliation and Reunification Commission and Roosevelt Johnson relinquished his appointment as minister. Relations with the governments of Guinea and Sierra Leone began to get worse as accusations were leveled by each government against Liberia for allegedly interfering in their internal affairs. Three radio stations were temporarily closed down by the Taylor government under the pretense that a new tax had been imposed and the stations must pay it or go off the air.[77] A large group of former NPFL combatants were turned into a special national police force known as the "SSS." The historical reference point for such a name was either lost on the Taylor government or ignored. True to it namesake, this group since its founding, according to Liberian citizens, has terrorized whole communities, publicly beaten individuals, destroyed property, and murdered innocent citizens.[78]

One of the most controversial examples of the SSS's outlaw behavior is the abduction and brutal murder of Samuel Dokie and his family in November 1997. According to published reports, Dokie and his wife, daughter, and niece were all picked up by the secret police from local county authorities where Dokie had gone for protection, begging the local official not to let the police take him when he learned that the SSS were looking for him. Dokie was later found decapitated. His wife and the children had been raped and all the bodies had been set a blaze.[79] The mutilated bodies were only discovered three days later. Many believe that the SSS were acting on orders from higher officials, especially since Dokie had worked closely with the NPP before switching over to the Unity Party of Ellen Johnson Sirleaf. In fact, the head of the SSS publicly admitted that he ordered the arrest of Dokie.

In the United States, during the period immediately following the July elections, many independent citizens and NGO efforts to assist with the transition to civilian government took place. One of the more watched events was a special Liberian/African American meeting held in Chicago, Illinois in May 1998. The meeting was organized by Rev. Jesse Jackson at his PUSH/Rainbow headquarters to discuss some of the most pressing challenges of national reconstruction in Liberia and to determine ways in which African Americans could support development and reconciliation efforts in Liberia. Several high-ranking members of the Taylor government attended as did a few thousand Liberian and African American citizens from all over the United States. The gathering was addressed by Susan Rice, the U.S. Assistant Secretary of State for African Affairs, and several members of the Congressional Black Caucus.[80] A subsequent weeklong conference on national reconstruction and the future of Liberia was organized in the Liberian capital city, Monrovia, and was also attended by Jackson, several hundred Liberians (many who were based in the United States), and a number of U.S. businesspersons. Jackson's apparently close but confusing relationship with Taylor has also been closely scrutinized by Liberian human rights groups. The Monrovia conference on the future of Liberia has been considered by most Liberians to have been a dismal failure as none of the popularly adopted resolutions or recommendations have been implemented by the Liberian government.

The September 1998 Clash

On September 18, 1998, Liberian security forces conducted a military assault on Camp Johnson Road in Monrovia. Hundreds of SSS officers and members of the police Special Task Force, joined by scores of irregular former combatants of Taylor's former faction, employed automatic weapons, rocket-propelled grenades, and mortars. In a seventeen-hour battle, as many as three hundred people were killed, many of them women and children. In the aftermath, according to reports including the State Department's human rights report on Liberia,

> The security forces committed many extrajudicial killings. Police shot and killed suspects in custody, and security forces on September 18

encircled and killed perhaps hundreds of ethnic Krahns who were affiliated with a faction that opposed Taylor during the civil war. Members of the SSS were implicated in the disappearance and apparent murder of a market woman. Security forces tortured, beat and otherwise abused or humiliated citizens.[81]

House-to-house searches and summary executions by government forces followed the gun battles. Krahn leader Roosevelt Johnson survived the attack and sought refuge in the U.S. embassy. According to the U.S. State Department,

> Krahn leader Roosevelt Johnson survived the initial attack and sought refuge in a Western embassy on September 19; police opened fire on Johnson and seven supporters in the entryway of the embassy, killing two members of Johnson's party, wounding other members of his party as well as two embassy employees. One hour later and three blocks away, several international NGO workers witnessed an execution of an unidentified male by security force members. Five senior officers and several junior officers of the Krahn-dominated Armed Forces of Liberia (AFL) were interrogated and tortured on September 21 at a military stockade in central Monrovia. They were then taken to a military base outside the capital and executed. The Government falsely claimed that the men had been caught in crossfire during the September 19 fighting. Eleven persons reportedly were tortured before being killed on October 1. Following these events, about 9,000 persons, most members of the Krahn ethnic group, fled from the country to neighboring Cote d'Ivoire.[82]

Thirty-three people were subsequently charged with plotting a coup against President Taylor. Twenty others who were also charged with treason were out of the country. Fourteen Liberians were convicted by a twelve-man jury of treason, which carried the death penalty, after a ninety-six-day trial.[83] Most of the defendants did not have adequate legal counsel and the state refused to provide resources to assist them with their defense and key state witnesses perjured themselves with inconsistent and contradictory testimonies. The prosecution spent a considerable amount of time trying to convince the jury that the trial was not a veiled attempt by the government to settle political scores by carrying out a witch-hunting expedition targeting the Krahn leadership. All fourteen of the convicted were from the Krahn ethnic group.[84]

Predictably, U.S./Liberian relations suffered a serious set back. In addition, the September clash led to the withdrawal of all nonessential U.S. personnel from Liberia and a suspension of all government-to-government assistance. Concerns exist inside the U.S. government, at the State Department, and in Congress, with respect to official Liberian involvement in the brutal conflict in Sierra Leon, the inde-

pendence of the judiciary that seems to be "hampered by ineffi-
ciency, corruption and a lack of resources,"[85] and the independence
of the legislative branch given the NPP dominance and sacking of
Senate Pro Tempore Attorney Charles Brumskin, who had emerged
as one of the clearest democratic voices in the country. Brumskin had
even led a senate resolution that authorized investigations into the
allegations that the Liberian government was involved with the
rebels in Sierra Leone and that called on the government to name its
ambassadors to Sierra Leone and Nigeria. Nevertheless, in the context of bombings at two U.S. embassies on the African continent, in
Kenya and Tanzania, the United States demanded an official apology
from the Liberian government and the United Nations appointed a
fact-finding mission to Liberia to look into the September assault at
the U.S. embassy in Monrovia. After months of acrimonious
exchanges a letter of regret by the Taylor government was forwarded
to the U.S. government. The United Nations also agreed to conduct
an investigation into the incident. The mission has taken place and a
report is still pending.

CHALLENGES OF DEMOCRATIZATION IN LIBERIA

Liberia is a country recovering from seven years of devastating ethnically based civil war that led to the country being fractionalized at every
level. During the war the state collapsed, more than two hundred thousand people were killed, thousands more maimed, and over one million
others were displaced out of an estimated three million citizens. The
democratization and national reconstruction processes, begun via the
July elections, have the arduous task of attempting to achieve two major
objectives in a short time-frame: (1) establishing and maintaining peace;
and (2) recreating a democratic nation-state in a country where the rule
of law was replaced by warlords and factions.

With a devastated economy, a traumatized population, an ethnically divided citizenry, and a president who was formerly proud to be
known as a warlord, Liberians have the challenge before themselves of
democratizing the country, establishing peace, and rebuilding a nation.
Numerous challenges and difficult choices exist in Liberia, causing all
those who would desire to assist to determine whether they will say
something or simply close their eyes and use "quiet diplomacy," essentially remaining silent in the face of well-documented atrocities, as has
been done in the past. It is clear that new voices need to be raised and
the "special relationship" redefined. Several of the more salient challenges that exist follow.

The Liberian Political Economy and Democratization

Liberia has a $1 billion dollar public debt and an external debt over $3 billion that has been defaulted because of the collapse of the state structure. The country's national budget in FY 1998 was only $64 million dollars. It is probable that international financial institutions will require the implementation of a structural adjustment program with the familiar harsh components of further devaluation of the Liberian currency, reduction of the civil service, and so on.

Followers of international politics are familiar with the reality that IMF and World Bank structural adjustment programs keep Africa tied to the dictates of the international financial and economic system. Some even believe that Africa's debt owed to the international financial institutions is the main factor that is causing Africa to become almost completely marginalized in the contemporary world economy.[86] In the past, the existence of structural adjustment rules of conditionality led many authoritarian African leaders such as Banda, Bokassa, Amin, Mobutu, and Babangida to create what is known as "facade democracy" in order to continue receiving aid. Liberia, under the Taylor government, has the challenge of rebuilding its devastated economy with the debt crisis looming over its head and the added difficulty of determining which currency will exist in a country that had three currencies based on factional division. Faced with massive debt, an estimated 95 percent unemployment rate, a decimated infrastructure, and reports that only $16,000 existed in the state treasury, led Taylor soon after being elected president to call for the country's citizens to "tighten their belts" and recognize it may be a long time before late salaries would be paid and citizens would be gainfully employed.

Furthermore, Elie E. Saleeby, Liberia's former finance minister, had the problem of solving the, "tale of three currencies." As reported in the December 1997 issue of *New African* magazine, Liberia had three currencies operating at the same time. Eighty percent of commercial transactions in the country are done in U.S. dollars. The remaining 20 percent is shared by Liberia's two local currencies, both called the "dollar" but with attachments. The Liberian dollar known as the J. J. named after J. J. Roberts, Liberia's first president, was introduced by the Doe regime in 1981. The other currency, called the Liberty, was introduced in April 1991 by Dr. Amos Sawyer's Interim Government of National Unity. That reality was further compounded by street-based money exchanger determining the exchange rate on a daily basis.

Realizing that Liberia was once a "collapsed state," there are any number of other major challenges to a democratic transition and democratic consolidation in the country. However, ethnic reintegration, the development of women and youth, the rebuilding of the infrastructure, reestablishment and strengthening of democratic institutions, the launching of a sustainable economic development program, and the resettlement of refugees and the internally displaced must top the list.

There are almost twenty ethnic groups dispersed throughout the country including: Bassa, Belle, Dey, Gbandi, Gio, Gola, Grebo, Kissi, Kpelle, Krahn, Kru, Loma, Mandingo, Mano, Mende, and Vai. These groups as they attempt to resettle in their original villages, have the awesome tasks of overcoming the ethnic genocide of the Civil War and attempt to rebuild their lives as neighbors alongside some of those responsible for the "ethnic cleansing" of their family members. Issues pertaining to reintegration can only be solved by recognizing both the differences of these groups and their commonalities. Bridging the gap of traditional tribalism is very difficult and will require years of reeducation and resocialization. Warring ethnic groups cannot be cast together in the name of nationalism or expected to abandon their opposition simply because their leader did not win an election. The important issue in the pursuit of establishing equality and harmony among diverse groups is not only political but also psychological. It is important that no groups feel permanently excluded from the decision-making process.[87] Shared power and shared heritage must be emphasized by grassroots education.

Detraumatization and programs that increase women's self-worth will be vital for Liberian women to overcome the history of brutality that allowed the systematic abuse and rape of over twenty-five thousand women throughout the seven-year war. Many of these women are raising children that remind them that they were savagely raped often numerous times by child soldiers who left them demoralized, plagued with sexually transmitted diseases, and a child with a rapist for a father. Women, who are the overwhelming majority population, also face an estimated 87 percent illiteracy rate and generalized social discrimination.

The work necessary to rehabilitate child soldiers is only just beginning. The sad truth is that many of the young people are psychologically and physically damaged to such a point that they may never be able to lead a normal life. Because some traditional programs for ex-combatants do not necessarily address all the needs of child soldiers, their conditions could continue to be a source of insecurity throughout the country, especially as the child soldiers grow up to adulthood.[88]

Reestablishing the state and democratic institutions will be a major challenge for some time to come. The independence of the legislative and the judicial branches of government still does not exist. In fact, in early 1999 Taylor purchased new vehicles for most congresspersons. The average salary for a member of the Liberian Congress is $40 a month. The restoration of the rule of law may well be the most difficult challenge of all. Even the physical infrastructure will take years to repair. Many of the buildings that once housed state institutions were occupied by thousands of displaced persons and are now slowing being renovated. More fundamentally, however, is the realization that many of those institutions were never run in a democratic manner even before the 1980 coup. The challenges in this area may end up being the most difficult to meet especially because of the overly centralized system of governance used by the Taylor regime, which still functions more like a command and control military structure rather than a modern democratic government. For instance, the judicial systems, and the rule of law were virtually nonexistent until recently, passports at one point could be purchased easily, and some of the country's most precious resources were being smuggled out of the country in a not so inconspicuous manner. The normal functioning of many institutions has been distorted and petty corruption is rife as most civil servants had gone years without being paid and are still not earning a living wage.

The lack of sustainable economic development and poverty alleviation programs are also major constraints to the democratization process in Liberia. The overwhelming majority of the population lives in abject poverty, earning less than one dollar per day. While per capita income figures do not exist, estimates of at least 90 percent of the population living in abject poverty are figures used by the United Nations Development Program. Moreover, also because of the war and migratory patterns a severe housing shortage exist in both the urban and the rural areas as homes were a favorite target of all the warring factions. The education system from primary to university is in desperate need of rehabilitation. In a number of communities the educational system is only just beginning to function again. Access to quality health care has all but disappeared. The John F. Kennedy hospital, once the best in West Africa, is operating at a minimum level with few medications or doctors. Food is generally scarce and the only clean water is provided by the European Union. Most of the land has not been farmed in years and because of the war farm animals are rare. Electricity exists only for those with generators. A serious national reconstruction and development program is necessary to be created and systematically implemented. Such a program would need to assign clear benchmarks that government can measure and report on progress. The creation of a business environment especially where Liberians can participate and thrive is also important. Currently, most businesses in the capital city are run by

Lebanese. At some point if business opportunities are not expanded for Liberians, tensions between Liberians and Lebanese (some who have lived in Liberia for a generation or more) will explode.

The resettlement and reintegration of refugee populations are a major democratic challenge. There remains large Liberian refugee populations in Guinea, Cote d'Ivoire, Ghana, and Nigeria. Their return to productive land is possible and some efforts have already started in this area. The roads and bridges are in extremely bad condition and remain a deterrent for many with the seed and farming tools. The resettlement and reintegration programs have to succeed or the country could face serious problems of national reconstruction long into the twenty-first century.

Finally, increasing political participation in the decision-making process may be a central benchmark by which to measure the pace of democratization in Liberia. Decentralization and revival of local and country government could be a key to this. After seven years of war and a decade of autocratic rule before that, the very politized population has been demoralized and is unsure of how to exercise its rights and responsibilities. Therefore, if civil society empowerment is to occur, Liberian citizens, community-based organizations, and other nongovernmental organizations will have to overcome a well-founded legacy of fear and intimidation associated with getting "too" involved in public life.

Related to successfully meeting of all the identified challenges is the need for thoughtful and mature leadership. Liberia's attempt at nation building and a democratic transition and consolidation effort will fail if mature leadership is not exhibited by the newly elected and appointed officials. A related challenge in that regard will be the need for the newly elected leadership to guard against the authoritarian tendencies that were an inherent part of the command structure developed during the civil war. If not checked from the outset this may prove to be at odds with the needed period of tolerance and reconciliation. For a number of political observers Charles Taylor himself is one of the main constraints to democratic development in Liberia. On May 14, 1999, Taylor sacked his entire cabinet and heads of state companies for them failing to attend a religious meeting and observing a three-day fast and prayer period that he had declared. Most were reinstated a day later but some were not, including the Ministers of Defense, Foreign Affairs and Justice. Internationally recognized Liberian human rights activist Kofi Woods has suggested that what exists today in Liberia is a criminal state and that Taylor therefore cannot allow for a independent legislature or a strong and independent judiciary. Whatever the case, if Liberia is to survive the various challenges of democratization and development have to be addressed.

AFRICAN AMERICANS AND POLICY OPTIONS
FOR DEMOCRATIC CONSOLIDATION

Despite notable individual acts of public diplomacy, and except for the anti-apartheid campaign against the racist minority regime in South Africa, organized African American support for democratic struggles in the international community during the immediate post–Cold War era has not been clearly articulated.

The Liberian case presents a number of unique opportunities for the African American community to launch a community crusade for the promotion of human rights and democracy in Africa. All of the issues that African Americans have been concerned with in the United States for much of the twentieth century are present in Liberia. Poverty, unemployment, full participation, sustainable development, the debt crisis, democratic governance, and the protection of human rights are all central issues for the consolidation of democracy in Liberia.

Several of the options open to African Americans have to first be considered against the background of what the Black community in the United States is well placed to do, current trends in United States foreign policy, and political realities on Capitol Hill. The Congressional Black Caucus is well respected and has a number of members who have visited Liberia and are very supportive of U.S. investment and aid while being knowledgeable of the complexities there. The caucus' point person on Liberia is former caucus chair and House International Affairs Committee member, Congressman Donald Payne. The special envoy for President Clinton on Liberia is Ambassador Howard Jeter. Jeter is a well respected and tested career diplomat who has a very good knowledge of Liberia and all the political actors. Vivian Lowery-Derrick, who is the Africa Bureau chief for USAID, knows Liberia and has been working on West African issues for over twenty years. Susan Rice, the assistant secretary of state for African affairs, has been involved with Liberian politics for some time. In addition, Rev. Jackson, the special envoy for human rights and democracy, has played a very important, albeit controversial, role in the Liberian political situation and has the potential to be a very positive force especially because of his relationship to the Clinton administration. There are also thousands of well-informed Liberian Americans in the United States who could be called upon to help educate African Americans about the current realities in a manner similar to what South African activists did during the anti-apartheid campaign period.

The following are a few options open to the African American community that could assist Liberia in its democratization and nation-state rebuilding process:

1. Devise and support community-based economic development projects in Liberia. The African American business community could take the lead in developing projects that would help to improve the human resources of the country. Additionally, skilled personnel exchanges could be arranged for short-term assistance needs. Investment could be in the safe and productive exploitation of many of Liberia's natural resources such as rubber, diamonds, gold, and timber.

2. Establish and maintain direct links between nongovernmental organizations. African American churches could establish material support projects and literacy programs through already existing networks. Historically it has mainly been White missionaries who have spread the gospel in Liberia and established institutions to assist in the alleviation of poverty and underdevelopment. The Black church is well positioned to play a huge role in this area. African American professional associations could commit to working with its counterpart in Liberia and develop innovative programs.

3. Develop academic and cultural exchange programs, especially in areas related to rebuilding state institutions. Historically Black colleges and universities could establish extension programs as well as faculty and student exchange programs. Such programs could be targeted to professional staff and personnel development for specific areas of work. Additionally, scholarship schemes could be established to assist with the development of young professionals in some of the critical areas of new information technology, solar energy, and agricultural sciences.

4. Monitor and expose human rights violations in Liberia. The protection of human rights should be high on the list of what can be done to support the consolidation of democracy in Liberia. The atrocities committed during the civil war must be documented and those responsible should be held accountable. Support for a truth and reconciliation commission is warranted. Short of that it may prove difficult for Liberians to put the past behind them or to have confidence that such violations will not occur in the future. Contemporary manifestations of harassment, intimidation, and criminal behavior by the security forces should be denounced and those responsible for extrajudicial executions brought to justice. In addition, those courageous human rights activists who have and can remain inside the country have to be defended and supported by the international community and especially African American human rights and social justice organizations.

It should be clear from the analysis that United States bears a tremendous responsibility for what has taken place in Liberia. Its support of the brutal Doe regime for close to a decade is inexcusable and cannot be ignored. Nevertheless, the end of the "special relationship" between Liberia and the United States has coincided with the end of the Cold War era. This period can be an opportunity for African Americans and others wishing to assist a country that can create a different future for itself. If the attention and assistance is not forthcoming, a true democratic transition and the possibility of democratic consolidation may be impossible. Moreover, if that is the case, the United States will continue to be called upon to provide humanitarian support, more than likely at a higher cost if an attempt is made to ignore the legacies of what has been one of Africa's worse tragedies.

NOTES

1. U.S. Department of State, *1998 United States Strategic Plan for International Affairs*, Washington, D.C., February 1998, p. 31.

2. Ibid.

3. Ibid.

4. Marina Ottaway, CSIS African Notes, No. 171, Center for Strategic and International Studies: Washington, D.C. April 1995, p. 1. For a breakdown on sectoral distribution of funding, see ibid., appendix 1.

5. Jackson was appointed in 1998 amid some fanfare and controversy. Many African American political analysts believed that any independence would be compromised. However, Jackson and others believed that the position would give him access to the highest foreign policy officials at the National Security Council, the State Department, the Department of Defense, and the President himself.

6. For a glance at some of the more important perspectives in the debate on democratization in Africa, see for instance the following works: Peter Anyang 'Nyong'o (ed.), *Popular Struggles for Democracy in Africa* (London: Zed Books/The United Nations University, 1987); Claude Ake, "Rethinking African Democracy," *Journal of Democracy*, vol. 2, no. 1 (Winter 1990), pp. 32–44.; Lual Deng, Markus Kostner, and Crawford Young (eds.), *Democratization and Structural Adjustment in Africa in the 1990s* (Madison: University of Wisconsin/African Studies Program, 1991); Llyod Sachikongye, *Democracy, Civil Society and the State: Social Movements in Southern Africa* (Harare: SAPES Trust, 1995); David Garnham and Mark Tessler (eds.), *Democracy, War and Peace in the Middle East* (Bloomington: Indiana University Press, 1995); Issac Shivji (ed.), *State and Constitutionalism: An African Debate on Democracy* (Harare: SAPES Trust, 1991); and Marina Ottaway (ed.), *Democracy in Africa: The Hard Road Ahead* (Boulder, Colo.: Lynne Rienner, 1997).

7. See, for example, Robert D. Kaplan, "Was Democracy Just a Moment?" *The Atlantic Monthly*, December 1997; and Fareed Zakaria, "The

Rise of Illiberal Democracy," *Foreign Affairs*, November/December 1997, pp. 22–42. The authors suggest that the global triumph of democracy was to be the glorious climax of the American Century but democracy may not be the system that will best serve the world, and that the rise of illiberal democracy's greatest danger other than to its own people is that it will discredit liberal democracy, thereby casting a shadow on democratic governance. Hence the United States should stop looking for new lands to democratize and new places to hold elections but try to consolidate democracy where it has taken root. For an alternative point of view, see Joel Barkan and David Gordon, "Democracy in Africa: No Time to Forsake It," *Foreign Affairs*, vol. 77, no. 4 (July/August 1998).

8. For an account of the first hundred days of the Taylor administration, see "Liberia: Special Report," *New African*, no. 358 (December 1997), pp. 1–21.

9. See Larry Diamond and Marc F. Plattner (eds.), *The Global Resurgence of Democracy* (Baltimore: John Hopkins University Press, 1993); Larry Diamond and Marc Plattner (eds), *Capitalism, Socialism and Democracy Revisited* (Baltimore: John Hopkins University Press, 1993); Larry Diamond and Marc Plattner (eds.), *Nationalism, Ethnic Conflict and Democracy* (Baltimore: John Hopkins University Press, 1994); and Larry Diamond and Marc Plattner (eds.), *Economic Reform and Democracy* (Baltimore: John Hopkins University Press, 1995).

10. John Williamson, "Democracy and the 'Washington Consensus,'" *World Development*, vol. 21 (1993), 1329–36.

11. Diamond and Plattner, *Economic Reform and Democracy*, pp. x–xi.

12. Several important analysis have been conducted in this area including the following: Carol Graham, *Safety Nets, Politics and the Poor: Transitions to Market Economies* (Washington, D.C.: The Brookings Institution, 1994); J. Healey and M. Robinson, *Democracy, Governance and Economic Policy: Sub-Saharan Africa in Comparative Perspective* (London: Overseas Development Institute, 1992); Jose Maria Maravall, "The Myth of the Authoritarian Advantage," in Diamond and Plattner (eds.), *Economic Reform and Democracy* (Baltimore: John Hopkins University Press, 1995), pp. 13–27; and Crawford Young, "Democratization and Structural Adjustment: A Political Overview," in L. Deng, M Kostner, and C. Young (eds.), *Democratization and Structural Adjustment in Africa in the 1990s* (Madison: University of Wisconsin/African Studies Program, 1991).

13. Jennifer Widner (ed.), *Economic Change and Political Liberalization in Sub-Saharan Africa* (Baltimore: John Hopkins University Press, 1994), pp. 1–5; and Samir Amin, "An Alternative to the Crisis for Africa and the Middle East: Autonomous Economic and Social Development in Democracy," *Bulletin of the Third World Forum*, vol. 10 (July), pp. 17–29.

14. Claude Ake, *Democracy and Development in Africa* (Washington, D.C.: The Brookings Institution, 1996), p. 158.

15. Samuel P. Huntington, *The Third Wave: Democratization in the Late Twentieth Century* (Norman: University of Oklahoma Press, 1991).

16. Samuel P. Huntington, "After Twenty Years: The Future of the Third Wave," *Journal of Democracy*, vol. 8, no. 4 (October 1997), pp. 4–5.

17. Ibid., p. 7.

18. Issac Shivji, "State and Constitutionalism: A New Democratic Perspective," in *State and Constitutionalism*, pp. 31–32

19. Ibid., p. 32.

20. Ibid., p. 33.

21. Liberia is a West African coastal country stretching across 43,000 square miles; about the size of Tennessee. The rainforest country is more than 66 percent rural and nearly 34 percent is urban. The population of Monrovia, the capital city, is about 40 percent of the nation's total. There are over twenty-eight ethnic groups in the country and over twenty local languages and dialects are spoken. The country is predominantly made up of followers of Christian and Muslim religions, and almost half adhere to some of the concepts of indigenous religions. The predominant agricultural crops are: rice, cassava, maize, yams, taro, peanuts, sugarcane, and assorted vegetables. Almost 25 percent of export earnings are from the commercial production of mainly tree crops—rubber, coffee, cacao, and oil palm products. Liberia is also wealthy in minerals such as gold and diamonds. For an excellent analysis of the child soldier phenomena in Liberia, see *Easy Prey: Child Soldiers in Liberia* (New York: Human Rights Watch, 1994).

22. Colonization was not widely supported by the leaders of the abolitionist movement such as David Walker, William Llyod Garrison, John Brown, Frederick Douglass, or Harriet Tubman. Nevertheless, it was widely debated as one of the best schemes acceptable to large segments of White American society including a young Abraham Lincoln. Therefore, the American Colonization Society was a very controversial organization, although it did received support for a number of diverse quarters for very different reasons.

23. A history of Liberia.

24. Ghana's Kwame Nkrumah, Egypt's Gabriel Nasser, Guinea's Sekou Toure, Tanzania's Julis Nyerere, and Algeria's Ben Bella were some of the members of the Casablanca group and leaders of the more radical African anticolonial movement. Ethiopia's Haile Selassie and Liberia's Shadrach Tubman were viewed as leaders of the Monrovia group. For a more detailed account of the politics of the period, see Immanuel Wallerstein, *Africa: The Politics of Unity* (New York: Vintage Books, 1969).

25. *A History of Liberia.*

26. Interview with Baccus Matthews, Monrovia, Liberia, April, 12, 1997.

27. Africa Confidential, "The Coup in Liberia."

28. Ibid.

29. Ibid.

30. Michael Clough, *Free at Last? U.S. Policy toward Africa at the End of the Cold War* (New York: Council on Foreign Relations. 1992). See also Robert Hoffman, "Colonialism, Socialism and Destabilization in Mozambique," *Africa Today*, vol 39, nos. 1–2 (Fall 1992).

31. Ibid.

32. It should be remembered, as Nzongola-Ntalaja, Ake, Cheru, and others have argued, that the democratic struggle in Africa did not start in 1989. Calls for a "second independence" began soon after many of the independence heroes

began to demobilize the mass-based organizations and citizens movements and either institute or maintain authoritarian policies reminiscent of the colonial era.

33. Lawyers Committee for Human Rights, *The Reagan Administration's Record on Human Rights in 1986* (New York: Lawyers Committee for Human Rights, February 1987), p. 86.

34. Lawyers Committee for Human Rights, *The Reagan Administration's Record on Human Rights in 1988* (New York: Lawyers Committee for Human Rights, January 1989), pp. 119–20.

35. Lawyers Committee for Human Rights, *The Reagan Administration's Record on Human Rights in 1985* (New York: Lawyers Committee for Human Rights, January 1986), p. 118.

36. Ibid., pp. 85–86.

37. Ibid., p. 86.

38. Ibid., p. 88.

39. Ibid., p. 89.

40. Ibid.

41. Ibid., pp. 89–90. Crocker would later admit that the biggest mistake made in U.S. foreign policy toward Africa during the Reagan administration was their Liberian policy.

42. Human Rights Watch, *The Reagan Administration's Record on Human Rights in 1988* (New York: Human Rights Watch and Lawyers Committee for Human Rights, January 1989), p. 119.

43. Quote from a prominent Liberian who served in the Executive Mansion under the Doe administration and continues to serve in the Taylor government.

44. A. Sesay, "Historical Background to the Liberian Crisis," in M. A. Vogt (ed.), *ECOMOG and the Liberian Crisis* (Lagos: Gabumo Publishing Co., 1992).

45. Whether the charges were true or not, the U.S. government apprehended Taylor and incarcerated him for a time.

46. Sesay, op. cit.

47. Ibid.

48. Ibid.

49. Interview with Paul Reeves, Monrovia, Liberia, May 20, 1997.

50. Sesay, op. cit.

51. *Human Rights Watch World Report 1993* (New York: Human Rights Watch, 1993), p. 21.

52. Human Rights Watch/Africa, *Easy Prey: Child Soldiers in Liberia* (New York: Human Rights Watch, September 1994), p. 53.

53. Bill Enoanyi, *Uncle Sam's Step Child* (Monrovia, Liberia: 1995).

54. *Amnesty International Annual Report 1997* (London: Amnesty International, 1998), p. 219.

55. Ibid.

56. The National Patriotic Front of Liberia (NPFL) became the National Patriotic Party (NPP), and the United Liberation Movement for Democracy in Liberia-Kromah (ULIMO-K) became the All Liberian Coalition Party (ALCOP).

57. The accredited parties were: Progressive Peoples' Party (PPP); the National Reformation Party (NRP); the Free Democratic Party (FDP); Liberia

National Union (LINU); Unity Party (UP); All Liberian Coalition Party (ALL-COP); National Patriotic Party (NPP); Alliance of Political Parties; Reformation Alliance Party (RAP); People's Democratic Party of Liberia (PDPL); United People's Party (UPP); National Democratic Party of Liberia (NDPL); and Liberian People's Party (LPP).

58. LEON *Final Report of the July 19, 1997 Liberia Special Elections* (Monrovia, Liberia: Liberia Elections Observers Network, September 1997), p. 11.

59. James Buckley, "Liberians Vote For Democracy," *Washington Post*, July 20, 1997.

60. Interview with Samuel Kofi Woods, Monrovia, Liberia, July 18, 1997.

61. The author observed this firsthand in front of the NPP headquarters during a visit to meet with Taylor supporters and NPP officials on July 8, 1997.

62. *New African* Special Report on Liberia, December 1997, p. 11.

63. This was one of the early electoral criticisms voiced by the NGO Refugee International, which had done a survey of refugee camps prior to the special elections being held. Refugee International estimated that at least half the eligible voting population was located outside of the country.

64. LEON *Final Report*, pp. 23–26.

65. Liberian combatants working with the Revolutionary United Front (RUF) had been accused of being in charge of the rebel/military alliance after having displaced the military leaders who originally staged the coup in the neighboring country. The recent peace accord that signaled the handing over of power back to the president by April 1998, was a definite outcome of the elections and Liberian membership in ECOWAS.

66. LEON *Final Report*, p. 10.

67. Ibid., p. 20.

68. Ibid.

69. *Human Rights Watch World Report 1993* (New York: Human Rights Watch, 1993), p. 24.

70. *African Voices* (Washington, D.C.: United States Agency for International Development, December 1997), p. 1.

71. *African Voices*, p. 4.

72. Ibid.

73. Ibid.

74. Ibid.

75. Ibid.

76. Briefing to the Security Council on Liberia by Mr. Felix Downes-Thomas, Representative of the Secretary-General in Liberia and Head of the United Nations Peace Building Support Office, March 11, 1999, pp. 2–3. Mr. Downes-Thomas' very favorable opinion of progress in Liberia also included his personalized view of security. He reported to the Security Council: "Monrovia is one of the safest cities in West Africa. I am able to drive myself around Monrovia without security escort at any hour of day or night."

77. Ibid.

78. Hundreds of well-documented reports to the Justice and Peace Commission from ordinary citizens have consistently suggested that the SSS are terrorizing the population.

79. U.S. Department of State, *Liberia Country Report on Human Rights Practices for 1998* (Washington, D.C.: U.S. Department of State, Bureau of Democracy, Human Rights and Labor, February 1998).

80. Jackson has been engaged with the Liberian democratization process for many years. He has also been called upon by the Clinton administration to help broker a peace agreement in Sierra Leone because of his close ties to Taylor.

81. U.S. Department of State, *Report on Human Rights Practices for 1998*, p. 2.

82. Ibid.

83. *Democracy Watch Newsletter*, vol. 1, no. 2 (March–April 1999), p. 1.

84. Ibid.

85. U.S. Department of State, *Report on Human Rights*, p. 7.

86. Kevin Danaher (ed.), *50 Years Is Enough: The Case against the World Bank and the International Monetary Fund* (Boston: South End Press, 1994).

87. See for instance Robert Neuman, "The Frailty of New Democracies," *Current Magazine*, September 1993, pp. 23–38.

88. Human Rights Watch, *Easy Prey: Child Soldiers in Liberia* (New York: Human Rights Watch, 1994).

CHAPTER 8

The Democratization
Trade in Haiti:
International Influence
since Duvalier

Lorenzo Morris

The struggle for democracy in Haiti as elsewhere is typically associated with the desperate uprisings of the overwhelmingly oppressed and impoverished masses that have spent most of their lives struggling to make ends meet. The news media images of urban violence, both liberating and repressive, make the strongest visual impressions when they are captured in the context of the powerless slum dwellers' efforts to survive. Yet it is the powerlessness of this group more than its desperation that has defined the emergence of the recent pushes toward democracy in Haiti. While the liberation from oppression may be the principal theme of democratic initiatives, it is liberation of the middle and upper middle classes in Haiti from political oppression that has defined the points of departure for political rebellion. It is not surprising that rebellion should come from those who do not enjoy access to power in the narrowly organized, dictatorial or oligarchical regimes that sequentially governed Haiti for more than a century. What is curious is that among the government's outsiders, those who have the least need for revolution and the most to lose should revolutionary fervor run its full course, are at the forefront of the uprisings.

It is not immediately evident that the relatively comfortable groups in Haiti should be among the first to demand a transformation in government. Why this would be the case is even less obvious. In the process of transformation, the downtrodden peasants, the starving, overcrowded slum dwellers of Cite Soleil and the streams of disparate boat people take center stage in the media's images of rebellions. For the most part, they are the ones who carry the rebellions to fruition, as the Aristide-Lavalas experience demonstrates. At the initial stages, however, the inspiration and provocation of the more middle-class instigators is generally overlooked.

A large part of that inspiration in Haiti, which surfaces in the 1985 prelude to the overthrow of Jean-Claude Duvalier, can be found in the role of foreign aid to Haiti. That is certainly not to say the intentional and self-conscious role of foreign aid but a role that it comes to play almost accidentally. International aid from varied sources was filtered and interpreted by the Duvaliers but it inevitably preserved the political implications that flowed from international power centers well removed from Port-au-Prince. Foreign aid in Haiti comes primarily from three sources: international agencies including the World Bank and American development associations; U.S. aid, particularly the Agency for International Development; and private, largely religious, organizations. Direct aid from other countries has been relatively small since the 1970s. More important, the flow of foreign aid has moved largely in concert with the inclinations of the primary aid providers, the United States and the World Bank as well as the International Monetary Fund.

An odd thing about international aid for a poor country is that it comes from organizations and countries that generally do not know the poor as well as the middle and upper classes in the countries they intend to assist. As it happens in Haiti the poor are only accessible to international wealth through the mediation of Haiti's upper class. There is only a small middle class to work with. The only alternatives in Haiti are the well-organized Catholic and Protestant missionary groups that are dispersed throughout the rural areas and central city slums. The Salesian Fathers, for example, from which Father Aristide emerged have long provided a variety of social services to the inhabitants of Haiti's slums. For U.S.-funded organizations among others such religious agencies are unacceptable intermediaries for their aid programs. As a consequence, American foreign aid is heavily filtered by local elites, independent and governmental elites, who inevitably profit politically as well as monetarily from the assistance.

Similarly, attempts to evade authoritarian regimes in constructing patterns of assistance for the purpose of promoting democracy may actually promote more "democratic" division than democratic diversity. In the 1980s the United States wisely sought to avoid indirect aid to the Duvalier regime by sending its assistance only to the private sector. But it could not effectively provide grants-in-aid to individual schools, for example, without encouraging a greater maldistribution of resources than already existed. The schools most likely to be identified for help and to have satisfactorily demonstrated their educational effectiveness were also the ones least likely to need American aid in order to continue functioning. As a consequence, aid is generally granted to "democratically oriented" associations whose leaders make the best impressions on American program evaluators. Obviously, public relations skills, international awareness, careful accounting, not to mention "good" English, work to the competitive advantage of this relatively elite set of local leaders.

At the level of governance the same kind of undemocratic biases are visible in the best-intentioned international initiatives to restore democratic rule in Haiti. In at least three important stages in the transition from the second Duvalier administration to the second Aristide administration, the international presence is crucial. International forces helped to tip the scales toward an emerging politically "moderate" upper class but the consequences of their actions were unanticipated popular insurrections. First, in 1985 the IMF and the World Bank joined arms in placing pressure on Duvalier to make modernizing social reforms for the purpose of inching toward a more participatory social structure. The effort failed but with interesting side effects. Second, in 1990 multiple international donors led by the United States and the United Nations along with the World Bank sought to ensure the first free elections in Haiti by promoting the candidacy of an internationally recognized "democratic" economist, Marc Bazin, for president. This effort was also a valuable failure. Third, in 1993–94 the international community led by the UN (UN Special Envoy Dante Caputo), the Organization of American States (Special Envoy Augusto Ocampo), and, of course, the United States sought to moderate the rigid military control of Raoul Cedras.[1] A more moderate Cedras would have been a respectable negotiation partner and transition leader. This effort failed and a small step toward democracy resulted.

IMPROVING DUVALIER'S PASSPORT IMAGE

Two decades of Duvalier dictatorship had completely effaced any direct experience with democratic governance for Haiti's weak but persistent opposition. Outside international pressure, therefore, had been viewed as a necessity by all those who expected a non-military coup d'état. As it turned out, international pressure was a crucial component in the February 1986 military replacement of Duvalier. It was pressure that had the odd, if not surprising consequences of provoking popular unrest and giving exceptional encouragement to the military. Still, internal economic and political conditions since 1980 gave an essential boost to popular revolutionary inclinations.

Of course, the revolutionary fervor and the taste for popular political transformation is grounded nearly as far back in Haitian history as in our own. Yet its roots were clipped before they could spread. Contributing to the failure of democratic impulses were both internal conflicts and the hostile embargo imposed almost two centuries ago by its more "democratic" neighbor to the north—an embargo that lasted until the democratic neighbor freed its slaves sixty years later. In large part, however, the internal legacy of French colonial inequality and the recurrent eruptions of internecine violence left authoritarian rule as the most likely path to national stability. Even populist, potentially democratic revolutions, such as one in 1957, quickly soured in the shifting environment of poverty and exploitive wealth.[2] In 1957 François (Papa Doc) Duvalier came to power with a commitment and a mandate to liberate the masses. He met with a relatively receptive American response—a response tempered by the belief that he would be a bulwark against the ghost of "communists future," then a prevailing foreign policy obsession. His behavior soon turned harsh, however, and the United States' open face turned away from him, though not necessarily in that order.[3] While Papa Doc's tyrannical rule is a peculiarly Haitian phenomenon, Haiti's long isolation from the international community and the fear of a hidden communist threat have distinct overtones of American foreign policy influence.

Still, it was not the first time that the democratic "godfather" to the north had unwittingly fertilized the seeds of political instability and authoritarian rule. With the end of the nineteen-year American occupation in 1934, Haiti's exposure to ethnocentrism and racial prejudice would be transformed into support for a harshly exploitive class system. In the years following the occupation, the United States developed significant elements of the Haitian physical infrastructure, including building the only major roads in use today. Unfortunately, U.S. aid contained no allocation for the development of electoral institutions. In fact, aid from all international donors served to discourage balanced economic development and internal investment.

"The International Monetary Fund has been an important actor in the aid community in Haiti," according to Weinstein and Segal.[4] In the last years of Duvalier it attempted through the new minister of finance, Marc Bazin, to promote a more balanced economy but encountered stiff resistance from the indigenous business elite. Jean-Claude Duvalier evidently hoped to cast himself at the center of Haiti's economic revolution. He proclaimed that "my father made the political revolution, I will make economic revolution."[5] His misperceptions of his father foreshadowed his own self-deception. In effect, the 1970s brought some economic modernization. For example, the number of industrial assembly plants increased from 25 in 1972 to 200 in 1980 when they employed sixty thousand Haitians.[6] In exchange for its receptivity to foreign, largely American, industry, Haiti received some tariff reduction and quota exemptions in the United States as well as insurance support for American investors from the United States Overseas Private Investment Corporation.[7] Duvalier agreed to bring some technocrats into his government, including Marc Bazin, who had strong ties to international manufacturing, agricultural business, and finance.[8] But by 1980 the slight sense of political liberalization that had accompanied this economic expansion had been destroyed. Duvalier was immobilized by his own contradictory policies, according to Cary Hector. Surrounded by conflicting pressures, he gave in to his repressive tendencies.[9] Many public critics of the regime were by 1980 already subject to arrest or exile.

Fortunately, the earlier attitude of indifference toward internal economic development by international agencies in Haiti had changed. Unfortunately, the aptitude and practices necessary to effectively transform an interest in development into meaningful economic progress was sorely missing. With the Reagan presidency, the return to indifference to Haiti's economic distortions became a shield for Duvalier. In many areas of development, among them agriculture, education, construction, and trade, the Haitian experience since the 1970s stands as a clear testament to the ineffectiveness of multinational foreign aid where the structure of government is archaically organized or rather disorganized under the crushing weight of oppressive corruption. By 1985 several international donors led by the World Bank and the IMF had placed considerable pressure on Jean-Claude Duvalier to "clean up" his governmental image and had sought to lay the groundwork for greater industrial investment in Haiti. The level and accessibility of basic education was so poor (an estimated 75 percent illiteracy rate) that any real business investment would be seriously constrained by the absence of a minimally prepared labor force.

Accidental Destabilization of the Dictatorship

The Duvalier government responded positively to the threat of a cut-off of international aid funds with what the Duvalier government doubtlessly thought would be a low-cost, high-impact improvement in Haitian education. A high impact was needed to persuade the international community that Baby Doc Duvalier could be popular, if not a populist like his father, without depending on foreign aid. A particularly low-cost program was needed so that millions of dollars could be siphoned off by the government agents from the aid money to subsidize the antidevelopment/reactionary military and paramilitary dependents on the "president-for-life." One of his solutions was simple. He declared a change of the medium of instruction in basic elementary and secondary education from French to Creole.

More than simply pleasing the international financiers, it was a response tailored to touch even the most disillusioned peasants. Across the country the majority of Haitian families had struggled for years to improve the lot of their children by sending at least some of their children to primary school. Few children ever remained in school for more than two or three years. The families often exchanged one child's schooling for that of another because they could rarely afford to pay for the continuous schooling of their children through the completion of primary school. A sure sign for the typical parents, however, that a substantial education had been acquired even without a diploma was knowledge of formal French. For the first few years of schooling, at least to the fourth grade, Creole was, of necessity, the primary language of instruction even where French was the goal for instruction. Later, as the children learned French from marginally prepared teachers working with scarcely any books, the language of instruction changed to the one spoken by the elite. Unfortunately, only the relatively well-off survived long enough in school to sample any of the equalizing benefits of education. By extending and legitimating schooling in the Creole language, therefore, Duvalier hoped to recast himself as more of a populist and an "education" president.

Nothing intended to democratize a country, however half-heartedly, is simple, as Michele (Ms Baby Doc) Duvalier may well have understood. She soon announced that no child of hers would ever be educated in Creole—a statement of preference, if not of fact. Her attitude, although without formal governmental authority, had major political repercussions. It made fairly clear to the Haitian masses that the elite did not consider this new form of education a vehicle for upward mobility. Rather than changing education in order to provide them greater access to the political and economic systems, they began to fear that they were being further removed from any real educational opportunity. At least, they could feel confident before then that the acquisition of French language competence by their children was a sign of achievement, a recognizable skill, and a step toward escape from the stifling deprivation of the Creole-only masses. Particularly, the small lower-middle class of Haitians who could afford to enroll in the private secondary schools reacted negatively. Among these students were the four students whom the military shot during a protest over the language of schooling, as well as other poor conditions, in Gonaives on November 28, 1985.

A protest demonstration of any kind in Haiti was extremely rare but one against a presidential policy was virtually unheard of. A demonstration in which schoolchildren were killed was also very rare and, apparently, beyond the toleration of the mass of Haitians. In the wake of the brutal slayings, the streets erupted in mass demonstrations in Gonaives and shortly thereafter in Port-au-Prince. Two months later, Michele and Jean-Claude Duvalier were on their way to take up "residence-for-life" in a completely French-speaking country.

To a large degree, a sense of upward mobility stimulated by the economic expansion of the late 1970s and early 1980s in Haiti may have magnified hopes for personal liberation through education among Haiti's newly emerging middle class. Such rising expectations help to explain the increased tendency toward protest in this period as well as the Duvalier regime's escalation of its repressive policies. Similarly, the renewed protests were probably mutually responsive. For example, the independent and influential Radio Soleil could be heard throughout the capital reporting the brutal slayings of the students but only in the early morning hours (before 6 a.m.) of the day following the demonstrations. By late morning the radio station was off the air and the only official news was "good news." Instead of submitting to this repression, however, multiple forms of communication and protest were inspired. Protesting suddenly became a popular preoccupation. It began in the relatively exclusive high schools, largely private, and spread to the streets. It steadily continued until Duvalier's departure. As the next minister of education, Rosny Desroches, observed, these chaotic conditions left no other choice for Haiti except another "American invasion."[10]

The irony of the overthrow of the twenty-nine-year-old Duvalier regime was first that it was stimulated by a symbolic attempt at democratizing education. Second, that attempt was provoked by the effort of international agencies, particularly the World Bank and the IMF, to improve and stabilize rather than unseat the Duvalier presidency. Third, Duvalier's own ineptitude and indifference, which normally fell more harshly on the very poor than on the wealthy or on the tiny middle class, offended the upwardly mobile poor and middle class. Fourth, he was eventually overthrown by a popular rebellion that would ultimately lead to the installation of a Creole language–oriented populist. This leader would incite the Haitian peasants and slum dwellers with promises to do for education what Duvalier had symbolically attempted to do before his political demise.

The irony of these unrequited democratic, but not-so-honorable, intentions does not end here with the 1986 unraveling of the Duvalier regime. In the denouement before his departure there were obvious domestic and international manipulations to prepare for the aftermath of the dictatorship. In the forefront of the struggle to prepare for the next government was the "Ti Legliz," the loose collection of little churches that had emerged along with several disorganized small political groups and rudimentary labor unions. The "Little Church" was a popular and powerful combination of local priests, nuns, and Catholic leaders not in the established Catholic hierarchy. It could easily be distinguished in its politics and economic status from the "Established Church," composed of virtually all the bishops and the Papal Nuncio who had been strongly allied with the Duvalier regime. Still, the church leaders paled as conservative champions in comparison with the army, which successfully supported the old leadership. In the winter of 1986, however, the army was not prepared to assert its national authority without outside support.

That outside support apparently came from the democratic powerhouse to the north. In fact, one journalist insists that it had been Oliver North's associates, on an Iran Contra–related trip to Port-au-Prince, that first encouraged the Duvaliers to take advantage of American Airline's international flight opportunities.[11] Whatever the details may be, it is clear that Duvalier fled the country under American protection much as one of the two military dictators who followed him to power did later. In fact, Prosper Avril, the second of the two follow-up dictators, fled to the United States on an American military plane. In spite of the strong taint of Colombian drug connections surrounding his subordinate Colonel Paul, Avril was taken into a kind of American protective custody.

What was there about General Henri Namphy, the other military dictator, and Prosper Avril that might have made them appealing to Haiti's democracy-oriented American allies? Had international support gone to the Ti Legliz, the future of Haitian politics would certainly have been different, probably more stable and less violent. But the military proved more attractive to international interests. Assuming, of course, that they did manage to appeal to American security interests, how could the United States and the Haitian military have sustained any kind of trusting relationship?

Some of the answers lie in the foundations of the Haitian military, especially its officer training. Their training has always been weak and irregular even by the most lax international standards. The weakness of officer training is perhaps best represented by the consistency with which general after general slips into paramilitary alliances and political intrigue. But the weakness of their training was probably hidden from public perception in the closed association of officers.

The officers were frequently beneficiaries or victims of long association dating back to officer training school. Rather than having been dispersed over a steady sequence of graduating officer training schools, the older officers were constrained to attend classes in one of the few graduating classes in the 1970s. Young officers often shared training, not only in Haiti but also in the United States, through specially sponsored American programs. In either case, the officers had all been exposed to North American military culture. They had apparently had just enough exposure to impress American representatives with their willingness to respect civil authority, but not enough to extend their respect beyond the stages of fear and resentment.[12] From the beginning, therefore, the military leadership was distrustful of independent civilian authority. Henri Namphy's barely disguised imposition of Leslie Manigat as president serves to demonstrate both the military's superficial respect for democracy and its overwhelming fear of it.

From the beginning of the post-Duvalier period in Haiti, the military had come to depend on superficial claims to democracy as both its basis of legitimacy and its primary foreign policy plank for appealing to or appeasing the United States. Each successive general or chief of police from Namphy through Avril to Raoul Cedras, the last military leader, stepped into the leadership role with claims of satisfying American demands for ultimately withdrawing the military from the presidential palace. In fact, Cedras had been preselected by the Bush administration and endorsed as the reliable enforcer of the rules during the election in 1990. Picked to replace General Abrahams, who had effectively protected the transitional presidency of Ertha Pascal-Trouillot, General Cedras was the American-sanctioned guarantor of free and fair elections in Haiti. He was placed in charge of the army during the elections and, as a result, retained the imprimatur of U.S. approval for some time thereafter.

A more important, though less tangible, seal of approval was placed on a former World Bank employee, Marc Bazin, by the international community. As a candidate for the presidency in 1990, he was initially treated as the leader and likely victor by the media. But as election day approached that seal of international approval became more an immobilizing weight dragging him farther down to a thorough defeat at the polls in December. Earning only 14 percent of the vote, he came in just ahead of the number of voided ballots in many districts. In contrast, Jean-Bertrand Aristide's 68 percent of the vote, earned with a defiant approach to U.S. electoral influence, was more than expected. Titid, as Aristide was popularly known, had managed to usurp through his populism the democratic label that the aloof and cosmopolitan Bazin was supposed to have been granted by his "worldly" connections. Understandably, in retrospect, everyone recognizes that even America cannot give democratic appeal away; it has to be earned. Burdened with his record of service to Duvalier as minister of finance, the mantle of rebellion could not sit well on Bazin's shoulders.

Leading the American effort to "give" democracy away was U.S. Ambassador Alvin Adams, an activist and dedicated promoter of the American creed. His activism worked well, but slowly, in pushing out General Avril, but poorly and ineffectively when he encouraged criticism from the Organization of American States of Aristide's human rights record.[13] Still, the United States largely financed the 1990 election. American election observers, led by former President Carter, quickly confirmed the democratic character of Aristide's dramatic victory. Fortunately for the United States, it could claim a role in subsidizing these fair elections in Haiti. Unfortunately, most international groups, including the United States, had deformed the focus of the democratic elections by backing a Haitian they could accept as one of their own. That meant that the Haitians could more readily see him as *not* one of their own.

Perhaps equally important, as an unfortunate relationship, is the legitimating role the American endorsement could play in the divided military. In spite of historical hostility to American intervention, U.S.-supported training of the Haitian military was widely respected. In the army, which provided one of Haiti's few avenues of upper mobility, access to such training or support for it was highly valued. The police may now be the path to upward mobility. In a society where social class is rather sharply defined, any alternative pattern of mobility is important. Thus, there was a traditional class (and color-related) division between the officers and regular soldiers in the army. Cedras' image of American influences could accordingly influence all those in the military who sought to break out of the traditional world. It is not surprising that Colonel J. Michel Francois, who seemed to have a closer connection with the common people, would lead the 1991 coup against Aristide and then turn leadership over to Cedras. Ultimately, then, the American dilemma in Haiti may be seen as an unintended affiliation with the most undemocratic of Haiti's claimed supporters of democracy. This affiliation was made more serious by the less public but widely believed link between the brutally regressive leader of FRAPH, Emanuel Constant, and U.S. intelligence agencies noted in Representative Conyers' 1997 report.[14]

If opposition to military rule in Haiti could be so ambiguously pursued, then American support for Aristide could also be understandably expressed with comparable maladdress. Even to reach its actual level of inept support, however, the Bush administration's preference for almost anybody but Aristide had to be turned around. Before the 1990 election there was little doubt that the United States, along with its closest European allies, preferred Marc Bazin. In fact, the day after Aristide's over-whelming electoral victory Port-au-Prince buzzed with credible rumors that the Bush administration representatives in Haiti were going to make accusations of electoral fraud indirectly implicating Aristide's Lavalas movement. Fortunately, the Carter delegation hastened to announce its firm conclusion, along with other observers, that the election had been fair. The Bush administration quickly joined others in celebrating the Lavalas success. Still, substantial skepticism about the sincerity of Amer-ican support for Aristide remained, a skepticism no doubt shared by mil-itary leaders, but for them any such doubts could only provide sources of encouragement for rebellion.

PROLOGUE TO ARISTIDE'S SECOND COMING

From the start of his campaign Aristide had made three significant promises affecting Haiti's relations with the United States and other for-eign entities. First, he had promised to reduce American influence over Haiti's affairs—a promise unlikely to endear him to the Bush adminis-tration. Second, he had promised to substantially raise Haiti's abysmal minimum wage. This promise might well have escaped negative interna-tional attention if it were not also seen as inconsistent with international monetary policy and trade. In fact, it appeared to some to be antitheti-cal to encouragement of American investment in Haitian industry.

In fact, Aristide's proposals were frequently seen as costly, if not dis-couraging, for international investors. His initial proposal to increase the minimum wage to fifty cents an hour from thirty-three cents was actively opposed by American and other international agencies.[15] Pre-sumably, investors would feel threatened by any labor-sensitive policy-making precedent. At the same time, long-established tariff protection for indigenous businesses were discouraged. Accordingly, the IMF and the World Bank demanded in Aristide's second administration that tar-iffs be lowered to attract imports. Tariffs were, therefore, lowered from 50 percent to 5 percent on many products.[16] Imports rose correspond-ingly. According to Rep. John Conyers' report, imports of rice from the United States, a Haitian product historically, went from less than 10,000 metric tons before 1986 to 162,000 metric tons in 1996.

An additional Aristide pledge to run the (foreign) drug dealers out of Haiti, should have boosted Aristide's stock in Washington. Unfortu-nately, that benefit may have been more than counterbalanced by the influence of drug money among Haiti's military and paramilitary. In this regard, Weinstein and Segal observe that "drug trafficking may be serv-ing as an alternative to bilateral aid" for some military officers.[17] The rise and fall of Colonel Jean-Claude Paul two years before the election under national and international accusations of drug-trade involvement provides evidence of such influence.[18]

The extent to which any of these aspects of Aristide's planning may have contributed to the military coup cannot be readily assessed because there are stronger factors in the background. Among the more persistent are the sharp class divisions in Haiti, which Aristide's movement seemed to threaten by its very existence. Ironically, the military straddled and accommodated this division with its own parallel class structure of officers and soldiers. Perhaps more ironic are the indications that there was more upward mobility for Haitians in the army than in civilian life.

Still, the upper class overwhelmingly disliked and feared Aristide before the coup and they continued to dislike him after his October 1994 return to power. The big difference was that the threat he embodied had been diminished by his three-year-long "Americanization." The business community could feel confident that U.S. influence over Aristide, both direct and indirect, would help provide support for their interests. The direct influence involves over a half billion dollars of promised foreign aid and comparable levels of trade and investment. An example of the aid benefit is provided by a 1996 USAID plan to triple its school lunch program in Haiti in order to feed 900,000 students.[19] Trade and aid together would, of course, be contingent on increased privatization, from which the business community hoped to benefit. In effect, planned growth in international aid and trade with privatization in the hands of international agencies could minimize Aristide's real control over the economy. Accordingly, journalist Kim Ives summarizes the 1994 IMF and World Bank jointly written plans for Haiti's "social and economic reconstruction" as follows:

Haiti commits to eliminate the jobs of half of its civil servants, massively privatize public services, drastically slash tariffs and import restrictions, eschew price and foreign exchange controls, grant emergency aid to the export sector, enforce an open foreign investment policy, create special corporate business courts where the judges are more aware of the implications of their decisions for economic efficiency, rewrite its corporate laws, limit the scope of state activity and regulation, and diminish the power of Aristide's executive branch in favor of the more conservative Parliament. In return, Haiti is to receive $770 million in financing, $80 million of which goes immediately to pay the debt accrued to foreign banks over the past three years since the coup.[20]

The indirect influence was probably more compelling for the socioeconomic elite. They see themselves, perhaps naively, as more compatible with American culture, style, and appearance than the destitute masses that rally to Aristide. As a result, they could be more optimistic about reaching an accommodation with their reborn president. Several critics view in Aristide's return the emergence of a "Lavalas bourgeoisie" that is technocratically oriented and very influential.[21]

On the other hand, the real strength of democratic regime, as well as the value of U.S. support for it, is told as much through its failures as through its successes. Simply put, it took only five days after the adoption of the U.N. Security Council resolution under U.S. pressure to establish its most menacing embargo, for General Cedras to call for talks with Aristide.[22] After three years of deception and stonewalling, a little statement of unambiguous pressure brought the junta to the table seeking settlement in June 1993. Only the uncertainty of U.S. enforcement can explain the junta's subsequent three-month waffling. Once again, a clear expression of force in the form of the Carter-led delegation and the U.S. Air Force was needed. While Carter, General Colin Powell, and Senator Sam Nunn warned the Cedras junta that they could save their lives but not their power, the menacing U.S. Air Force made the threat of imminent invasion inescapable.

Yet, as had happened before during the 1915–34 U.S. occupation, this invasion brought hope for democracy while ignoring much of the necessary organizational development and governmental resources that would be affected by the invasion. The Haitian military structure was effectively protected through the rather questionable attempts to transform it into a police force, improving and modernizing it.[23] At the same time, grassroots organizing and popular pro-Aristide developments received no comparable encouragement and no subsidy. Of course, Aristide supporters received valuable protection through the surveillance of the American soldiers but protection can lead to atrophy as well as development. Promised U.S. aid was a long way off and would only indirectly support Aristide's political base.

As a consequence, the most sincere American effort to support Haitian democracy had succumbed to its historical political ambiguities. The United States returned the elected leader to the halls of the presidential palace while it subsidized much the same military located in the same fortresses, in the same neighborhood as the palace, from which the popular leader had been overthrown. The partially American-trained army that overthrew Aristide in the first place has since been partially retrained as police by Americans.

Still, the real success of American support for Haitian democracy may emerge from the sometimes clearer vision of ordinary Americans and Haitians who continue to confront the recent injustice and authoritarian behavior directly. They demand simple justice and a democratic hearing. Perhaps, a rumored internationally sponsored "truth commission" to examine the junta's abuses will give vent to those demands. In the meantime, a striking reminder of individual American contributions to human rights came in the court-martial case of U. S. Army Captain Lawrence P. Rockwood. Captain Rockwood insisted on inspecting a notorious Haitian prison even though his army superiors had not authorized it. In explaining his actions he said:

> I found it difficult not to conclude that the U.S. government could not to some degree be held ethically, morally or legally responsible for human rights violations being carried out with the knowledge of the command, in the direct proximity of its forces, and being executed by Haitian military police whose activities, under an agreement of "cooperation," were being supervised by U.S. forces with the flagrant exemption of the known criminal activities in Haitian confinement facilities.[24]

The captain calls to mind the moral and humanitarian motives for the American intervention while complaining about the impracticality of the American military's rules for implementing their goals. Unconsciously, however, he became an extreme example of the modes of implementation. Although he had to disobey his superiors in order to make official plans for democratic support realistic, others have carved opportunities out of the ambiguities in international aid policies. Like the rebellious Haitian students under Duvalier, Haitian peasants have pushed for more logical and humanitarian intervention.

CONCLUSION

From the beginning of the American occupation the television showed the audiences at home where the real support for democracy comes from. It does not come from a coherent and well-developed strategy for stabilizing the democratic electoral and judicial procedures. Nor does it come from an effective American system for substituting trained police for a corrupt paramilitary. It comes from the unplanned and unsystematic initiatives of individuals and groups acting in response to immediate pressures and crises. These responses may be unsystematic, yet they are probably "systemic." That is to say, they grow out the domestic national goals where the best interests of American business and labor are respected and where balanced development is promoted. When these latent values supersede narrow multinational economic directives, the national-human interests of Haiti benefit. Similarly, when Haitian leaders, whether Aristide or Andre Preval, take control of their country's economic development, they are in a better position than all outsiders to protect the nation's political development, its fairness and equity. International political aid must always be limited.

The incentives to reinterpret international policy, from a more humanitarian perspective are built into the traditional popularism of Haitian politics. That same populist tendency which once led to authoritarianism can also lead away from it. Ironically, the United States draws on the democratizing aspects of that background but it generally does so only inadvertently as if democracy itself were an unintended benefit of political instability.

NOTES

1. Kim Ives, "Haiti's Second U.S. Occupation," in Deirdre McFadyen and Pierre LaRamee (eds.), *Haiti: Dangerous Crossroads* (Boston: South End Press, 1995), p. 81.

2. Elizabeth Abbott, *Haiti: The Duvaliers and Their Legacy* (New York: McGraw-Hill, 1988), p. 47.

3. Anne Hiliare Jolibois, *Démocrates et Démocratie* (Port-au-Prince, Haiti: Bibliothèque Nationale d'Haiti, 1994), p. 192.

4. Brian Weinstein and Aaron Segal, *Haiti: The Failure of Politics* (New York: Praeger, 1992), pp. 121–23.

5. Jolibois, *Démocrates*, p. 191.

6. Cary Hector, "Haiti-U.S. 1946–1996: 50 Ans de Relations Haitiano-Americanianes," *Le Diplomate*, vol. 1, no. 2 (September 1997), p. 7.

7. Ibid.

8. Christopher Clement and Natalie Cherot, "The Neoliberal Crisis in Haiti: 1994 to Present," paper presented at the annual conference of the International Studies Association, Miami, Florida, October 17–19, 1997, p. 10.

9. Hector, "Haiti-U.S. 1946–1996," p. 8.

10. Greg Chamberlain, "An Interregnum: Haitian History from 1987–90," in McFadyen and LaRamee (eds.), *Haiti*, p. 18.

11. Amy Wilentz, *The Rainy Season* (New York: Simon & Schuster, 1989), p. 22.

12. Michele Zebich-Knos, "Religion, Coup Politics and Development in Haiti," paper presented at the annual meeting of the American Political Science Association, Chicago, September 1992, p. 13.

13. Chamberlain, "An Interregnum," pp. 38–39; McFadyen and LaRamee, *Haiti*, pp. 4–5.

14. John Conyers, "CODEL Conyers Haiti Trip," Report to the Committee on the Judiciary, U.S. House of Representatives, August 1997, p. 11.

15. Marx Aristide and Laurie Richardson, "Haiti's Popular Resistance," in McFadyen and LaRamee (eds.), p. 191.

16. Conyers, "CODEL Conyers Haiti Trip," p. 16.

17. Weinstein and Segal, *Haiti*, p. 100.

18. Wilentz, *The Rainy Season*, p. 172.

19. Conyers, "CODEL Conyers Haiti Trip," p. 16.

20. Ives, "Haiti's Second U.S. Occupation," p. 117.

21. Ibid.

22. David Park and Farah Chery, "The Haitian Crisis: A Review of Neglect and Chaos in International Decision-Making," *Congressional Black Caucus Foundation Policy Review*, vol. 1, no. 2 (November–December 1994), p. 32.

23. Conyers, "CODEL Conyers Haiti Trip," pp. 1–3.

24. "The Duty to Disobey," *Washington Post*, February 5, 1995, pp. C1–C2.

CHAPTER 9

Afro-Creole Nationalism as Elite Domination: The English-Speaking West Indies

Percy C. Hintzen

BACKGROUND

Political nationalism has provided the ideological underpinnings for overthrowing colonial domination. It has provided, also, the blueprint for the development of a postcolonial society. Its legitimacy was argued on the basis of the rights of the colonized population to sovereignty, national autonomy, self-determination, and freedom from repressive domination. At its heart, it was a contestation of colonial constructions of difference.

Those suffering under the yolk of colonial domination in the English-speaking Caribbean were, for the most part, descendants of slaves transported originally from Africa. In Guyana and Trinidad, they were replaced on the plantation by indentured servants brought primarily from India after emancipation in 1838.[1] Today, East Indians comprise an absolute majority in Guyana and the largest racial group in Trinidad and Tobago. Everywhere else in the English-speaking Caribbean, with the exception of Belize with its large indigenous Amerindian population, descendants of African slaves comprise over 90 percent of the population. This number includes the group of colored descendants of unions between the Black slaves and White colonizers.

During the sixteenth century, a system of European domination and absolute control quickly established itself, unhindered by indigenous challenge. The native populations of Caribs and Taino-Awaraks were quickly decimated to the point of total extinction in most island territories very soon after their first contact with the European explorers and conquerors. Their disappearance was hastened by continued resistance to European conquest, by the spread of new European diseases for which they had no natural protections, and by the consequences of land seizure for colonial production. Thereafter, the European colonial plantocracy and officials easily prevailed against the persistent, even though localized and discontinuous, rebellions organized by the African slave population throughout the period of plantation enslavement. East Indian workers mounted similar challenges to the terms of their contractual obligations in Trinidad and Guyana.

ANTICOLONIALISM AND THE INTERNATIONAL CHALLENGE TO WHITE SUPREMACY

Mobilization against the colonial administrative, managerial, and ownership elite became more persistent and organized during the twentieth century. The terms of nationalist contestation were shaped by the reality of the overwhelming predominance of the Black descendants of enslaved West Africans in the island territories under British colonial control. West Indian nationalism was shaped by the latter's struggles for self-definition and self-determination. It was informed by the internationalization of a newly developed racial consciousness during the first three decades of the twentieth century. The imposed assertions of White supremacy that legitimized European colonial domination were being challenged in new international discourses of racial identity.

Racial struggle and the quest for racial equality had taken on a new urgency in the twentieth century after the defeat by Ethiopia in 1896 of an Italian conquering army in the Battle of Adowa. This was followed by the victory of the Japanese over the armies of Czarist Russia in 1904. These two events gave impetus to ongoing localized challenges to White supremacy that were occurring among the colonized populations of Africa, Asia, and the Caribbean. Europe's predispositions to war and conquest were beginning to erode claims of the superiority of White civilization. In the eyes of the colonized, the distinctions emerging in a new discourse of scientific racism between the "civilized" and the "savage" were being contradicted by these predispositions. The fratricidal tendencies of European "civilization," which became particularly glaring in the conduct of the First World War, contributed much to the erosion of the myth of White supremacy as a basis for legitimizing colonial domination.

An emerging Black universal consciousness began to take institutional form in the organization of a fledgling Pan-African Congress in

London in 1900. It grew quickly, under the inspired leadership of the American W. E. B. DuBois. In 1919, the Congress was able to mount a highly successful and credible alternative to the Paris Peace Conference that had been convened to set the terms of peace after World War I. The intention of the Congress was to force the insertion of issues of racial domination into international policy-making .

Challenges to colonial domination occurring in the West Indies were contributing integrally to the new international currents informing the development of a new consciousness of African universal identity. During the first decade of the twentieth century, direct connections were established between Black West Indians and Booker T. Washington in the United States. A number of Black West Indians attended a world conference held at Washington's Tuskegee Institute in 1912. There, they became highly influenced by Washington's ideas. Some, including Agustus Parkinson of Barbados, began to directly advocate a modification of the educational systems of their colonies in keeping with the Tuskegee model.[2]

The Jamaican, Marcus Garvey, was perhaps most influential in the development of African identific consciousness during the first three decades of the twentieth century. Between 1909 and 1914, Garvey became exposed to labor radicalism during stints in Panama, Costa Rica, and London as a West Indian migrant laborer. After being introduced to Pan Africanism in London, he returned to Jamaica in 1914 to form the Universal Negro Improvement Association (UNIA). The Association received its philosophical underpinnings from a combination of ideas gleaned from the labor movement of Europe, from Pan Africanism, and, in particular, from the influence of Booker T. Washington. The UNIA grew rapidly, developing branches in the West Indies and in the United States of America. At the invitation of Washington, Garvey traveled to the United States, where, between 1916 and his deportation in 1927, the UNIA developed into a formidable international Black nationalist movement with branches in the United States, the Caribbean, and Africa. Total membership exceeded 5 million in 1927. At the UNIA's convention held in Harlem in 1920, attended by twenty-five thousand delegates, a Declaration of Rights of Negro People of the World was drafted demanding self-determination, political and legal equality for Blacks, and the liberation of Africa.[3] More than anything else, the UNIA became an organizational manifestation of a new universal understanding of diasporic intimacy among the Black populations of the world. It was this understanding that began to inform the development of nationalist consciousness at the various levels of sociopolitical organization.

The development of racial consciousness on an international scale continued unabated during the third decade of the century, fueled by the formation of new race-based international organizations. The League against Imperialism was launched as a "non-White counterforce to the League of Nations" in 1927 at an international conference held in Brussels. It was developed in response to the steadfast refusal by the League of Nations to address the issue of racial equality in its charter and deliberations. The delegates to the conference represented a multinational multiracial alliance opposed to the principle of racial domination in national and international affairs. Opposition to the league also came to be reflected in race-specific organizations such as the League of Coloured Peoples (LCP) formed in London in 1931. Both organizations served as examples of mounting calls for racial equality and of emerging challenges to White racial superiority at the national and international levels.[4] They represented the formalization of efforts aimed directly at challenging colonial domination. By the end of the decade, branches of the LCP began to show up throughout the West Indies

International currents against colonialism were being fed during the thirties by the two emerging superpowers of the Soviet Union and the United States. The Soviet Union had begun to take an intense interest in Europe's colonial possessions indirectly through the Red International of Labour Unions of which a Black Trinidadian, George Padmore, was a leading official. It developed an even more direct involvement through the Negro Bureau of the Communist International of Labour Unions, which Padmore headed, and through the International Trade Union Committee of Negro Workers, an offshoot of the Red International of Labour Unions, for which Padmore served as secretary.[5] The development of an international alliance of Black labor fed directly into anticolonial nationalist organization in the West Indies. West Indian leaders of an increasingly powerful labor movement began to develop strong ties of affiliation with socialist and communist labor organizations in Europe. These affiliations, developed largely through West Indian intellectuals in London, led, eventually in 1945 to the founding of the Caribbean Labour Congress (CLC) as a broad association of trade unions and their affiliated parties in the English-speaking Caribbean. The parent body of the CLC was located in London. An influential segment of its leadership, many with direct ties to the Communist Party of Great Britain, began advocating an anticolonial agenda of radical social change for the West Indies. Its affiliates included the Britain's socialist Trade Union Congress and the British Labour Party. The main thrust of the CLC was in the securing of an independent Federation of the West Indies.

It becomes clear, therefore, that, in combination, anticolonial sentiments in Europe, particularly among socialist and communist political organizations in Britain, and the activism of the Soviet Union had influenced the nationalist efforts in the region in deep and profound ways. The willingness of both to recognize and acknowledge the integral ties between racial domination, international capitalism, and the structure of colonial exploitation appealed to the nationalist leadership. In British Guyana, one of the central figures in labor organization in the region, Hubert Nathaniel Critchlow, affiliated his union with the Socialist International and, by 1930, was calling for a socialist reconstruction based on workers' struggle to overthrow capitalism. In 1932, Critchlow visited the Soviet Union.[6]

The profound effect that the socialist and communist challenges to capitalism had upon the development of West Indian nationalism is unquestioned. Many of the region's leaders who went on to head post-independence governments were members of the CLC. These included Grantly Adams of Barbados (who went on to become prime minister of a West Indian federation), Michael Manley of Jamaica, and Cheddi Jagan and Forbes Burnham of Guyana.[7] But racial nationalism was an inevitable conflict between the expression of racial nationalism and international socialism. The multiracial vision of an international proletariat that stood at the heart of socialist ideology conflicted sharply with the emerging development of a universal Black consciousness. Once the latter became the basis of the anticolonial struggle in Africa and the Caribbean, then the door was open for a rejection of socialism. In the thirties, international events were to bring the contradiction to a head in a way that profoundly shaped the development of West Indian nationalism. Ultimately, these had the effect of curbing radical expression and of bringing to the center of nationalist discourse new conceptualizations of identity informed by images of an African "diasporic intimacy."[8] The appeal in the colonies of arguments for a class struggle began to erode with the rising tide of fascism in Europe. The new racial discourse strengthened the appeal of those advocating the contestation of colonialism on racial grounds. It contributed, also, to an erosion of the appeal of White morality and of its claim to occupancy of the center of civilized discourse. The class-based challenges to capitalism emanating from Europe began to lose their appeal. The weak reaction of radical Europe to Mussolini's invasion of Ethiopia in 1935 provided confirmation that the paramount basis of identity was race. This notion was reinforced by the complicity of White governments in their failure to act in the League of Nations against Italy. The invasion galvanized Black opinion throughout the world. Marcus Garvey, the preeminent Black political leader in Jamaica, declared Mussolini to be the "arch barbarian of our times." An American Committee for Ethiopia and an International African Friends of Ethiopia were formed in England and joined with the LCP and the Pan-African movement to condemn the invasion. In the

West Indies, the invasion gave birth to a new Black "Rastafarian" nationalist movement, which took its name from Haile Selassie's given name Ras Tafari.[9]

The profound shift in ideological direction and in affinities from class to race was immediately evident among those West Indian intellectuals in Britain who had become the driving force behind the development of nationalist thought. Particularly important in this regard were C. L. R. James and George Padmore from Trinidad. Before the invasion, the two were deeply involved in British left-wing politics. They had become very influential in efforts at developing and supporting the anticolonial agendas of socialist and communist political organizations in Britain. Padmore's communism had led to a particularly close relationship with the Soviet Union. Even before Mussolini's invasion, both had begun to develop suspicions about the commitment of the European left to colonial liberation. The reaction of the left to the invasion brought these concerns to a head. Padmore broke with Russia over its refusal to observe sanctions against Italy. Eventually, the break extended to communism itself. Joined by James, Jomo Kenyatta of Kenya, and other Black immigrants from Britain's colonies, he formed the International Africa Friends of Abyssinia. This signaled the beginning of a new ideological direction that placed Africa at the center of a discourse of identity and nationalism. The intellectuals most responsible for shaping the character of West Indian nationalism were at the very center of this development. Their new understandings translated directly into the reformulation of West Indian nationalist expression. The shift to notions of a universal African consciousness as the basis of the struggle against colonialism was institutionalized in the formation of an International African Service Bureau, and later of the Pan-African Federation.[10] It signaled a new emphasis on international Black organization in efforts aimed at securing national sovereignty for Black countries. The shift was formalized in 1945 at a Pan-African Congress held in Manchester. Many of those in attendance, including Jomo Kenyatta and Kwame Nkrumah, were to return to their respective countries to lead independence movements.

Thus, by the late thirties, the basis was laid for the insertion of Pan-Africanism into the development of nationalist consciousness in the predominantly Black colonies of Europe located in Africa and the Caribbean. From then on, nationalist campaigns were to be based on the independent organization of persons of African descent. In the colonies themselves, attention shifted to racial mobilization. The emphasis on the colonial metropole came to be placed on the development of country-focused independence movements. The issue of generalized challenges to colonialism itself was left to radical left movements such as the Movement for Colonial Freedom, formed in 1954. This represented the culmination of efforts by disparate anticolonial movements in Britain to mobilize for independence for Britain's colonies. Included among the groups represented in the movement were labor unions, students' groups, and socialist and communist organizations. They were joined by progressive members of the British Labour Party, who gave the movement clout in the British Parliament. The aim was to bring an end to British colonialism as a "moral" imperative.[11] This internal campaign against colonialism in Britain created the space for the development of racialized nationalist challenges. The nationalist movements in the colonies and their country-based metropolitan organizations were freed from the burden of making strategic racial compromises with metropolitan allies. Such alliances would have been rendered imperative without the independent development of ideological challenges to colonialism that drove British anticolonial opposition.

It was the influence of Pan-Africanism as defined and shaped by the Pan Africanist Congress and its predecessors that informed the development of Afro-Creole nationalism in the West Indies. Pan Africanism became the basis for the contestation of White supremacy as the linchpin of European colonialism.[12] Its influence gave rise to a conceptualization of the West Indian state as the institutional embodiment of Black nationalist aspirations for sovereignty and self-determination

Pan-Africanism provided the ideological framework for the contestation of White supremacy upon which rested colonial legitimacy. The growing institutional and ideological separation from the radical movement in the metropole had profound consequences for the direction taken by the nationalist movement. The relationship between colonialism and capitalism itself went largely uncontested among the large majority of the nationalist leaders. This allowed the United States to begin to exercise the most profound influence upon West Indian nationalism. American involvement with West Indian nationalism emerged out of a combination of strategic concerns, economic interests, and domestic political calculation. These propelled the Untied States into a dominant role in a developing tripartite relationship that included Great Britain and its West Indian colonies. It is out of this relationship that the character and limits of West Indian nationalism were established.[13]

U.S. NATIONALIST INVOLVEMENT

During the interwar years, the United States became firmly convinced that the emergent pattern of neomercantalism in European colonial relations was detrimental to its economic interests. Support for the anticolonial movements in the region was seen as a means of breaking this mercantilist hold. There were also domestic political pressures for U.S. intervention. Economic crisis and political turmoil in the West Indies were creating pressures for migration of West Indians to the United States. Many of the new migrants settled in New York, attracted by opportunities developing in the service and commercial sectors of that city. They quickly became inserted into American racial politics at a time of growing strategic dependence by the Democratic Party upon the Black vote. Their very presence engendered deep concern and sympathy among African American voters for the plight of West Indians who remained at home under the yolk of British imperialism. Black support for the anticolonial cause was heightened by an ongoing economic crisis and its resultant turmoil in the region. There were also strategic geopolitical considerations that weighed heavily upon U.S. policy in the region. The growing political turmoil in Europe that preceded World War II compelled the United States to increase its strategic presence in the Caribbean for its own protection. All of these concerns propelled the United States to take a special and active interest in the region and to pay particular attention to Britain's West Indian colonies.[14]

American direct intervention in policy-making in Britain's West Indian colonies was formalized during World War II. It came in the wake of a decision made in August 1940 to provide destroyers to an embattled Britain in support of that country's war with Nazi Germany. In exchange, the United States demanded the right to locate military bases in the colonies. Direct American influence was exercised through an Anglo American Caribbean Commission formalized in 1942. The establishment of the commission was part of a broader effort to place ultimate responsibility for the protection of the entire hemisphere directly in U.S. hands in the event of a German victory in Europe. An agreement to this effect was signed with leaders of the independent states of the hemisphere. It gave the United States the right to assume, unilaterally, trusteeship of the colonies of any European power defeated by Germany should the latter attempt to transfer to itself sovereignty of such colonies.

The United States used the Anglo American Caribbean Commission effectively to further its anticolonial interests. Immediately it embarked upon a campaign of intense criticism of Britain's colonial policies. Such criticism was informed, less by enlightenment, and more by profound concerns over the destabilizing consequences of resentment against European rule. In the view of the United States administration, it was this very resentment that explained the rapidity of Japan's advance into Europe's Asian colonies. The anticolonialism of the United States stemmed, also, from domestic political and security concerns. There were fears that civil disorder in the West Indies would trigger civil unrest at home among the West Indian population and their African American supporters, particularly in the city of New York.[15]

Thus, the United States became inserted into West Indian colonial discourse as a defender of nationalism. Its involvement began to have a profound effect upon the orientation and ideological character of the West Indian nationalist movement. The Democratic administration placed itself in a position to shape the political currents of the region and to establish strategic political ties with its nationalist leaders. With this involvement, opportunities for surveillance and intelligence gathering increased considerably.

With the defeat of Germany, the foreign policy of the United States had to respond to a new and different set of concerns. The strategic and economic considerations that drove its earlier policy of anticolonialism began to disappear rapidly in the face of profound changes occurring in the postwar international environment. Developing postwar economic relations between the United States and Europe began to eat away at U.S. anticolonial predispositions. Anticolonialism in the prewar era was driven by the desire of American policy-makers to gain access to the markets of Europe's colonies and to exploit their investment opportunities. At the end of the war, mercantilist barriers were dismantled as the United States assumed the major role in the postwar reconstruction of Europe. Increasingly, the economic interests of the United States were becoming tied to the ability of Europe to maintain its exploitative relationships with its colonies. The economic devastation of the war led to increased dependence by the colonial powers upon the latter's economic surpluses. A strong, stable, and resurgent Western Europe was central to the ability of the United States to assert its superpower status as the leader of the capitalist world. U.S. capital invested in postwar Western Europe thus became increasingly vulnerable to decolonization. With this, the economic motivation for its anticolonial policy vanished.[16]

There were, also, profound changes occurring in U.S. politics at home that were acting to diminish significantly Black influence on national decision-making. The new postwar Republican administration was not dependent upon the African American vote as was its Democratic predecessor. Moreover, it had very few ties to the African American community. There was little incentive, therefore, to consider the concerns of the Black population in shaping postwar foreign policy. Anticolonialism was being affected also by a resurgence of racist views that were beginning to hold sway in the United States. Such views began to feed into generalized notions about the unfitness for rule of non-European peoples. Additionally, the McCarthy era of virulent anticommunism at home began to affect negatively anticolonial policy abroad by provoking extreme intolerance for nationalist movements even mildly critical of the Western capitalism or of the United States.

All the above signaled an end to the economic, strategic, and domestic political considerations that drove the anticolonial policies of the Democratic administration of the thirties and forties. With the assertion of its role as leader of the free world in the postwar environment, containment of communism became the driving principle of U.S. foreign policy. It became, also, the basis of support for or opposition to nationalist movements in the ex-colonies.

Nonetheless, any predisposition for intervention against anticolonial movements in Europe's colonies was constrained by the realpolitik of the emerging Cold War. New considerations were beginning to impinge on U.S. foreign policy. The emergent Soviet Union was providing considerable support to anticolonial movements in Europe's former colonies. The United States was cast, in a new ideological campaign aimed at winning the hearts of the new nationalist movements and regimes, in the role of a repressive reactionary power. In this climate, any support provided by the United States for a return to the colonial status quo had to be tempered by geopolitical and geostrategic calculations. Such support came with the real possibility of confirming the role of the United States as a neocolonial power. What emerged in U.S. foreign policy was the practice of supporting those nationalist leaders with an explicit commitment to anticommunism and to a pro-Western agenda. At the same time, the United States embarked on an aggressive policy of active intervention against the radical and progressive leaders of anticolonial campaigns in Europe's colonies.

Historian Cary Fraser argues persuasively that it is within the context of this new U.S. policy of communist containment that the boundaries of West Indian nationalism came to be defined. A potential conflict with Britain over support for the nationalist aspirations of its West Indian colonies was defused in the face of the declining economic importance of the latter. With the economic burden of supporting these colonies growing, Britain began making preparations for ending its colonial responsibilities in the region. It began to promote a plan for federation as a formula for securing their political independence. With independence inevitable, United States policy in the region shifted to ensuring an anticommunist agenda for the postindependence governments. It did so through active intervention.

U.S. intervention in the region was justified on a number of counts. It had become acutely aware of the role of radicals, many of them known Marxists, in the region's nationalist movements. Avowed socialists had managed to gain political power through elections in British Guyana in 1953 and again in 1957. The left wing within the political leadership in

Trinidad had become highly influential in the shaping of political policy. It had managed to shape a campaign to force the United States to give up a portion of one of its remaining military bases for the location of the capital of a proposed West Indian Federation. Undergirding all of this was the turn taken by the Cuban revolution in 1961. America was unprepared to brook another Cuba in the Western hemisphere.

Concerned over the presence and influence of the radical left in the region, the United States began to act decisively to define the limits of West Indian nationalism. With the active support of Great Britain, a campaign was mounted to expunge any hint of radicalism and anti-Americanism from the nationalist agendas of West Indian political movements. With American policy driving Britain's actions and decisions, the West Indian nationalist movement took on a decidedly anti-communist and pro-West character. This phase of U.S. interventionism, argues Fraser, marks the passage of the British West Indies into the U.S. sphere of influence.

THE CLASS BASIS OF AFRO-CREOLE NATIONALISM

West Indian nationalism was shaped, also, by the historical unfolding of the domestic political economy. At the beginning of the thirties urbanization and proletarianization were creating conditions for the development of a trade union movement. Trade unions were being organized out of massive mobilization campaigns for better working conditions. Even in Guyana and Trinidad, with their large and growing East Indian populations, the African population was at the center of these mobilization efforts. The movement was being fed by the economic crisis of the depression. Beginning in 1935, worker dissatisfaction finally exploded into debilitating riots that persisted throughout the English-speaking West Indies until 1939.[17]

Developments in Europe were acting to legitimize the role of professionals and intellectuals in the organization and leadership of the growing working-class movements. West Indian intellectuals residing in Britain had become allied with their European counterparts as champions of progressive causes. The emergence of the British Labour Party provided a great deal of legitimacy to these causes. Progressive members of the West Indian middle class became encouraged to support similar mobilization efforts in their respective colonies.

During the twentieth century, the size and strategic significance of the West Indian middle strata increased considerably. This was partly in response to an infusion of foreign capital for large-scale plantation agro-production, agro-industry, mining, assembly and packaging operations, refining, import substitution, and the like. The expansion of the middle strata was spurred also by growth of state administration. The demand for an intermediate strata of functionaries engendered by these developments provided Blacks and coloreds who had managed to acquire skills and education with the wherewithal for their eventual emergence as a powerful political force for change. Most important among this intermediary group were the professional and salaried urban workers holding state and private sector jobs.

The assumption of leadership positions in worker movements was a considerable departure from the historical practice of this colonized middle strata. It represented a shift from the prior strategy of seeking inclusion in the circle of the colonial elite as a basis of increasing the power and influence of its members. With colonialism and its system of White supremacy under attack, efforts to be included at the apex of a defunct and illegitimate system lost credence and instrumental appeal. Such efforts were replaced by strategies aimed at capturing positions of leadership in a new world order of independent sovereign nations. This was to be acquired through constitutional means. Self-determination became the new focus of political behavior among the politically active segment of this domestic middle strata.

As early as the second decade of the twentieth century, members of the middle strata were making demands for devolution of power to representatives of the colonized populations. Organized efforts began with the formation of a Representative Government Association in Grenada. Founded by Theophilus Marryshow, a journalist, the association embarked on a campaign for an independent West Indies. In 1919, Marryshow's inspiration led to the founding of a similar organization in Dominica under the leadership of attorney Cecil Rawle. These efforts spurred the development of regionwide movement launched at a conference in British Guyana in 1926. The conference was attended by political and labor leaders from throughout Britain's colonized West Indian territories. It was at this conference that the ideology and organization of West Indian Afro-Creole nationalism was fashioned and formulated.

By the latter half of the thirties, local political leaders were making strident calls for self-government and eventual independence. These leaders came predominantly from the ranks of the middle-strata elite. They were also predominantly Black and colored. They included Barbadian attorney Sir Grantley Adams, Jamaican colored businessman Alexander Bustamante—the son of a White planter, colored Jamaican attorney Norman Manley, and Black oilworker Uriah Butler of Trinidad. The sole racial exception was Portuguese Trinidadian publisher Albert Gomes. Nathaniel Critchlow from Guyana and Uriah Butler from Trinidad were the only nationalist leaders attending the conference with working-class backgrounds. Significantly, by the fifties, Gomes, Butler, and Critchlow had all faded from the political scene.

The nationalist leadership quickly established itself as a vanguard on the cutting edge of the development of the new ideology of nationalism. Its strategic insertion into the politics of anticolonialism rested, almost exclusively, upon its ability to mobilize support from among the lower strata of workers and peasants. With the exceptions of Guyana and Trinidad with their large, predominantly rural East Indian population, these lower strata were overwhelmingly Black. An appeal to racial identity, under such circumstances, made political and strategic sense. Fashioned by an increasingly anticolonial and anti-White middle-class leadership, it was such an appeal that began to shape the character of the nationalist movement in the region.[18]

In its formulation, therefore, the ideology of Afro-Creole nationalism came to integrate lower-strata challenges to colonial and European domination with the aspirations to power of the middle-strata elite. The "racial understandings" that informed this nationalist movement differed in significant respects from the ideologies of Pan-Africanism developing in Europe and North America. In the West Indies, there was little by way of commitment to notions of the new commonality rooted in an African "diasporic intimacy."[19] The emerging context of the struggle was different in the colonies. So were the prerequisites for mounting a successful anticolonial campaign. Increasingly, these campaigns became dependent on strategic support provided by one or the other of the two emerging superpowers. A rejection of colonialism on purely racial grounds was incompatible with strategic dependence on one or the other of these White superpowers.

Afro-Creole nationalism was critical if mass support for the political agenda of the emergent elite was to be secured. It was to the understandings of this Black working class that the nationalist appeal was pitched. As such, the rituals and symbols that were embraced by the movement were not explicitly anti-White. They incorporated instead aspects of the expressive culture of this domestic lower strata, including their patterns of speech and dress, their forms of worship, and the like. Ritualistic embrace of these local forms served as a visible indicator of the willingness of the middle strata to reject their own aspirations for colonial elite status, thereby legitimizing their anticolonial credentials.

NATIONALISM AND NEOCOLONIAL ACCOMMODATION

In the postwar era, new forms of capitalist organization were beginning to signal the demise of colonialism and the emergence of neocolonialism.

Through its challenge to colonial domination, nationalism was creating conditions for insertion of these new forms into the domestic political economy of the former colonies. The United States was located at the undisputed center of an emerging neocolonial reality. In the West Indies, Afro-Creole nationalism became the legitimizing principle for the penetration of these neocolonial forms. Colonialism was rapidly becoming an impediment to the development of more intensive forms of exploitation in the peripheral economies. This, more than anything else, explained the prewar attack mounted against it by the United States. New developments in global capital were engendering new patterns of international capitalist relations. These demanded significant changes in the political economies of the colonies. The emergence of the United States as the financial and technological superpower within the industrialized capitalist world and as the world's major market was the force driving these transformations. The relations of empire between the European colonial powers and their non-European colonies were becoming replaced, rapidly, by a new focus of international relations centered upon the United States.

In numerous respects, the nationalist movements paved the way for accommodating the new demands of neocolonialism. Sovereignty freed the new postcolonial leadership from obligations imposed and maintained by colonial power. There were enormous benefits to be derived from a reorientation of their countries' economic relations away from the colonial metropole and toward the United States. The latter had become catapulted to a position as the world's dominant economic and financial power.

During the fifties, West Indian nationalist leaders began to employ their increasing autonomy to effect a reorientation in their international relations. They began a gradual shift in their economic and political relations toward the United States. A potent signal of this shift was the formulation of plans for the implementation of a "Puerto Rican" model of development patterned after the model of "industrialization by invitation" that informed the bootstrap policies of the United States in Puerto Rico.[20] Such a development was the predictable outcome of the deepening ties of dependence with the United States. It was intensified further by a developing tourist industry based on North American visitors that was becoming indispensable to the economic well-being of islands such as Barbados and Jamaica. Additionally, the United States was beginning to absorb a growing number of West Indian immigrants under conditions of growing unemployment and underemployment in the region. North American migration was becoming critical to the region's efforts at poverty alleviation. Remittances from these migrants were proving important as additional sources of income and economic support.

The nationalist leaders were faced with the reality of raised expectations promised in their anticolonial campaign. Popular participation in politics, engendered by the nationalist campaign and institutionalized by the insertion of democratic representative government, brings with it demands for economic betterment. Those at the bottom come to expect, therefore, significant improvements in their life conditions. Such expectations of improvement give considerable legitimacy to efforts by nationalist leaders to institute changes in economic and political arrangements in pursuit of modernity. Thus, the development of ties with the world's economic superpower made considerable sense in such a pursuit.

Nationalist ideology and aspirations produced a governing elite whose position of power came to be legitimized increasingly by its qualifications as "modernizers." As the embodiment of Afro-Creole aspirations, this elite came to be popularly understood to represent the "will of the people." In exercising this "will," understood in terms of the need for development, they entered into a new pattern of neocolonial domination and dependency. This became manifest in a shift in relations of dependency to the new global superpower of the United States. Such a shift in orientation served more than pragmatic functions. It represented also a powerful symbol of self-assertiveness for the country's new and emergent nationalist leadership. A new neocolonial reality became hidden under the symbolic camouflage of the exercise of sovereign right of international association.[21]

NATIONALISM AND THE COLD WAR AGENDA

Economic pragmatism led, naturally, to the development of political ties with North America. The new pattern of neocolonial dependency brought in its wake an imposed pro-capitalist agenda that placed severe limits and imposed strict conditionalities on domestic and international policy. This came with profound ideological implications as the nationalist leaders lined up behind the United States across the Cold War divide. Anticommunism became a justification for the constriction of freedom and for the setting of limits on democratic participation. This emergent postcolonial construction began to take shape even before the granting of independence. Once inserted into the Cold War discourse, nationalist leadership in the region quickly imposed the litmus test of anticommunism as a legitimizing principle of political participation at any level. Without exception, it was the anticommunist leadership that led the governments of the region to independence during the sixties and seventies. Radical members of the nationalist movement found themselves isolated and abandoned as the new anticommunist agenda began to unfold. Those who attempted to break out of the ambit of the United States and of the strictures of anticommunism all found themselves suffering from a near consensus of opposition among the postcolonial leadership of the region. Moreover, persistent and pervasive efforts at destabilization by the United States received the covert, and sometimes, overt support of the region's nationalist leadership.

In pursuit of their ideological agenda, nationalist leaders were prepared to violate the very principles of democracy and self-determination for which they had fought in their anticolonial campaign. They rallied around an anticommunist coalition of the Peoples' National Congress and the United Force in British Guiana in the early sixties. These two parties had become engaged in a violent campaign against the colony's democratically elected and legitimate government of the Peoples' Progressive Party (PPP). The campaign against the government was conducted with the orchestrated support and intervention of the United States and Great Britain. Both governments had declared the leadership of the ruling party to be communist. Reeling from a combination of covert activity, constitutional fiat, and violent confrontation, Cheddi Jagan, the colony's prime minister, was forced to yield to demands for an imposed settlement that guaranteed the ouster of his party from power. A change in government in 1964 ushered in a period of brutal undemocratic rule that lasted until 1992 and left in its path economic ruin and racial turmoil.[22]

In Trinidad, the Peoples' National Movement's (PNM) explicit rejection of socialism at its formation in 1956 proved not enough to satisfy the litmus test of anticommunism. While in office, its leadership became embroiled in a conflict with the United States over the use of the naval base at Chaguaramas for the capital of the West Indian Federation. The intervention of Britain on behalf of the United States forced a purging by the ruling party of its radical leadership and secured a denunciation of communism by its leader, Eric Williams.[23] In exchange, a constitutional arrangement was signed with Britain that guaranteed the party's continued political power and the country's independence, which was quickly granted in 1962. The PNM remained in power until 1986 before losing in elections to a coalition of moderate and right-wing parties in the face of ongoing economic crisis.

Thus, the insertion of Cold War ideology into Afro-Creole nationalism created the conditions for control of governing institutions by anticommunist political leaders, supported by powerful international actors. All the leaders who came to power during the sixties did so while announcing their commitment to a moderate ideological position and to a pro-capitalist program of development for their respective countries. In 1961, Alexander Bustamante came to power in Jamaica by engaging in a virulent attack on communism, Cuba, and the West Indian Federation. In the process, he swept the socialist-leaning government of Norman Manley out of power. He was rewarded with full self-government. In 1962, Eric Williams was granted independence for Trinidad and Tobago after declaring communism as "one of the evils facing his country."[24] With independence came an explicit commitment to capitalist development linked to North America. The governments of Barbados, Guyana, Jamaica, and Trinidad and Tobago, all of whom were granted independence in the sixties, embraced the credo of "industrialization by invitation" as the basis for their development. They aggressively pursued efforts to attract foreign industry while opening their economies to free trade and providing guarantees of profit repatriation and protective legislation to foreign investors.

The pattern of support by Britain and the United States for leaders embracing moderate and pro-western ideological positions was replicated throughout the region. Such support allowed Vere Bird in Antigua and Barbuda to dominate the colony's politics. In 1967, Bird became its first premier under a constitution of self-government. His economic program was based on the attraction of foreign investors in light industries and tourism. Support for anticommunists allowed the moderate George Price in Belize to continue to dominate the colony's domestic political affairs. In Dominica, it created the conditions for the success of moderate Edward LeBlanc in ousting the committed socialist Phyllis Alfrey from the leadership of the Dominica Labour Party. LeBlanc led the party to electoral victory in 1961. Immediately, government was given increased powers. In 1967, under a new self-governing constitution, it was granted Associated Status with Britain. It was British support for conservative Herbert Blaize that allowed him to dominate the legislative affairs of the colony after gaining power in 1962. In 1967, Blaize became the colony's first premier after the granting of Associated Statehood with Great Britain. In Montserrat, William Bramble's change in strategy from agitation against the colony's economic elite to one of accommodation was rewarded with a political victory for his Labour Party in 1961. He immediately instituted a program of economic development based upon active promotion of foreign-financed tourism and of attraction of foreign capital. In St. Lucia, conservative George Compton's United Workers Party won an electoral victory in 1964. Under his leadership the country was granted Associated Statehood in 1967. His economic program, like the others, embraced aggressive attraction of foreign investment.

Thus, in the sixties the political leaders heading every single government of the British West Indies were uniform in their declared willingness to tow the line imposed by the United States. They fully embraced a pro-western, vehemently anticommunist ideology. Were they not prepared to do so, they would have found themselves facing formidable international opposition directed from and dictated by the United States. This reality sparked the observation by Eric Williams, the former prime minister of Trinidad and Tobago, in pointing to Vietnam and the Dominican Republic, that a campaign would have been mounted against any leader who espoused views that were antithetical to the plans of the United States for the region.[25]

THE CHALLENGE OF THIRD WORLDISM

During the sixties, the legitimacy of governing elite was integrally tied to discourses of development and sovereignty. The meaning of independence was shaped by expectations of modernity contained in popular understandings. It was shaped, also, by expectations of self-determination and racial equality. Under conditions where such expectations remained unrealized, legitimacy becomes threatened. Conditions in the domestic and international environment at the end of the seventies began to pose precisely such a threat.

New challenges to the policies and practices of the United States, domestically and internationally, were becoming evident in reassertions of discourses of race and imperialism. Such challenges were beginning to manifest themselves in the domestic civil rights movements of the fifties and sixties in the United States. Internationally, they were being raised in the wake of that country's Cold War interventionist policies. These were occurring during a period when the rigidities of Cold War demarcations were becoming compromised by new understandings and interpretations of "North-South" relations. Cold War ideology was being superseded by discussions of a new "Third World" commonality. With this, the issue of racial domination became telescoped onto the stage of international relations between the northern and southern countries. International relations were becoming collapsed into discourses of racial domination and subordination.

The insertion of "Third World" understandings into the ideological debate and of racial understandings into the arena of international relations was becoming increasingly evident. The development of Arab socialism under the Nasser regime in Egypt was beginning to legitimize challenges to Western capitalism on racial grounds. The direct intervention of American troops in Vietnam in 1965, and the bombing of Laos and Cambodia served, symbolically, as a manifestation of a new racialized imperialism. This was the most visible of a pattern of ubiquitous involvement of the United States against popular "Third World" challenges to colonialism and imperialism.

Popular opinion in the newly constructed "Third World" quickly turned against the United States, which was beginning to be viewed as the architect of the new racial imperialism. All the signs in the new "North-South" confrontation began pointing to the moral and strategic superiority of the "South." The signs were everywhere, and were becoming particularly evident in the growing success of progressive nationalist movements in Africa, in the defeat of the French by the Vietnamese nationalists in 1954, and in the victory of the Front for National Liberation against the French in Algeria in 1962. Almost everywhere there were indications of an escalating and winnable struggle against a racialized neocolonialism. This was highlighted, particularly, by the initiation of armed struggle in the Portuguese colonies of Guinea-Bissau and Angola. The Sharpeville massacre in South Africa underscored the continued paramountcy of race in human relations, international and domestic.[26] This evidence of a newly racialized struggle was not confined merely to instances of western interventionism. The split in 1960 from the Soviet Union by China and the emergence of the latter as an international power in its own right began to complicate notions of communist solidarity. It inserted issues of race into radical debate as China became a major force in the new "Third World international."

Such were the ingredients that went into the construction of a new "Third World" common identity. It emerged out of a newly reconstructed sense of a common history rooted in colonialism and in other forms of racialized domination by the White industrialized North. The common experience of domination was forging a unity of interests among the countries of the South. This experience demanded the development of a common strategy of confrontation as the new prerequisite for solving endemic social, economic, and political crises of the newly understood "Third World." The ideology of Third Worldism signaled a growing consensus that the problems facing less developed countries were directly attributable to their historical relations with the industrial north.

The emergence of Third Worldism was not independent of political challenges to capitalism in the colonial metropole. The victory of the socialist Labour Party in Britain in 1964 and its period of tenure until 1970 was mirrored in political developments throughout Western Europe. Progressive governments capturing power in Western Europe were embarking upon a process of reorganization of their respective societies along anticapitalist principles. As democratic socialism began to sweep Western Europe, demands by the United States for strict adherence to anticommunism began to lose their moral force. Anti-imperialist currents were being felt in the United States as well. Anticommunism as a justification for a policy of intervention in the Third World was under increasing challenge in growing popular opposition to the Vietnam War and to military intervention in Southeast Asia.

The practices of racial segregation in the United States were beginning to telescope themselves onto the international arena in the debate on racial imperialism. Links were being made between the policy of U.S. international intervention and increasing assertions by America's people of color for civil rights. The practice of racial imperialism abroad and racism at home began to underscore and support claims made for the existence of a racialized international division of labor.

Third World solidarity was given an additional boost by the growing rapprochement between the superpowers across the ideological divide. In 1971 President Nixon visited the U.S.S.R. to signal the beginning of U.S.-Soviet détente. In 1972 he visited China to cement a yearlong effort out of which emerged a normalization of relations. With détente, the barriers of ideology that may otherwise have foreclosed development of political and economic relations among Third World countries began to erode.

The West Indies was becoming inserted into this new international climate of Third Worldism at a time when the benefits of the developing relationship with the United States was being questioned. Economic and political ties with the United States were not producing the anticipated returns in developmental transformation. Indeed, the period of nationalist assertion was accompanied by growing unemployment and poverty.[27] The new international climate combined with the dashed expectations for economic betterment to cast doubt on the strategy of linkage with the United States at a time when new arguments of racial imperialism were beginning to challenge claims that such a strategy reflected a demonstration of self-determination.

By the late sixties there was in the West Indies a discernible swing in mass opinion toward alternative understandings of sovereignty and self-determination. It was fueled by Black power and antiwar demonstrations raging in the United States. The foreign policy of the United States soon came to be understood, popularly, as an extension of its practice of racial oppression against its Black population at home. West Indian governments advocating continued ties with the United States and uncritical support of western capitalism soon found themselves under attack by advocates of "Black power" in the region. In 1968 the government of Jamaica was forced to take action. Walter Rodney, a citizen of Guyana, had gained regionwide prominence for his rejection of capitalism and neocolonialism. In his writings and speeches, he explained the roots of both in an internationalized racial division of labor. While a lecturer at the University of the West Indies in Jamaica he began to conduct a "Black power" campaign against the government by organizing segments of the Jamaican lower classes. Fearing his growing popular appeal, the government of Jamaica revoked his right to work in the country. The decision provoked debilitating riots that almost crippled the conservative regime of the Jamaica Labour Party.[28]

By 1970, Black power challenges to pro-U.S. governments seemed to be sweeping the region. In Trinidad, radical trade unionists joined with university students to create a mass movement that mounted a severe challenge the moderate pro-capitalist regime of Eric Williams. Their campaign of mass mobilization escalated when factions of the army, led by radical junior officers, mutinied in support of their cause. The Williams government survived the crisis only after the intervention of a loyalist coast guard and veiled threats of a U.S. military intervention.[29]

Radical nationalist leaders throughout the Third World were given considerable breathing room with the election of Jimmy Carter to the presidency of the United States in 1976. A commitment to human rights placed the Carter administration in conflict with corrupt right-wing regimes being opposed by radical insurgency movements. The pronouncements of the Carter administration against civil rights violations provided tacit support for the leaders of these movements. With the appointment of Andrew Young as U.S. Ambassador to the United Nations, there was less strident opposition to Third World socialist movements fighting campaigns of national liberation.

The reduction in the stridency of the U.S. campaign against radical movements in the Third World came at a time of a discernible shift in the policies and programs of political leaders in the West Indies. It was reflected in mass rejection of the capitalist policies of the sixties and of the practice of establishing exclusive ties with the United States. After 1971, the Forbes Burnham government in Guyana increasingly and publicly identified itself with the nonaligned movement and with Third World socialism. Its foreign policy position became stridently anti-American and the regime developed strong ties with Cuba and China. By 1975, a series of nationalizations of foreign concerns contributed to acquisition by the state of 80 percent of the country's economic assets.[30] Governments intransigent to calls for change were swept out of power. In Jamaica, the Peoples National Party under Michael Manley, won a landslide victory over the conservative Jamaica Labor Party (JLP). The victory was secured in a campaign that promised fundamental socioeconomic change informed by the principles of democratic socialism. Manley pledged the elimination of class barriers and class privilege, "real" sovereignty and self-determination at the international level free from the dictates of external powers, and local control of the domestic economy that was free from the dictates of foreign investors.[31] In 1970, Mau-

rice Bishop returned to Grenada and joined with radical activists Kenric
Radix to forge a popular movement against the right-wing government
of Eric Gairy. In 1979, his socialist New Jewel Movement seized power
from the corrupt right-wing regime and established relations with Cuba
and Eastern Europe.

The yet-to-be-independent smaller islands were also swept away in
the tide of Third World radicalism. In Dominica, the government of
Patrick John had to resort to a brutal campaign against popular political dissent to maintain power against popular calls for radical reform.
In St. Lucia, the St. Lucia Labour Party (SLP) began a process of internal radicalization after George Odlum returned from Great Britain to
eventually become its Deputy Leader. The party was able to attract
enormous popular support.

During the seventies, the space for the exploration of alternative
political and economic strategies was created in an international environment that challenged United States hegemony. Increasingly, the U.S.
was cast as the international leader in a new form of racialized neocolonialism. During the second half of the seventies, an economic recession added to its weakened international position despite a growing conservative climate that favored a more aggressive international policy to
combat the spread of radicalism.

GLOBALIZATION AND THE END OF NATIONALISM

By the beginning of the eighties, an international debt crisis, generalized
conditions of economic recession and crisis, and a resurgence of the
Cold War created a new environment that forced a reformulation of
nationalist discourse. The economic crisis was fueled by an inflationary
explosion between 1973–74 that produced a doubling of commodity
prices and a quadrupling of oil prices. The crisis contributed to an
increase of 43 percent in the costs of Third World imports from industrialized countries. Serious declines in prices of commodity exports and
significant drops in demand began to place severe pressure on the ability of the Third World economies to earn foreign exchange.[32] The accu-
mulation of huge current account deficits forced drastic cut backs in
imports, and considerable declines in incomes and economic activity.
Huge deficits accumulated during the period were offset by relatively
easy access to foreign exchange support made available through accumulated financial surpluses of oil-exporting countries. Foreign exchange
support was made available by the International Monetary Fund (IMF)
through an oil facility set up to fund oil-related balance of payment
deficits. For the English-speaking Caribbean, foreign exchange surpluses

accumulated by Trinidad and Tobago, an oil producer, became available for deficit financing of current accounts imbalances for most countries in the region.

Between 1979–80, a second "oil shock" produced another series of dramatic increases in oil prices fueling another international recession that rocked the Western economies. The resulting escalation of interest rates in international financial markets and decreased demand for export commodities placed enormous additional pressure on foreign exchange. Debtor countries, borrowing at flexible interest rates or seeking to refinance loans, were faced with enormous, unpredictable interest payments. Under the threat of default by major borrowers in 1982, international banks made a decision to suspend or limit loans to many beleaguered Third World economies. Countries in the region, rocked by severe economic crises, were forced to turn to the IMF as the agency of first resort for financing balance of payments deficits. Quickly, the IMF was joined by the World Bank in making demands for enormous concessions in exchange for assistance to beleaguered LDCs in a program of structural adjustment. These adjustments imposed a regime of strong controls on domestic demand, cuts in state expenditure, devaluation, export promotion, economic liberalization, and concessions aimed at attracting foreign investors.

The burgeoning middle classes and urban lower classes, who had emerged as the most strategic political force in the English-speaking Caribbean, were most profoundly affected by the ensuing economic crisis. As their lifestyles became threatened, their support shifted to leaders whose programs seemed to have the best chances of attracting foreign investment and foreign exchange supports. Popular support shifted to those political leaders willing to aggressively pursue a program aimed at attracting foreign financing. A consensus emerged that the leaders best suited to run the country were those able to develop strategic ties with international actors in a position to deliver badly needed economic assistance.

In the early seventies, the democratic socialism of Jamaica's Michael Manley came to typify new understandings of nationalist self-determination. Manley was the first to suffer the consequences of the changes in the international economic and political environments. Soon after 1976, his Peoples National Party (PNP) became the target of political and economic destabilization efforts by the United States. President Jimmy Carter's dovish approach to the Third World was coming under increasing attack by a resurgent conservative movement led by Ronald Reagan. In Jamaica, escalating debt, capital flight, and divestment of foreign capital from the domestic economy was fueling a growing economic crisis. In its efforts to secure balance of payments support, the Manley government was forced to approach the IMF and to accept conditions of economic reorganization that were anathema to the party's espoused ideological position. The conditionalities imposed were more stringently applied by the IMF as a means of ensuring a reversal of policies rooted in the principles of socialism.[33] In the process, wittingly or unwittingly, the IMF became another component in an interventionist campaign aimed at supporting the pro-capitalist, pro-western opposition.

The program of "stabilization" called for by the IMF demanded a devaluation of the country's currency and massive cuts in state expenditure. These exacerbated economic conditions, causing further erosion in popular support for the ruling party particularly among the country's middle classes. A propaganda campaign succeeded in placing the blame for the crisis on Manley's socialism and upon his ties with Cuba. Quickly, a majority of the voting population became convinced that the strengthening of relations with the United States offered the best hope for crisis resolution. Majority support shifted to the Jamaica Labor Party headed by conservative Edward Seaga. The archetypal conservative pragmatist, Seaga had assumed the leadership of party in 1974 with a reputation as an economic wizard developed during a stint as minister of finance and planning between 1967 and 1972. He was unequivocally committed to the capitalist model of development based on the attraction of foreign private investment. He was strongly pro-western and pro-American. And he was able to rely on the support of the Carter administration as well as upon American conservatives, particularly Ronald Reagan, who, as a presidential candidate, took special interest in Jamaica's affairs.

Seaga's JLP won an electoral victory on December 15, 1980, after a violent and ideologically charged campaign. The victory presaged the demise of the nationalist agenda as West Indian political leaders in the eighties were forced to deal with the realities of a new globalism. The conditions of participation in this new international political economy conflicted fundamentally with the principles of nationalism forged earlier in the century. Political leaders were forced to make a number of concessions anathema to this nationalist agenda. These concessions struck at the heart of notions of sovereignty and self-determination.

The new globalism was accompanied and supported by a resurgence of the campaign of U.S. interventionism. This came with the end of rapprochement and with the "heating up" of the old bipolar rivalries of the Cold War. Cold War interventionism in the region strengthened the positions of conservative political leaders who could now anticipate, expect, and demand U.S. support. Those unwilling to accept the new conditions imposed on domestic and international policymaking had to be prepared to face the consequences of a policy of U.S. retaliation aimed at the demobilization of leftist groups, neutralizing leftist political leaders, and destabilizing leftist governments in the region.

The conservative tide became evident throughout the English-speaking Caribbean as politicians strongly devoted to export oriented capitalism, the reestablishment of strong ties with the United States, and liberal economic policies came to dominate the region's political systems In Antigua, the welfare and labor oriented George Walter's Progressive Labour Movement (PLM) was voted out of power in 1976, despite winning the popular vote. His successor was veteran politician, Vere Bird, who headed the rival Antigua Labour Party (ALP). Bird's economic policies emphasized the attraction of foreign investment, particularly in the tourist and export-oriented sectors of the economy. In April 1980, Bird's popularity gave his party an overwhelming victory at the polls. He continued to dominate the country's affairs after leading it to independence in November 1981.

In Barbados, Tom Adams' strong advocacy of capitalist policies and of a staunchly pro-American foreign policy while leader of the parliamentary opposition paved the way for a dramatic electoral victory by the Barbados Labour Party in 1976. His government vigorously pursued policies based on the attraction of foreign capital and the development of local capitalism.

In Belize, the government of the moderate George Price was buffeted by an economic crisis that had become particularly severe by 1979. His Peoples United Party managed to hold on in that year's elections and took the country to independence in 1981. But in 1980, the opposition United Democratic Party (UDP) made the decision to elect to its leadership the conservative pro-American Manuel Esquivel whose ideology placed heavy emphasis on free enterprise and the encouragement of foreign investment. Under Esquivel's leadership, the UDP won a sweeping victory in the country's first postindependence elections held in 1984.

In Dominica, political chaos, caused partly by declining economic conditions and partly by brutal repression of political radicals, resulted in the collapse of the regime of Patrick John in 1979. Out of an ideological amalgam of dissidents emerged the extremely conservative and pro-American Mary Eugenia Charles, who led her Dominica Freedom Party to electoral victory in July 1980. Like the other regional conservatives, her political platform was grounded in a firm commitment to private enterprise, to the attraction of foreign investors, and to a strong aversion to socialism.

In Montserrat, despite a successful economic program and a commitment to welfare policies, the government of Percival Bramble lost power in 1978 to John Osborne. Osborne's victory came in the wake of a blistering attack on his predecessor's welfare program, which he berated as socialist. His ardent support for the free enterprise system and for the attraction of North American investors to the country galvanized the country's local business community around him.

In Saint Kitts and Nevis, the dominance of progressive Robert Bradshaw from the 1940s until his death in 1978 was not enough to stop the conservative tide. In 1980, a coalition government of the Peoples Action Movement (PAM) and the Nevis Reform Party gave his Labour Party its first electoral defeat since its formation in 1946. Under the premiership of conservative Kennedy Simmonds there was a decidedly more moderate turn to the policies of the colony, which was granted independence in 1983.

In St. Lucia, the government of George Compton suffered a defeat in 1979 after fifteen years in power. Compton's loss to the Saint Lucia Labour Party (SLP), whose guiding light was the radical George Odlum, appeared to be one of the instances (with Guyana and Grenada) where the conservative tide was being bucked in the region. Nonetheless, ideological factionalism within the SLP, under the leadership of moderate Alan Louisy, provoked a political crisis that forced a 1982 election. This time, the electorate turned, once again, to Compton, attracted by his policies of industrialization by invitation and the attraction of foreign investments in the tourist sector.

The appeal of the conservative leaders was bolstered by a propaganda campaign that highlighted the demonstrated political and economic failures of the region's two socialist governments: the Burnham regime in Guyana and the Manley regime in Jamaica. There was abundant evidence of the demonstrated resolve of the United States to oppose, neutralize, and destabilize progressive governments, organizations, and groups and to provide support for their pro-capitalist, pro-western counterparts. The ties between these conservative regimes and the United States were so complete that many joined the latter in a military invasion of Grenada to oust its radical government in 1983.

The United States made abundantly clear its willingness to provide economic and political support to its regional allies. In return for its strong and unwavering support for the policies advocated by Reagan's administration, the JLP government in Jamaica became the recipient of a tremendous amount of U.S. bilateral assistance. U.S. support and backing cleared the way for the transfer of a considerable amount of multilateral assistance to the country, particularly from the IMF. Additionally, the Reagan administration poured significant amounts of resources into the development of a program of economic assistance for its Caribbean allies. Using the argument of supporting its "vital interests" in the region, the U.S. administration pushed through Congress a Caribbean Basin Economic Recovery Act. Known as the Caribbean

Basin Initiative (CBI), the act was signed into law in August 1983. Included in its provisions were duty-free access of the products of selected countries to U.S. markets. Apparel assembled in these countries were provided special access to the U.S. markets through a textile initiative. Special tax benefits and investment incentives were made available to potential and actual U.S. investors in the region. And the United States provided backing for bilateral support for the region from other countries, particularly Canada, Mexico, and Venezuela.[34] The United States also doubled its aid to the region as reflected in an increase from 6.6 to 13.6 percent of its overall economic assistance budget going to the Caribbean between 1980 and 1984.[35] Most of the increased allocations were targeted for use by the private sector, to provide critical balance-of-payments support, for infrastructure projects, and to support training and scholarship opportunities. The choice of countries to be included in the CBI initiative was determined on strictly ideological grounds. Guyana, Grenada, and Nicaragua were pointedly excluded.

The policy employed by the United States against progressive governments that retained power during the eighties was to use the might of its economic power to generate, sustain, and deepen economic crisis. It was precisely such a strategy that forced a change in ideological direction upon a socialist PNC regime in Guyana. Desmond Hoyte, successor to President Forbes Burnham, took the opportunity of his death in 1986 to adopt economic and foreign policies that were more consistent with U.S. designs for the region. By 1987, Hoyte's change of ideological direction began paying dividends in the form of bilateral and western multilateral assistance, which was in short supply during the Burnham presidency.

The carrot of economic and developmental assistance was accompanied by the stick of the threat of military intervention. The United States increased its military presence in the region and publicized this increase by holding military exercises (Big Pines I and II) and joint maneuvers with some of the region's armed forces. The infrastructure for this significantly expanded U.S. military presence was constantly upgraded after 1981 particularly at its bases in Honduras. It provided support for a guerrilla campaign against the Sandinista government in Nicaragua. It invaded Panama in 1989 to oust the intransigent government of Manuel Noriega. And in 1983 it mounted an invasion to oust the radical pro-Cuban and pro-Soviet government of Grenada. The invasion was the culmination of retaliatory efforts by the United States aimed at political and economic destabilization during the entire term in office of the radical New Jewel Movement (NJM). The NJM had come to power by coup d'etat in Grenada in 1979.

Conservative governments under challenges by guerrilla campaigns in the region were provided with massive amounts of military assistance in demonstrations of the willingness of the United States to intervene in support of its ideological allies. This was particularly the case for the governments of El Salvador and Guatemala, both under siege from radical guerrilla groups. Honduras became a staging ground for a guerrilla campaign mounted by the American supported contras against the radical Sandinista regime in Nicaragua. Military intervention and military support became visible indicators of the reassertion by the United States of its hegemonic role in the Caribbean and Central America and its return to a vigorous assertion of its national and regional interests.

The policies of the new conservative leadership have focused upon the development of export-oriented activities, many in specially erected industrial parks and export processing zones (EPZs). Domestic agriculture has plummeted and there has been an increasing emphasis upon the exports of traditional agricultural commodities. There has also been a heavy emphasis on tourism. The result has been a more intense integration of the political economies of the region into the global system of manufacturing and finance and a deepening reliance upon experts with the technical and managerial competence by both the public and private sector. This has produced significant changes in the composition of the governing elite. Located at the center of this new elite is a political executive that has become highly dependent upon the transfer of resources from western international governmental and economic actors for its power. It relies upon the group of technical experts for establishing and managing the new realities of economic globalism. They have become responsible for securing resource transfers from private and public international financial institutions, both bilateral and multilateral, into the domestic political economy. These experts are indispensable to the government's efforts at reorganizing and managing a political economy in the process of neoliberal transformation. They are recruited from a growing group of international elite with unrestricted means of geographic and even sectoral mobility. Their employment opportunities depend upon their willingness to be constantly on the move seeking the salaries, privileges, prerequisites, and chances of promotion provided by multilateral agencies and transnational organizations with seemingly limitless access to resources. The political, technocratic, and managerial elite is joined by a new grouping of merchants involved in importation and wholesale and retail activities. Local manufacturers are forced to turn their attention to export processing activity producing on a subcontracting basis for companies based in the industrialized economies. Tied increasingly to the international system of manufacturing as subcontractors, they are forced to undertake the labor-intensive aspects of a disaggregated system of international manufacturing. To make profit, they are forced to maintain low labor costs, wages, and salaries in their own peripheral political economies.

The new global agenda is intensified further with the escalating dependence of Caribbean political economies on tourism. Its success depends upon the attraction of foreign investment in growing tourist industries, the reorganization of economic activity, the retraining of the work force to cater to international, and particularly western, tastes, the destruction of local architectural forms and their replacement with "modern" western forms for tourist accommodation, and the commodification of local culture to suit western palates.

All of the above act to create conditions for the undermining of the nationalist agenda. As the focus of the new elite shifts to sectors of the political economy that cater to the demands of international finance and manufacturing, resources are diverted from satisfying the needs of the local population. Governments turn to international NGOs as they seek to reduce spending on health, education, welfare, and social security. These NGOs attempt to fill in the breach as workers become displaced from wage-earning activities, and as real wages become significantly depressed.

Those without formal connection to this new global reality are forced to rely increasingly upon their own efforts to secure access to international resources, directly and indirectly. Many become heavily reliant upon remittances transferred from abroad by relatives. Others begin to engage in small-scale, semilegal or illegal activities in the "informal sector" servicing the needs of the new domestic and international elite or filling in gaps left in the process of economic transformation. Typically, the informal sector comes to include an enormous amount of nonconventional activities including petty trade, smuggling, gambling, thieving, outworking, personal services, and the like. Most important in the West Indies is the involvement in the local and international drug trade and in male and female prostitution. These activities are directly associated with the tourist industry.

Thus, nationalism with its aspirations for sovereignty and self determination becomes meaningless and irrelevant. It is replaced by popular glorification of the behavior and practices of the North Atlantic, and particularly North America. These include the pathologies of western capitalism such as drug consumption, gang violence, environmental degradation, and the privileging of profit over welfare and social security. There has been an avalanche of outmigration, particularly to North America especially of the skilled and educated. Domestic capital and savings have been, legally and illegally, exported abroad to purchase and support northern lifestyles.[36] As a consequence and for all intents and purposes, the nationalist domestic agenda has been abandoned.[37] The explanation for its abandonment is that it no longer serves the interests of the regional elite who were its ideologues.

NOTES

1. Slavery was abolished in the British colonies in 1833. It was followed by a five-year period of "apprenticeship" where the former slaves were required to remain on the plantation under conditions similar to indentureship.

2. F. A. Hoyos, *Builders of Barbados* (London: Macmillan Caribbean, 1972), pp. 98–100.

3. see P. Hintzen and W. M. Will, "Garvey, Marcus Mosiah," in Robert J. Alexander (ed.), *Biographical Dictionary of Latin American and Caribbean Political Leaders* (New York: Greenwood, 1988).

4. See P. G. Lauren, *Power and Prejudice: The Politics and Diplomacy of Racial Discrimination* (Boulder, Colo.: Westview Press, 1988), pp. 76–101.

5. See S. Howe, *Anticolonialism in British Politics* (Oxford: Clarendon, 1993), pp. 84–89.

6. A. Chase, *A History of Trade Unionism in Guyana* (Georgetown, Guyana: New Co., 1964), pp. 50–53.

7. See Howe, *Anticolonialism*, pp. 210–13.

8. P. Gilroy, *The Black Atlantic: Modernity and Double Consciousness* (New York: Penguin, 1993).

9. Lauren, *Power and Prejudice*, pp. 118–22.

10. See Howe, *Anticolonialism*, pp. 84–86.

11. Howe, *Anticolonialism*, p. 234.

12. See P. Hintzen, "Reproducing Domination: Identity and Legitimacy Constructs in the West Indies," *Social Identities*, vol. 3, no. 1 (1997): 47–75.

13. See C. Fraser, *Ambivalent Anti-Colonialism: The United States and the Genesis of West Indian Independence, 1940–64* (Westport and London: Greenwood, 1994).

14. See ibid., pp. 9–53.

15. Ibid., pp. 55–89.

16. Ibid., pp. 93–121.

17. See West India Royal Commission 1938–39, "Statement of Action on the Recommendations," Cmd. 6656, London, 1939.

18. See P. Hintzen, "Structural Adjustment and the New International Middle Class," *Transition*, Issue 24 (February 1995), pp. 52–74.

19. Gilroy, *Black Atlantic*.

20. See J. R. Mandle, *Persistent Underdevelopment: Change and Economic Modernization in the West Indies* (Amsterdam: Gordon and Breach, 1996), pp. 57–71.

21. See Hintzen, "Structural Adjustment."

22. P. Hintzen, *The Costs of Regime Survival: Racial Mobilization, Elite Domination, and Control of the State in Guyana and Trinidad* (Cambridge and New York: Cambridge University Press, 1989), pp. 52–56; N. Sheehan, ""C.I.A. Men and Strikers in Guiana against Dr. Jagan," *New York Times*, February 22, 1967; D. Pearson, "U.S. Faces Line Holding Decision," *Washington Post*, May 31, 1964; S. Lens, "American Labor Abroad," *The Nation*, July 5, 1965; A. Schlesinger, *A Thousand Days* (New York: Houghton Mifflin, 1965), p. 779.

23. *Trinidad Guardian*, October 1, 1961; S. Ryan, *Race and Nationalism in Trinidad and Tobago* (Toronto: University of Toronto Press, 1972), pp. 197–203.

24. *Trinidad Guardian*, October 1, 1961.

25. E. Williams, *Economic Transformation and the Role and Vision of the PNM*, an address to the PNM Annual Convention, Trinidad, 1974, p. 28.

26. See G. Chaliand, *Revolution in the Third World* (New York: Penguin, 1978), pp. 17–24.

27. Mandle, *Persistent Underdevelopment*, pp. 79–92.

28. See O. Gray, *Radicalism and Social Change in Jamaica: 1960–1972* (Knoxville: University of Tennessee Press, 1990), pp. 145–65.

29. Hintzen, *Costs of Regime Survival*, pp. 78–84.

30. Hintzen, *Costs of Regime Survival*, pp. 65–69.

31. See M. Manley, *Jamaica: Struggle in the Periphery* (London: Third World Media, 1982), pp. 25–91.

32. See N. Girvan, "Swallowing the IMF Medicine in the 'Seventies,'" in C. K. Wilber (ed.), *The Political Economy of Development and Underdevelopment* (New York: Random House, 1984), p. 169.

33. See Girvan, "Swallowing the IMF Medicine," and Manley, *Jamaica*, pp. 149–203; P. Anderson and M. Witter, "Crisis, Adjustment and Social Change: A Case Study of Jamaica," in E. LeFranc (ed.), *Consequences of Structural Adjustment: A Review of the Jamaica Experience* (Kingston: Canoe Press, 1994).

34. See G. Shultz, "Caribbean Basin Economic Recovery Act," statement before the Senate Finance Committee, April 13, 1983.

35. Ibid.

36. See K. McAfee, *Storm Signals* (London: Zed Books in Association with Oxfam America, 1991).

37. P. Hintzen, "Democracy and Middle Class Domination in the West Indies," in C. Edie (ed.), *Democracy in the West Indies* (Boulder, Colo.: Westview Press, 1993).

PART III

Shaping a New Diplomacy

CHAPTER 10

Defining National Security: The African American Stake in U.S. Defense and Foreign Policy Formulation

Ronald V. Dellums

I believe that the clearest expression of a society's values will be illuminated by the fiscal priorities established in its national budget. The choice between guns and butter—investment in the military versus investment in meeting human needs—will demonstrate a nation's commitment to the universality of educational opportunity, the health of its communities, infants and seniors, the quality of its housing, and the access of all of its citizens to employment and economic opportunity.

Assessed in this light, budget choices made during most of the past fifty years of United States history fail the moral test of government. The creation, perpetuation, expansion, and maintenance of a permanent war economy well past the end of the Cold War has wrought social and economic havoc throughout society.

For years, my community of Oakland, California, has endured the constant anguish of the premature and often violent deaths of many of our most precious community gifts—our young people. This plague has had a disproportionate impact on the African American community, although its horrors are not exclusively our province.

On a large scale, our children suffer from a plague of hopelessness that has led predictably to self-destructive behavior. Their cynicism and frustration are bred from the results of a declining public commitment to social investment: poor schools; overstressed teachers; deficient and deteriorating housing; inadequate health care; and other elements of a collapsing infrastructure.

These "physical" traumas have been aggravated by a palpable retreat from the struggles for racial equality and economic equity. Young people see few jobs to which they can aspire as adults; they cannot escape or ignore the diminution of opportunities to compete for mainstream economic success.

These realities have conspired to produce a fatalism about the future that has, in turn, threatened the durability of life. Too many of our children have taken to killing each other for fleeting economic advantages on the street, in part because they believe literally that they have no future as adults.

For decades before and during this crisis, this same community—like similar communities across the nation—has borne witness to and undertaken a struggle to demand the full participation of persons of the African American community (and the Latino, Native American and Asian American communities) in the political, economic, and social institutions that govern our lives in the United States. Our community birthed the revolutionary activism of the Black Panther Party, alongside ploddingly slow but measurable progress in the struggle for inclusion in the mainstream body politic.

The goal of each aspect of this struggle was not just to assert the full measure of our dignity and citizenship. It was also to feed and clothe our children, provide medical care to our communities in order to end the scourge of infant death and other preventable diseases. It was to provide meaning, comfort, and sustenance for our elders, and to generate the economic activity that would provide work for those for whom our civil rights activism had opened doors previously slammed shut.

These were the issues that confronted me as a young elected official of the Berkeley City Council. As a psychiatric social worker and job development specialist by profession, I understood both the opportunities and limits of the federal war on poverty. The primary limit was the waning commitment to social programs concomitant with the increasing financial commitment the federal government had to make to prosecute its ill-advised war in Southeast Asia.[1]

Therefore, I found powerful resonance when Dr. Martin Luther King Jr. chose to involve himself in the movement against United States involvement in the Southeast Asian war that was raging in Vietnam. Dr. King expressed the metaphoric insight that the bombs dropping in Vietnam were exploding in the ghettos and the barrios of America, thus providing graphic characterization of the effect of the nation's misplaced priorities. Dr. King clearly saw that urban America and its residents were being destroyed through financial abandonment—what later would become known as "benign" neglect—as surely as if the napalm denuding the forests of Vietnam were levelling the buildings of Detroit and other cities.

Despite the acuity of his vision, however, he was criticized in the African American community for "diluting" his focus on the civil rights movement. Instead, his clarion call should have awakened our leaders to the risks a society generates when it eschews funding the solutions to social problems in pursuit of international military adventure. Any effective civil rights struggle must be accompanied by an "economic" rights struggle that seeks to ensure that opportunities exist behind the doors that may be opened.

Dr. King came to speak at the University of California campus in Berkeley just after I had been elected to the Berkeley City Council. His presence and speech triggered in me a profound responsibility to act, both to end the war and to alter the Cold War mentality that was robbing our community of critical resources. He confirmed what we confronted every week in council: our city's ability to deal fully with its economic and social problems would be forever thwarted so long as the federal government was preoccupied with siphoning scarce financial resources away from our urgent domestic problems and pouring them instead into fighting the Southeast Asian war and, more broadly, the larger Cold War.

A bumper sticker slogan popular during the late 1960s and early 1970s captured this tension aptly: *Won't it be a great day when our children's schools have all the money they need, and the Pentagon has to hold a bake sale to buy a bomber!*

Given the social upheaval of the sixties, the risks associated with a failure to achieve change in our national priorities in 1967 seemed urgent and grave; that urgency and gravity has been increased by an order of magnitude in the ensuing thirty years.

SITTING AT THE TABLE

When I first was sworn into the United States Congress in 1971, I sought a seat on the Education and Labor Committee. With my background both as a local government official and as a psychiatric social worker and job development consultant, I had worked with all of the so-called Great Society programs of the 1960s. I felt that I could bring this expertise to bear on recrafting national policy within the domestic agenda. I hoped to bring improvement to the best these programs offered—such as the principle of "maximum feasible participation of the poor"—while shedding the worst (the often inflexible bureaucratic approach to problem solving). I was determined to wage a fight to achieve the necessary funding to ensure these programs' success.

Instead the House Democratic leadership gave me a seat on the Foreign Affairs Committee. My frustration simmered, until I recalled Dr.

King's words about the correlation between domestic initiative and the orientation of foreign and defense policy.

I had just been granted a seat at the table that would help establish those international policies. I could help both to end the Vietnam War and to reorient our Cold War foreign policy. From this fulcrum, I could help to deliver resources so urgently needed to solve our domestic problems.

Over the next two years, I realized that our military policy—overseen by the Armed Services Committee—was the tail that wagged the dog of foreign policy. This was especially so with regard to federal expenditures. The military consumed, and still does consume, 15–20 times more resources than our foreign assistance programs. It was the bull that chased other programs off the field.

Any change in security policy significant enough to have a meaningful impact on the domestic investment pot would have to be within the military field and not under the jurisdiction of the Foreign Affairs Committee.

In response to this realization, I petitioned the House leadership for a transfer to the Armed Services Committee. After a hard-fought battle led by the Congressional Black Caucus, I secured a seat—over the objection of the committee chairman—as the committee's first African American member. The ensuing twenty-five-year odyssey—one that would include a stint as the committee chairman—was an often lonely voyage. But it proved beyond a doubt to me the wisdom of Dr. King's prophecy: one had to contend successfully on the battlefield of ideas in the national security arena in order to produce opportunity in the domestic policy arena.

I intended to master the defense policy process; to be able to prevail on its terms and in its esoteric frame of reference. No more would "experts" and colleagues be able to say to me: "Oh Ron, if only you understood how dangerous the world is and how important these military programs are in response to them. Then you would understand why we must sink these resources into the military account and cannot afford to transfer them to our domestic needs."

Slowly and with increasing credibility, we were able to put forth arguments and, in some cases, prevail. As a result, resources were not squandered on dangerous or unnecessary programs such as the MX-mobile missile (which was never built as a mobile missile system); the Pershing II missile deployment in Europe (which was abandoned); the megabillion dollar "Star Wars" program (never built); the comprehensive "strategic homeporting" for the Navy (significantly curtailed at considerable savings); or the B-2 bomber program (reduced from scores of planes to only 21). These victories were achieved because they were the right policy and because vibrant mass movements gave weight and credibility to the arguments that were being made within the Congress. As a consequence of these victories, money that would have been spent on these programs was available for other military programs and pressure was reduced to raid even more the civilian accounts that were being drained to finance the military expansion.

Despite these sporadic programmatic successes, the military budget increases of the Reagan era in the 1980s shifted the federal budget debate in our nation so dramatically that we have yet to recover from it.

In his first budget message to a Joint Session of the Congress, then President Reagan announced from the House Floor that he would reduce federal domestic spending by approximately $50 billion, ostensibly to help bring the federal budget into balance. In that same speech he deferred broadcast of a defense plan. When the plan was sent up to Congress a few weeks later, it bore a price increase of $50 billion. No budget savings had been realized by the domestic cuts. Instead, there had been a straightforward transfer of resources from the domestic agenda to the military. Under Reagan, we were going to beat plowshares into swords!

Dr. King could not have asked for a more brilliant illumination of the linkage between domestic and military spending. He could not have envisioned a clearer sign that, despite the end of the Vietnam War, the bombs being built to fight the Cold War were still exploding in cities across America. Millions of Americans, and especially African Americans, would slip into economic marginality as the military spending spree shredded the domestic agenda and ultimately the federal safety net.

In fiscal 1998, the annual federal interest payment that would be needed to finance the enormous national debt that arose during this period—from the combination of increased military spending and ill-advised tax breaks for the well to do—is larger than the annual budget deficit. Imagine how differently the balanced budget debate (if we would have had one) would have proceeded in the mid-1990s without this debt burden consuming such an enormous share of the annual federal tax dollar.

It fell to the Congressional Black Caucus (CBC) to accept President Reagan's invitation to produce an alternative. We mounted a challenge to this fiscal insanity with our annual "alternative budget" submittal. With supreme confidence in our purpose, the CBC placed before the Congress a budget[2] that sought to prevent the fiscal madness contained in the Reagan budget and to return some semblance of proportion, balance, and efficacy to federal budget policy. The core fiscal elements of the effort were to reverse the disastrous tax and military budget provisions of the Reagan-era budgets, and invest the savings in solving our core domestic problems.

We labored in relative obscurity year after year—applauded only by devotees of the congressional process who watched the proceedings of the House Floor on CSPAN, as we valiantly argued against the insanities of nuclear first-strike policies, "Star Wars," and the military interventionary posturing contained within the ambit of the Reagan-era military strategy. We were after all the "Black" caucus, and military policy was a special province from which the pundits and newscasters habitually excluded us. It was the domain of the "experts" and I—still the only African American member of the defense oversight committee—was doubly impugned as a left-leaning "peacenik" from Berkeley.

Whatever expertise we were grudgingly granted over the policy prescriptions we offered to cure the devastating social ills afflicting the nation was quickly overwhelmed by the fear of colleagues to be associated with our "devastating" cuts in the military account. In the guns versus butter debate, it was not considered wise to vote against guns.

Even so-called "progressive" allies in the peace community—clamoring for leaders to build upon what would become the success of the nuclear freeze movement—reserved judgment until they could "see the numbers," a lack of faith it is hard to imagine would have been evidenced against non-minority leaders of such an effort.

The political leadership that had emerged from the African American Members of Congress on this budget struggle was the core of resistance to the Reagan-administration effort to destroy the victories won during the New Deal and Great Society eras. We were the only members willing to draw the explicit connection between increased military spending and the growing desperation within our communities. We were Dr. King's apostles, attempting to warn with the same clarity of analysis that his inspired perceptions had offered a generation before.

Now, as we approach the next century, with the end of the Cold War firmly in place and the pressures of the balanced budget agreement newly upon Congress and the president, an opportunity has arrived to force a new national security debate. All policymakers are now confronted with the explicit trade-offs spoken of by Dr. King thirty years earlier. No more letting the debt pop up to cover the purchase of a new plane. Every dollar spent on the military is now literally a dollar that will not be spent on one of the other two legs of our national security triad: a strong domestic economy with a well-trained citizenry living in healthy communities; and an engaged foreign policy that can bring diplomatic resolution to conflict and promote the sustainable economic development and respect for self-determination and human rights that are the fundamental prerequisites to regional and international stability.

The resolution of those trade-offs will determine the course of our nation for decades—indeed generations—to come. The African American community has as much, if not more, at stake on the outcome as any in this country. The degree to which we rise to the moment and assert the full measure of our citizenship to participate in the establishment of military and foreign policy will be the degree to which these priorities will be resolved in a manner that may restore hope to our children and vitality to our communities.

I am not so arrogant as to believe that there is a monopole view within the African American community on issues of peace and conflict, military deployment, foreign assistance, and the participation of the United States in world affairs. Indeed, even within the Congress, the several dozen African American members have differing views over United States involvement in issues of arguably African American concern as, for example, the use of military forces to secure an end to mass starvation in Somalia or to restore a democratically elected government to Haiti; the continued enforcement of the United States economic quarantine against Cuba; and the degree to which economic sanctions should have been employed against apartheid South Africa.

Differences abound when one gets to policy issues that have parochial impact such as the purchase of B-2 bombers (at $2 billion per plane) and other weapon systems or the establishment of yet another round of base closures. Notwithstanding this fact, I believe that African American leaders and scholars can contribute enormously during this fleeting moment of opportunity to redefine United States national security strategy, and the funding priorities underlying its implementation. Our communities are among those in the most pain, and it is we who understand better than most how deeply our national security is threatened by the fragility of our social fabric.

REDEFINING NATIONAL SECURITY

Many of my congressional colleagues, both on and off the National Security Committee (the new name for the once Armed Services Committee), argue that the "most important" function of government is military defense and that it is deserving of every penny that can be thrown its way. As a result, programs are funded for millions, sometimes billions, of dollars a year that would not withstand for an instant the scrutiny that is given to a wide variety of domestic programs.

In my view, the Constitution's framers did not believe that military spending deserved such prominence or deference. In the Constitution's preamble, they ascribed the purposes for producing that framework document, and the governmental structure and authorities contemplated, in the following manner:

to form a more perfect Union, establish Justice, insure domestic Tranquility, provide for the common defence, promote the general Welfare, and secure the Blessings of Liberty to ourselves and our Posterity.[3]

Defense is surely there, but so are justice, the general welfare, and domestic tranquility. Despite their recent military struggle for liberation from a potentially belligerent and still powerful Crown of England, the framers saw defense neither as "number one" nor as a singular priority for successful nation building.

They understood, in a way missed by most policy-makers during much of the long Cold War, that the security of the nation depends also on internal coherence, community, a proper respect for justice and liberty, and the well-being of our people. Despite the limits of the framers' vision—especially with regard to race and slavery, conquest, class, and gender among others—they knew enough to anticipate the dangers both of a permanent military state[4] and of the failure to provide for coherent domestic policies in support of nationhood.[5]

The arrival of the Cold War and its permanent military establishment, nuclear weapons, secrecy, and erosions of liberty, have posed one of the clearest challenges to the balance of priorities and power that the framers set out. Whatever debatable wisdom there was in the national security strategy of the Cold War, there were clear adverse consequences. Not the least of these were the tremendous economic distortion that occurred, especially during the last two decades of the Cold War, and the threat that such distortion now causes to our national integrity.

Without debating the merit of the Cold War strategy here, suffice it to say that we are now clearly past that period and have been for a decade. Any global threat has clearly receded; the Warsaw Pact is disbanded (and its members seek admission to NATO); the Soviet Union has disintegrated; and Russia and the United States seek to implement an awkward partnership.[6]

Yet in 1998 the basic military strategy of the United States remains the same as it was during the Cold War: Be prepared to go it alone, if necessary, to fight major wars anywhere in the world, at anytime, with minimum periods of mobilization. Recently, President Clinton even enunciated a nuclear weapons policy that explicitly contemplates using these unique weapons against non-nuclear threats to our security—a return to Cold War thinking as well.[7]

Our current security environment both allows and demands that we revisit—from root to the highest branch—the predicates and policies of U.S. national security strategy. Into that debate, the African American community must seek to right the balance, to reorder the priorities, and to change the very character of how our nation thinks about its national security and the elements of which it is constituted. We can contribute to a more informed understanding of both the *opportunities* and threats that exist in our changed world.

In order to succeed, a national security strategy must fully articulate and support the contributions to national security of both foreign assistance programs designed to promote regional and international stability and investments made in traditional "domestic" accounts for education, infrastructure improvements, and science research and development. If it does not, it is doomed to fail in the terms of the references for success set out in the Constitution's preamble.

Certainly instability and danger remain in various parts of the world, including Russia and other nations of the former Soviet Union, the Balkans, and portions of central and western Africa. The Persian Gulf and the Korean peninsula merit continued attention because of the significant possibilities for open warfare among nations in those regions.

Humanitarian crises and instability throughout the globe will properly continue to require the involvement of military forces—including participation by the United States—at least in the near term. Military modernization in China, Southeast Asia, Latin America, and elsewhere—including within the United States—provide reasons for concern that a post–Cold War arms race could, of its own weight and momentum, create new regional instabilities or the potential for belligerence where they do not currently exist.

To the degree that these challenges will need to be responded to militarily, such actions should be undertaken through the mechanisms of the United Nations security council or recognized regional organs such as the Organization of African Unity or the Organization of American States. The United States should act as a colleague that can, perhaps, bring special military skills to the table once the international community has agreed on the requirement for, the scope of, and the method of international intervention.

Even without making such an explicit commitment to an internationalized process of determining whether, when, or where to bring military force to bear on a problem, the United States could scale back its military simply by fully acknowledging that there exist very few potential military problems of any scale for which we would not enjoy significant allied contributions to the effort. And we should not be trapped into the belief that the challenges noted above, only partially military in nature, will ultimately need to be resolved by the application of military force. Diplomacy, economic development, and arms control implementation are among many other strategies that can defuse the potential for armed violence long before there is even the possibility for such to arise. The success of such strategies may be undermined by continued high levels of U.S. military spending.

We need to view these security challenges in their economic, cultural, and diplomatic frames of reference as well. As I often noted throughout the Cold War, conflicts and instability that are economic, political, social, and cultural in their origins cannot be solved by the application of a superpower's military might. They need to be solved by resort to economic and political engagement that respects social and cultural traditions within the framework of internationally recognized human rights.

When analyzed and understood in these terms, it becomes clear that investments in robust programs for sustainable economic development and timely diplomatic activity in behalf of crisis intervention and conflict resolution will make an enormous contribution to United States national security.

Beyond budgetary issues, though, we must also recognize that inconstant support by the United States for the expansion of democracy and respect for internationally recognized human rights—a hallmark of the Cold War–era military alliances that were entered into by successive administrations—contributes ultimately to instability.

For example, for decades a succession of U.S. administrations offered tacit support to the apartheid regime in South Africa, and to similar regimes in southern Africa, on the theory that chaos and instability would befall those nations were majority rule and nonracial governments to emerge. Similar laxity characterized policies implemented toward regimes in central Africa, the poison of which still persists to this very day. Purportedly we pursued these alliances to preserve our access to strategic materials necessary to our military-industrial-ideological competition with the Soviet Union and China.

Similarly, in Central America and the Caribbean, we supported dictators, fought against insurgencies, and supported narrowly based political oligarchies in an effort to control the political success of communism in the hemisphere. Our current policy of seeking the economic isolation of Cuba is an antiquated remnant of that bygone era, reminiscent of the destabilization of the Allende government in Chile.

The resulting death and destruction, migration and social disruption could have been avoided had programs such as the Alliance for Progress paid more attention to linking aid to democratization and a respect for human rights, and less attention to which governments paid lip-service to the anticommunist cause.

In Asia, of course, we fought two large and costly wars to contain communism—the first under United Nations auspices in Korea and the second when we seized the fallen colonial banner of the French in Indochina and were led to the same military doom that befell that colonial power. Other covert activities throughout the region have left their mark as well, precipitating massive death and large-scale instability.

The common thread of all of these engagements was the perceived need to fight communism on all fronts, simultaneously and to the death. The animating feature of U.S. foreign policy during the era was the belief that lurking behind local turmoil was the threat of Soviet advance. We have clearly emerged from that era.

It seems reasonably true for the near term that the security issues that will most occupy the attention of the world community have to do with the local consequences of ethnic and nationalist (or religious) conflict and their threats to either regional stability through war or terror or the human rights of a nation's citizens. We no longer need worry that these conflicts may erupt into a global conflagration, with large-scale force on force conflicts that would inevitably lead up the escalation ladder to nuclear exchange.

Are there lessons from the Cold War era, however, that are worth bringing forth into this new security environment? What foreign policy elements of a national security strategy can be implemented that will work to achieve positive and enduring benefits from the current strategic environment? What should be avoided, if we are not to create instability where we might otherwise forestall it?

The powerful success of the global anti-apartheid movement in creating conditions that led to the end of the racialist system in South Africa offers one important lesson. Within the United States component of that global movement, significant and powerful moral issues animated the opposition to the U.S. government policy of "constructive engagement," which was, as noted above, pursued to advance U.S. strategic interests in the region by ensuring relations with the government of the Republic of South Africa.[8] The movement demanded that the United States abandon military/economic alliance modality as a basis of relations with that nation, and replace it with a substantive policy that corresponded with the values of racial equality and self-determination.

As the principal congressional advocate for comprehensive economic sanctions against the regime, I understand full well the power of the moral argument, resting as it did on the such extraordinary principles. It simply was unconscionable that a nation professing adherence to both principles could so actively facilitate the perpetuation of a regime that abhorred both. Because the principles were so clear, and the movement demanding adherence to them so widespread, the Congress implemented modest U.S. economic sanctions against South Africa, over the objection and veto of President Reagan. It was clear within a couple of years that we would succeed in imposing even more severe sanctions on that immoral regime.

All of this was accomplished during the height of the Cold War arms build-up and against the backdrop that a claimed "evil empire" was still locked in mortal global combat with the United States. Clearly the world did not succumb to totalitarianism when we put the principles of democracy and human rights ahead of military convenience. In fact, I would argue that the world became more stable and the potential for peace, democratization, and stability were enhanced by such a course.

Many professed at the time that such a course would fail to loosen the grip of the apartheid regime and would harm only the Black majority in South Africa. History has proven them wrong. Beyond that, I believe history has also demonstrated that forceful diplomacy backed by economic sanctions can help to facilitate radical political transformations without resort to massive violence. There should be no question that, without sanctions, the inevitable cataclysmic military conflict that would have occurred in South Africa as the Black majority sought to secure its rightful place in their nation would have surely led to massive killing and forestalled for decades any possibility of the racial reconciliation that the government of President Nelson Mandela has thus far pursued with some success.

Whatever the future for South Africa, as it strives to bring fruition to the potential of its new democracy and economic opportunity to those so long held in subjugation—and the recalcitrance and resistance of the formerly dominant White minority is a strong negative force—the chance exists at least that this continuing transformation can be kept relatively nonviolent.

As a result of the rapid consolidation of political power by the Mandela government, South Africa has been able also to play an increasing role in the stabilization of the whole of southern Africa and a leadership role in continental security affairs. The moral authority of its leadership may facilitate the creation of regional mechanisms for conflict resolution and containment, and for a growing demand to respect the human rights of the continent's citizens.

Thus, one critical element of a successful U.S. national security strategy in this new era must be to align its foreign policy with its stated national principles. This will require, at the same time, that we refrain from failures of leadership that result from bad practices. United States removal from the jurisdiction of the International Court at the Hague in the face of legal claims brought against it by Nicaragua (for mining harbors) and the refusal for so long to ratify important international human rights instruments are just two examples from the Cold War era that retarded the advance of the rule of law internationally and the stability that such rule can encourage.

On the other side of the divide of the Cold War from the South Africa sanctions effort are a series of peacekeeping efforts that propelled the United States into new and unchartered waters. During the Cold

War, it was unthinkable that the United States and the Soviet Union could be utilized in large-scale peace operations. How could they be trusted to set aside their global conflict in most circumstances.[9]

As a result, our military did not know how to think about the strategy and tactics of such activities when the end of the Cold War opened this as a possibility for United States involvement. They were there to "do the big one." Indeed, those who were used to opposing the interjection of U.S. force in the internal affairs of other countries were intellectually unprepared to grapple with the nuance of using U.S. forces to enforce peace or to end genocide.[10]

In Somalia, Haiti, and Bosnia, we have stumbled through the post–Cold War transition period, learning along the way the inappropriateness of applying the strategies of the Cold War to the problems of this new era. As we emerge from the transition period into an as yet unknown future, we must try to apply the lessons of both eras to the problems we will confront in the future.

In sending military forces to Somalia, both the United Nations and the United States sought to provide a secure environment for food distribution in order to stop widespread starvation caused by the use of food as a political weapon. This laudable and successful endeavor was aborted when both the United Nations and the United States chose to make one of the factions to the underlying civil conflict the "enemy." Once the "hunt for Aideed" began, the humanitarian mission was transformed and doomed to fail. Lives were lost and the mission scrapped. Inculcated during the Cold War to define "bad guys" and "good guys" (with often odd characterizations developing as to whom we placed in which category), we learned the hard way in Somalia the maxim of peacekeeping: take no sides; make no enemies.

In Bosnia, this tension abounded as European-led peacekeepers sought to implement a UN mandate that might provide an end to the intercommunal violence in that newly devolved nation of the former Yugoslavia. Despite acts of ethnic violence committed on all sides to this three-sided struggle, the United States in particular sought to condemn the Serb faction more heavily. Our instincts were to apply military force against one side, a strategy that was feared by the nations on the ground who understood that their "peacekeepers" would be linked to the warfare against one faction and thereby become imperiled—as had U.S. forces in Somalia. Even now, the uneven application of the economic assistance program that is a key element of the strategy to build a durable peace in the region threatens the potential success of the effort.[11]

It is notable that the "Dayton Accords," negotiated in Dayton, Ohio, among the Bosnian Muslim, Serb, and Croat elements of the former Yugoslavia and signed in Paris, contained numerous provisions designed to facilitate economic reconstruction and reintegration of the war-torn communities. There was clear recognition that sustainable economic development coupled with a respect for ethnic rights and self-determination (autonomy) could provide a recipe for long-term stability. Peacekeeping was simply the means to separate the warring parties long enough for grudges to recede and stakes in the peace to build up.

Having witnessed the steady development of peaceful relations among the nations of Western Europe twice belligerents in this century, it should come as no surprise to any that a strategy that combines economic development, a respect for self-determination and national integrity, the implementation of confidence-building measures about military intentions, and an observance of the expanding principles of international human rights can contribute much to the goal of regional stability. For it is not so much that "democracies don't fight wars against each other" (after all, Hitler came to power through the ballot) or that economic intercourse per se is sufficient to forestall conflict (witness again the twentieth-century wars between trading partners), but that a comprehensive framework of international law and practice can create the conditions that give rise to stability and confidence in that stability.

In contrast, the Alliance for Progress economic program failed to provide stability in Central America. Its failure can be linked to its lack of commitment to press for the growth of democratic practice and widespread economic opportunity.[12] In addition, it became subsumed as part of a larger counterinsurgency effort led by military forces hostile to revolutionary change and, in the end, it reinforced the conflict in class relations that gave rise to the original conditions of instability.

What do these observations hold for the future? The United States must expand its national security strategy to embrace more fully a set of responsibilities to promote sustainable economic development, arms sale restraint, and the respect for self-determination and internationally recognized human rights. It must commit itself to the jurisdiction of those laws and treaties that have codified these principles and it must learn to act more consistently in concert with international organs in the determination as to when and where to employ military forces to solve problems.

The problem of U.S. isolationism has never been a national unwillingness to be active in the world. It is, rather, that the nation has usually insisted on acting unilaterally—that is, in isolation from others. Our military is organized, equipped, and sized because of this penchant. A change in national orientation about the unilateral use of military force can lead to significant reductions in military expenditures, which in turn can liberate resources toward these other national security requirements.

Given their relative scales (true foreign assistance programs receive less than $10 billion in annual appropriations while the military program budgets remain above $250 billion), even modest reductions in U.S. military spending that are invested in these foreign assistance programs could have a dramatic and positive impact on international stability. As other nations look at the United States as a reduced threat to their well-being and constrain their military modernization programs accordingly, this in turn could create the conditions for further military reductions that will, again in turn, free up more resources.

For those who worry about a "power vacuum" into which belligerents may move, it must be remembered that these military reductions must be coupled with a willingness to promote and enhance regional and international security mechanisms that rely upon coalition forces acting under international mandate. Clearly, the United States in collaboration with the other nations of the world can move effectively to prevent or reverse true aggression; and more than enough military capability exists in the world to undertake the humanitarian and peace operations that are the more likely requirements of the coming era.

At the end of World War II, and throughout the Cold War, the United States squandered opportunities to build such an effective international architecture for nuclear and conventional disarmament, comprehensive nonviolent decolonization, conflict-resolution mechanisms, and economic development strategies that would lead to more stable regional environments. As we emerge from the end of the post–Cold War transition, we must not ignore similar opportunities.[13] Otherwise we will reap more of the same: additional decades of arms races that impoverish our nation's communities and those of others, and contribute to regional instability and conflict.

Some will argue that the proceeds of reductions in military spending should be spent exclusively on the domestic front and not shipped overseas. I would assert that the measure of the "peace dividend" invested domestically will be significantly increased by making leveraged strategic investments in international stability through increased involvement in promoting sustainable development. As a strategy, it has proven itself in Western Europe and Japan. There is no reason such a strategy cannot succeed as well in Africa, the Caribbean, Asia, and throughout the Americas and the balance of Europe.

A RIGHT-SIZED FORCE

The federal resources for an expanded foreign policy leg of our national security strategy are to be found in the current overinvestment in our military budget. Finding such savings, though, is not solely a budget issue. At its heart it is a strategic issue, a question of defining what military resources need to be available to the nation to meet its legitimate needs for defense and to participate in internationally sanctioned coalition efforts to control the spread of violence. To arrive at an appropriate resolution of this issue we must ask: What threats and opportunities exist toward which our military should be organized? What military strategy ought it be organized to implement? What ought it be able to accomplish on its own, that is, without the assistance of coalition partners? How might a military force that could meet these requirements be sized, trained, equipped, and organized?

Only when we have some sense of the answer to these questions can we set out to calculate the savings achievable through such a reorganization.

Given that the major "military" threat to the United States is the Russian nuclear weapons arsenal and the risks of a terrorist attack by a weapon of mass destruction (chemical, biological, or nuclear), it is imperative that we be organized to meet that threat—and to eliminate it if possible.

The clearest pathway to eliminate the danger posed by the Russian arsenal and its components is to negotiate further deep reductions in the two national stockpiles and to continue the active collaboration to secure and dispose of nuclear materials that we are undertaking with the Cooperative Threat Reduction program. To the degree we need to worry at all about deterring a threat of Russian attack, orders of magnitude lower numbers of nuclear weapons would suffice. Thus, we should move to START III negotiations and press for negotiations toward pure deterrence levels. And we should be prepared to take unilateral initiatives at downsizing our arsenal to provide confidence to the Russians that they can proceed safely with such an action plan. We should not be inventing new military requirements for these weapons as we move beyond planning for large-scale nuclear war with either the Russians or the Chinese.

With regard to a terrorist attack, it should be apparent to all that a nuclear response to a terrorist attack against the United States would be futile. Whom would we strike with such indiscriminate power? With regard to the battlefield use of chemical or biological weapons, we have more than sufficient conventional power to deter and or respond to the use of such weapons. We should spend less time focused on whether to make a nuclear response and instead invest more resources into troop protection gear and other safeguards. By refusing to be lured into a "tit-for-tat" response mentality—that is, if you use a weapon of mass destruction, we'll use one as well—we can increase our leverage in the arms control and diplomacy arena. It is in that arena that we can make our greatest strides to prevent such attacks.

We should avoid massive expenditures on national ballistic missile defenses that would have the complicating effect of potentially spurring larger-scale modernization of nuclear weapons contained within the militaries of Russia or the People's Republic of China. Modest missile defenses that do not defeat the deterrent capability of the nuclear powers will allow us to move into the endgame negotiations to eradicate the arsenals of the five nuclear powers—and any others—and institute a global regime to forestall the introduction and use of these weapons in the future.

Currently, planning guidance requires the United States to be able to prosecute alone two major conflicts nearly simultaneously and to participate in peace operations and "operations other than war." More realistic implementation planning both with regard to the pace of deployment and the contribution of coalition partners would allow the United States to reduce the size of its active forces (especially ground forces) in favor of more reliance upon reserve forces. That such a military choice is more consistent with the framers' view that the nation's military would be staffed by citizen soldiers is an added bonus.

In addition, such a planning posture would allow for more graduation in the levels of military preparedness of our units. We would avoid having to maintain as many units at such high states of readiness. We could afford to reduce the overseas presence requirements that currently stress our naval resources and demand an overaccelerated ship-construction program.

Further downsizing of our military infrastructure, including the Department of Energy nuclear weapons infrastructure, would be possible beyond even today's ability if we were to make the nuclear and conventional force reductions described above.

Finally, we can afford to stop purchasing highly expensive advanced armaments that were designed to fight now departed foes identified during the Cold War. As noted above, we face no major conventional military threat. A strategy of continued investment in research and development in future technologies will more than suffice as a hedge against the potential emergence of a global peer competitor with hostile military intentions. Large-scale expenditures on often exotic technology runs the risks both of purchasing hardware that will not best meet an emergent threat and of triggering a new cycle of an advanced arms race with disastrous budgetary and security consequences.

The savings associated with even modest adjustments along these lines easily exceed $50 billion per year. Doubling our true foreign assistance programs from $10 billion to $20 billion per year would leave $40 billion per year for investment in the domestic leg of our national security triad. Trebling our foreign policy commitments to $30 billion per year would leave an additional $30 billion for domestic investment. As I have indicated above, I believe that investments in international stability in this range can lead to a security environment that can support even more dramatic reductions of military spending in the long run.

Of course, additional savings above this $50 billion could be safely achieved even in the short run.

What would it mean to have $30–$50 billion a year to invest in rebuilding our communities? Current federal budget policy, for example, commits approximately $5 billion per year to community development; $15 billion to elementary, secondary, and vocational education and $10 billion to higher education; and $10 billion to ground transportation.

Every dollar that is spent in these programs hires a teacher, a recreation counselor, a bus or train operator, a construction worker, and so on. The dollars spent on these efforts will be recycled over and over in our communities, leading to new businesses, economic opportunity, and, ultimately, hope for the future. And the salaries and wages earned will contribute to an increase in local tax revenues and a decrease in dependency on local social welfare programs. The economic synergy would be large.

Savings from the military account of the scale discussed above can make an enormous difference in the federal commitment to working with our local communities to solve their pressing problems. Such an investment can give hope to our children and bring peace to our communities. The African American stake in helping to shape the contours of the national security debate, to understand its dimensions, and to place appropriate price tags on its elements—military, foreign affairs and domestic—is not a side issue to be approached only when other issues have been addressed. It is at the core of the needs of our community; it is at the core of our identity as citizens of the United States; and, it is at the core of our identity as a people with a history on two continents.

NOTES

1. For a more thorough examination of the connection between military spending and its effect on domestic investment see Ronald V. Dellums, "Welfare State vs. Warfare State: The Legislative Struggle for Full Employment," *The Urban League Review*, vol. 10, no. 1 (Summer 1986): 49–60.

2. That first alternative budget submitted in 1981 for the fiscal year 1982 debate began an annual commitment to put a national budgetary agenda in

front of the Congress. With only one exception, the CBC has submitted an alternative every year since that initial effort.

3. Constitution of the United States.

4. See, for example, article I, section 8, clause 12: To raise and support Armies, *but no Appropriation of Money to that Use shall be for a longer Term than two years*; (emphasis added) and Amendment III: No Soldier shall, in time of peace be quartered in any house, without the consent of the Owner . . .

5. The broad mandate set out in article I, section 8, and especially the power "to regulate Commerce" set out in clause 3 of that section and the "necessary and proper" powers established in clause 18 were clearly intended to provide the federal government with sufficient power to ensure the well-being of the new nation.

6. It is the Russian nuclear arsenal that poses the only current threat of large-scale military damage against the United States. The United States has a profound interest in crafting military policies that provide confidence within Russia that a continued downsizing of the nations' nuclear arsenals is in its national security interest. A significant number of current congressional initiatives in national security are inconsistent with managing such an important relationship, including especially a cavalier disregard toward the Anti-Ballistic Missile Treaty to which Russia is the successor state in interest.

7. This ill-advised shift in policy occurs at a time when we should be aggressively collaborating with the other nuclear powers to move toward the elimination of these weapons as is required by under article 6 of the Treaty on the Non-Proliferation of Nuclear Weapons, the so-called NPT, to which the United States is a party. The invention of a new mission provides further concerns to other nations about the efficacy of this commitment and threatens the success of other high-priority national security goals of the United States, such as the entry into force of the Comprehensive Test Ban Treaty that would end underground nuclear weapons testing.

8. Constructive engagement was not an invention of the Reagan administration. It had been an enduring feature of U.S. Cold War policy since the Truman administration at least. For a good discussion of the ongoing Cold War conflict between the United States commitment to democracy and self-determination on the one hand and its willingness to back colonial power and racial minority government on the other, see, for example, Thomas J. Noer, *Cold War and Black Liberation: The United States and White Rule in Africa, 1948–1968* (Columbia: University of Missouri Press, 1985), especially chapter 2, "Race and Containment."

9. The experience of the United States and Russian troops serving side-by-side in Bosnia in the peacekeeping effort that grew out of the Dayton Accords is a notable example of what opportunities are created by the end of bipolar conflict in the post–Cold War era. Each side brings a different but important element of credibility to the communities whose security is aided by the peace operation. In a similar vein, it will be critical to secure the involvement of the People's Republic of China if there is to be any successful diplomatic resolution of the conflict on the Korean peninsula. It would be tragic to allow a new bipolar superpower conflict, either with Russia or China, to unravel the dramatic potential that this era allows.

10. Because of the events in Somalia, Haiti, and Bosnia, I asked a group of theologians from various religious backgrounds to sit down and discuss with me their views on the morality and philosophy of peace operations. It was an extraordinary opportunity for me to shed my Cold War baggage and to seek to understand the moral dimensions of the international obligation to resist aggression and genocide.

11. See, for example, Charles G. Boyd, "Making Bosnia Work," *Foreign Affairs*, January/February 1998, pp. 42–55.

12. See, for example, Walter LaFeber, *Inevitable Revolutions: The United States in Central America* (New York: W. W. Norton, 1983), pp. 148–60.

13. It bears mentioning that United States actions undoubtedly will have an effect on the military modernization strategies of both the People's Republic of China and Russia. Neither currently poses any significant military threat to the United States (save possibly for the large strategic nuclear arsenal of Russia). Yet U.S. military expenditures and organization could drive each to make investment decisions that in turn will drive a further U.S. response. This cycle/countercycle of military investment can be avoided now, through scaling back U.S. procurement plans, reducing force levels and operational tempo, and working with both nations to establish further transparency and confidence-building measures. Notwithstanding such reductions, the United States would have more than sufficient military force for its own defense and for participation in coalition efforts organized in response to aggression, genocide, or humanitarian crises.

CHAPTER 11

A Personal Road to Diplomacy

Ronald D. Palmer

I gave an impassioned speech at Howard University in 1979, on the history of Blacks in diplomacy and the need for HBCUs like Howard to do more in preparing students for careers in international affairs, particularly in the Foreign Service. In a rather wide-ranging text entitled "The Road to Diplomacy" and I discussed Howard's impact on my career to a degree, but I have decided in the present essay to expand the treatment of my personal preparation in the hope that it may be useful to others preparing students and perhaps even inspire someone as I was inspired.

I went to Detroit in 1947 to finish high school, which I did in 1949. My mother tells me that my high school counselor thought my independent and self-assured temperament would get me into trouble with the law, since my bearing clearly showed that I didn't realize that I had been born into the lowest caste of society and I carried myself above my station. He said such aspirations were unrealistic and would lead me to frustration and inevitable conflict with the established order. I should be satisfied to go into the automotive factories like the other young Black men.

He implied that Whites were superior to Blacks not the other way around, as I seemed to believe. I was actually suspended from high school for nearly a week because I held my head high and refused to be intimidated. Since I had done nothing wrong, except to be myself, eventually some of my teachers must have intervened because I was reinstated.

Somehow, four years of football and basketball helped me keep my discipline. A brilliant English teacher forced me to learn to work up to my potential and made sure I was prepared for college work. She made me do four times the work she assigned to other students. I had to learn and recite in class to her satisfaction the four Hamlet soliloquies. The

others only had to learn one. I had to write four times as many compo-
sitions as the others, including autobiographical essays. Her constant
questions to me were, "Who are you? What will you become?"

I came to Howard in January 1950 on a road that led away from the
assembly line at Ford's River Rouge plant in Detroit where I had been
laid off, six months after graduating from high school in June 1949.

I went to Ford because I didn't know what else to do. I had been a
footballer and I had been encouraged by a former teammate to join him
in matriculating at Detroit's Wayne University to seek to play ball there
on an athletic scholarship. However, I had already decided by then to
give up sports and to become a serious student because I knew I wanted
to be a diplomat. I had been motivated by the fact that Ralph Bunche
had won the Nobel Peace Prize in 1950. I also admired Secretary of State
Dean Acheson because he was constantly involved in important conferences in London and Paris and I thought I would like to do that one day
myself. The fact that Acheson was always so well dressed was not lost
on me either. I noticed that dipomats could be as sharp as Duke Elling-
ton and Billy Eckstine—my other well-dressed heroes. My problem was
that I didn't know how to get started on the road to diplomacy. So since
Ford was hiring, I thought I would work for a while and save some
money while trying to figure out my next step.

I was surely the most hopeless assembly-line worker Ford ever
hired. I worked on a drill-press at the head of a transmission line. I took
casings and put them in my machine to drill bolt holes. Unfortunately, I
often put the casings in wrong and they cracked so the entire line had to
be shut down. This made me very popular with the other workers on the
line, who could lounge and laugh while my machine was being repaired.
The foreman developed a noticeable tic, however, caused by the shriek
of the metal casings when they cracked in my machine. Doubtless, Ford
was as relieved as I was when an October recession caused production
to be reduced and led to redundant employees (me) being laid off.

I discovered quickly that unemployment was a horrific experience.
Standing in long lines of workers seeking jobs clarified my mind rapidly.
I needed to leave Detroit as soon as possible. Seeking ways to do so, I
even applied to join the French Foreign Legion. Fortunately, my ex–coal
miner Uncle James Eliron Roberts had become a medical doctor by
going to Howard and he and my mother's other brothers Horace
Molvin Roberts, Henry Clay Roberts, and Russell Edward Roberts had
established a commercial laundry in Washington and they invited me to
join them in the business. My monetary compensation would be limited
but the firm would pay for my tuition and books at Howard. Early in
the week of December 15, 1949, I received a call from the French Consulate saying my application to join the Foreign Legion had been

accepted, but I was able to decline since I was departing for Howard and Washington on December 15. The Foreign Legion was recruiting at that time because of the war in Indochina. I missed that. I entered Howard in January 1950 and was required to join the ROTC so when the Korean War broke out in June 1950 I was exempted from the draft so I missed that war also.

Instead, I found my vocation of study in evening school at Howard. One night in class during that winter I felt my brain stir like some dormant muscle and I realized that some sort of transformation was taking place and I could think logically, quickly, and imaginatively. I found I had a gift for the French language. I liked economics and even statistics. I proudly took classes in political science in classrooms where Ralph Bunche had taught. I visited his former office at Howard and sat in the chair where he had sat. Alain Locke, Everett Dorsey, E. Franklin Frazier, John Hope Franklin, Rayford Logan, and others gave me encouragement and nurtured my desire to become a diplomat. I became a good student and graduated with majors in economics and French.

When I started Howard in 1950, there were four Black U.S. diplomats: Clifford Wharton, who entered the Foreign Service in 1924; William George, who entered in 1929; Rupert Lloyd, who entered in 1941 as a clerk and became officers in 1945; and Charles M. Hanson, who passed the examinations in 1948 and relieved Lloyd in Monrovia. I heard about Rupert Lloyd in 1953 from his in-laws John and Sadie Harlan and their daughter Jacqueline. By then Lloyd was assigned to Paris. The Harlans encouraged me to take the Foreign Service examination. The examination materials emphasized that the Foreign Service recruited, assigned, and promoted on merit principles. If merit were the criterion, I knew I could compete.

I had no idea of the history of past discrimination, where merit had decidedly not been the criterion for recruitment, assignment, or promotion. I had no idea of the distance that had already been travelled by those who had gone before me. I took America's promise for granted.

When I began my studies, Howard's campus had a highly international atmosphere. Howard had the highest percentage of international students of any American college or university. Additionally, the university was still enchanted by the successful tour by the Howard Players of Scandinavia and Germany in 1948. The Howard Choir, led by Warner Lawson, performed annual concerts with the National Symphony Orchestra of such international music as the Choros Number 10 of Brazil's Villa-Lobos, the Carmina Burana of Carl Orff, and Beethoven's Ninth Symphony.

Like some other historically Black colleges and unversities, Howard had a small colony of able Jewish professors who were refugees from

Nazism. They made Dante and Faust and Kurt Weill and China and Japan and Europe accessible to me. Howard had an intimate relationship with India at that time resulting from Mordecai Johnson's great admiration of Mahatma Gandhi. There were teachers from Haiti, Puerto Rico, and elsewhere in the Caribbean. I was infatuated with France and followed eagerly the experiences of Mercer Cook and Franklin Frazier in Paris, as reported by Ollie Stewart in the *Afro-American* newspaper. They were Fulbright Lecturers. I decided to become a Fulbright Scholar when I got my B.A.

I made my application and faced a committee headed by Rayford Logan and consisting of Mercer Cook and, I believe, Alain Locke. They grilled me unmercifully but nominated me for the award. I arrived in France in September 1954 and met Ollie Stewart, who took me in hand and mentored me. He helped me find my way. Stewart thought I was too young and inexperienced to deal with luminaries there then such as Richard Wright and James Baldwin and the Jean-Paul Sartre and Simone de Beauvoir coterie. I never met them. Instead, Ollie steered me toward the less exotic crowd of Blacks who made Gaby and Haynes' Café Americain their headquarters in Pigalle. I met African American dancers, singers, musicians, the cast of "Porgy and Bess," and others. My American student friends and I also were regular patrons of Gordon Heath and Lee Payant's club on the Rue de l'Abbaye where the duo sang French and American folksongs.

I dived into French life and quickly learned of the confusion and disillusionment that had been created by the French defeat by the Vietnamese in May 1954 at Dien Bien Phu. The defeat had brought Prime Minister Pierre Mendes-France to power and he had declared an end to France's overseas role in Indochina and had started Morocco and Tunisia on the road to independence. France still maintained its historic colonial role in Africa and African students were numerous. France had turned its imperial energies to Algeria after losing Indochina, and the Algerian question was deeply agitating French public opinion.

I was assigned to the Institute of Political Studies at the University of Bordeaux in October. I went to lectures on subjects that interested me but I kept a rigorous schedule of eight hours of daily study to prepare for the Foreign Service examination.

I had taken it in the late summer of 1953 in the old three-and-a-half-day format. I passed the French test but my composite score on the other parts of the examination (American history, economics, English, data analysis, and general background was 58 as I recall—with 70 being a passing score). My grade indicated I could pass the examination but I was aware that I needed intensive work to become more informed on American topics such as history, literature, geography, and culture.

The U.S. consulate in Bordeaux had a USIS Library and I became one of its most dedicated users. I read all of Ernest Hemingway, F. Scott Fitzgerald, William Faulkner, John O'Hara, James T. Farrell, John Dos Passos, Langston Hughes, Richard Wright, T. S. Eliot, Gertrude Stein, and all I could of other writers. I knew jazz but I didn't know America's other classical music so I listened to recordings of works by Norman Dello Joio, Howard Hansen, Walter Piston, William Schuman, Aaron Copeland, Roy Harris, George Gershwin, and others. I even gave lectures on Gershwin and his music.

I followed a methodical program of study of each century of American history in as much depth as I could. I read French and European history in French. Professor Morisot of the University of Bordeaux was the mentor of the Fulbright students. We visited him once a month or so and he kept judicious and avuncular note of our progress. I have seen the report he made on me when I underwent a background security investigation in 1956 after passing the Foreign Service written examination in December 1955 and the oral examination in February 1956. He had realized how serious I was and he was aware of how hard I was studying. I owe him a great debt.

About midway through my academic year in Bordeaux, I received a notice about fellowships being offered for M.A. study by the School of Advanced International Studies (SAIS) of John Hopkins University in Washington, D.C. I submitted an application and had an oral interview in Paris in the spring of 1955. I won a fellowship that paid all costs, including room and board, and gave me a small monthly stipend.

I entered SAIS in the fall of 1955 and passed the Foreign Service examination in its new one-day format in December. After passing the oral examination, I promptly decided to finish the two-year master's program in a year and a half. The SAIS authorities disagreed but I was determined.

The program reqired M.A. comprehensive examinations in American foreign policy, international economics, international law, and European diplomatic history as well as examination in one's area of regional specialization. Mine was East Asia. My professor was Paul Linebarger, a China specialist.

A language examination was necessary but I already had French. This suggested to Linebarger that I should start working on Indochina and later the entire Southeast Asian region. My date for entry into the Foreign Service was established for February 1957. I spent 1956 in the most painful and arduous period of study I have ever experienced but I passed the M.A. oral comprehensives in January 1957 and entered on duty, as scheduled, in the February Foreign Service Officer Class of 1957.

After training at the Foreign Service Institute, my initial assignment was as Laos-Cambodia Analyst in the Division of Research for the Far East in the State Department's Office of Intelligence and Research. This period was from June 1957 to August 1959, during which I worked on an important project with the distinguished diplomat Marshall Green. I began full-time language study in Indonesian in August.

I went to Jakarta in 1960 as the junior member of the Economics Section of the U.S. embassy. Jack W. Lydman was my boss and helped me become a professional. I went to Kuala Lumpur, Malaysia, in October 1962, also as an economics officer. The tour was aborted in June 1963 because of my wife's illness. Kent Goodspeed, Francis Underhill, Don McCue, and Ambassador Charles Baldwin helped me through a difficult time.

I returned to Washington to work in the State Department's Operations Center of the Executive Secretariat. Deputy Executive Secretary Jeanne Davis, who was a "talent scout," recommended me to Assistant Secretary Lucius Durham Battle Jr. as his staff aide. Luke Battle gave me a strategic bureaucratic perspective. His successor, Harry C. McPherson Jr., gave me a strategic political perspective.

McPherson was responsible for my 1965 assignment to Copenhagen as cultural affairs officer. Ambassador Katherine Elkus White had me write speeches for her and she and her husband joined me in exploring the exciting Danish cultural world. I learned how to be an ambassador from her. In 1967, she helped me win an assignment to the United States Military Academy at West Point as the State Department Faculty Member and Assistant Professor in the Department of Social Sciences.

Colonel George (Abe) Lincoln, the legendary head of that department, tried to help me gain an intellectual perspective, including sending me to Vietnam in the summer of 1968 to explore my doubts about the war.

I was reassigned to the State Department in 1969. By now, Marshal Green was Assistant Secretary of State for the Far East and he put me on the Philippine desk as deputy to Richard E. Usher, a gentle and intelligent leader. Dick Usher gave me wide freedom to undertake and manage an historic study of changes needed in the 1947 U.S.–Philippine Military Bases Agreement mandated by Henry Kissinger, then in the White House.

This work led to Ambassador Henry E. Byroade's choosing me in 1971 to hold the critical position of political-military officer to oversee implementation of the Bases Agreement in Manila. Byroade had learned an effective delegation of authority management style from General George C. Marshall and was a marvelous, relaxed, and shrewd diplomat. Byroade, his deputy William C. Hamilton, and others such as Frank Maestrone, Frazier Meade, and Byroade's successor William Sullivan guided me in this difficult job from 1971 to 1975.

James M. Wilson Jr., coordinator for humanitarian and human rights affairs, selected me as his deputy for human rights in 1975. In this job, Jim Wilson was like a father to me. I had help also from Sandra Vogelgesang and Winston Lord of the Policy Planning Staff; Charles Runyon of the Legal Bureau; Warren Hewitt in the United Nations Bureau; Assistant Secretary for Inter-American Affairs William Rogers and George Lister of his staff; Under Secretary of State for Political Affairs Philip C. Habib; Under Secretary for Management Larry Eagleburger; congressional staffer John Salzburg; and many others. By now, Henry Kissinger was Secretary of State and I was one of the last ambassadors he selected.

My ambassadorial career began in Togo in 1976. I had a high-energy staff led by Deputy Chief of Mission William B. Young. We had great support from Assistant Secretary of State for African Affairs Richard Moose. We had the best Peace Corps in the world and one of the best small embassies.

Director General of the Foreign Service Harry G. Barnes Jr. and the assistant secretary for personnel named me to head the Foreign Service personnel office in 1978. This assignment enabled me to work closely with Deputy Director General Nancy Rawls and a superb staff led by deputy Arthur Woodruff.

I succeeded Ambassador Rawls when she became ill and relied heavily on Andrew Steigman, who took my former position. Harry Barnes and Joan Clark, his successor, were stellar instructors in the mysteries of personnel management. We had great support from Under Secretaries for Management Ben Read and Richard Kennedy. Secretary of State Cyrus Vance took a close interest in personnel questions, especially the recruitment, retention, and promotion of minorities and women.

I was chosen to be Ambassador to Malaysia by Richard Kennedy and Secretary of State Alexander Haig when the Reagan administration began. I had known Haig at West Point where he was deputy commandant of the Corps of Cadets. The 1981–1983 assignment to Kuala Lumpur was one the high points in my career. Deputy Chief of Mission Lyall Breckon, Don McConville, Paul Blackburn, Don Steinberg, and others were the key to the success of the mission.

From 1983 to 1986, I was assigned to the Center for Strategic and International Studies (CSIS) as a Visiting Scholar. I worked for Amos A. Jordan who had succeeded Colonel Abe Lincoln at West Point. Bill Taylor and Reggie Brown, with whom I also had taught at West Point, were CSIS colleagues. Looking back, this assignment was a key factor in preparing me for my subsequent academic career. I was able to write a book at CSIS. There is no doubt that my extended CSIS stay kept me out of the Foreign Service mainstream too long and away from the promotion-enhancing jobs that, perhaps, I should have sought. On the other hand, I was happy in the work I was doing. I thought it was valuable and useful and I have no regrets.

In due course, my CSIS work did come to the attention of the White House and the Department of State and I was selected to be Ambassador to Mauritius in the 1986–1989 period. The island was beautiful. The people were hardworking, intelligent, and stimulating. The culture was rich, deep, and varied. I had a good team. We carried out our mission with dash, dispatch, and skill. Again, I had the honor of leading one of the best small embassies in the Foreign Service. Who could have asked for more?

The facts of life are, however, that small embassies do not lead to promotion. I reached the limit of my time-in-grade in 1989 and retired happily. I found what I had sought in the Foreign Service: opportunity, a full life in interesting places, professional and personal growth, extraordinary people with whom to work, and great satisfaction. I was not as successful as I might have been, I was no Ralph Bunche or George Kennan, but I loved my career, and I did the best job I could do.[1]

I found that we need Black diplomats in the same way we need Black teachers, and linguists, and classical scholars, and doctors and lawyers and engineers, musicians and military officers. Diplomats need to be trained in the same long and meticulous way that other professionals are trained. A higher priority for training of Blacks in international affairs is needed because government service is not the only outlet now for persons with such training. More than 60 percent of persons with graduate degrees in international affairs are now employed in business, journalism, not-for-profit firms, NGOs, and the like. Few careers lack an international component these days.

I challenged Howard University in 1979 to become more active in preparing Blacks for the Foreign Service. Three Howard students passed the Foreign Service examinations in 1969. None passed in 1978; one passed in 1977. Indeed, despite Black interest in the Third World and specifically Africa, only fourteen Blacks out of 7,273 takers of the written examination passed the 1977 examination and only nineteen Blacks out of 9,637 takers passed it in 1978.

As for Howard, in the period 1970–1978, these were the facts:

Year	Takers	Passers	Year	Takers	Passers
1970	2	0	1975	18	0
1971	1	0	1976	33	1
1972	5	1	1977	16	1
1973	18	1	1978	21	0
1974	14	0			

In the period 1970–1978, 120 Howard students took the Foreign Service examination—four passed it. In the period 1960–1969, six Blacks passed the exam, including three Howard students, out of three hundred Blacks who took the exam in that decade. I was the only Howard student to pass the exams in the decade 1950–1959 and only the second Black to do so in the postwar period.

A reorganization of the Foreign Service personnel structure took place in the 1955–1957 period resulting in the moving of certain officers into the Foreign Service Officer (FSO) category. When I entered in 1957, the Black officers were Clifton Wharton, Rupert Lloyd, William George, Charles Hanson, David Bolen, Orville Lewis, and John George, all of whom had served in Monrovia. Others were James Parker, Clinton Knox, Wiliam P. Boswell, Terence Todman, and Leslie Polk. Ollie Ellison entered in 1958 and James Baker and Joyce Garrett in 1960. There were seventeen officers in 1961 when the Kennedy administration began.

By 1966 in the Johnson administration, there were still only nineteen Black FSOs. They included Clinton Knox, James Baker, David Bolen, William Boswell, Ollie Ellison, Yvette Fonveille, Richard Fox, Benjamin Goode, Charles Hanson, Archie Lang, Lloyd Lee, Roscoe Lewis, James McRae, Robert W. Miller, James Parker, Samuel Pinckney, Leslie Polk, Cecil Richardson, Terence Todman, and me.[2] Clearly, something had to be done to increase the number of Blacks in the Foreign Service and the method chosen was to eliminate the written examination and administer the tough oral examination to candidates. Those who passed were given five-year reserve officer appointments. By their fifth year they had to pass another stiff oral examination to obtain tenured status. A recruiting target of twenty Blacks a year was established in 1967. Even so progress was slow. The targets were not met in the Nixon-Ford administration. The Carter administration took a more aggressive approach and not only made it a priority to attain yearly recruiting targets but also undertook to fulfill unmet targets of earlier years.

By 1979, the total of officer-level Blacks had reached 202 persons out of a total of about 4,000 officers. Of these 103 had career status; 99 were officer candidates who faced the second oral exam. Another 48 Blacks were officer-level specialists. In 1978, 43 minorities were recruited out of a total of 112 persons who entered on duty. However, it was already apparent that affirmative action would come under sustained attack. There were problems also in getting the quality of entrants desired. A disproportionate share of Blacks have lacked the mastery of writing skills the career requires.

There were 202 Foreign Service Officers in 1979, of these about half were tenured officers and half were untenured reserve officers who had to pass an oral examination in a stipulated period. There were about four thousand Foreign Service officers at that time and there were fourteen Black ambassadors.

For the record: There were 223 Black generalist Foreign Service Officers in FY 1981; 242 in 1983; 254 in 1985; 257 in 1986; 286 in 1987; 273 in 1989; 279 in 1990; 269 in 1991; 268 in 1992; 263 in 1993; 249 in 1994; 248 in 1995 and 245 in 1996. Blacks have consistently totaled about 5 percent of the Foreign Service. From smaller bases, totals of Asian Americans and Hispanics has risen to now approximate the total of Blacks.

Having challenged Howard in 1979, I sought more recent statistics regarding the performance of Howard students on the Foreign Service examination. These are the data:

Year	Takers	Passers
1992	23	1
1993	27	2
1994	25	0
1996	31	2

A pessimistic view of the data is that few Howard students continue to pass the examination. An optimistic view is that more students are taking it.

The intuition I had in 1979 that affirmative action was in for serious trouble was borne out. The vigor of Black recruitment diminished in the Reagan, Bush, and Clinton administrations. Additionally, Asian Americans and Hispanics have competed strongly with Blacks for Foreign Service positions. Table 11.1 shows the trends.

TABLE 11.1
Foreign Service Hiring of Minority Junior Officer Candidates, 1978–1997

Year	Total	Blacks	Asians	Hispanics
1978	162	33	NA	NA
1979	183	21	NA	NA
1980	251	30	NA	NA
1981	257	21	NA	NA
1982	189	24	NA	NA
1983	170	19	NA	NA
1984	220	15	NA	NA
1985	293	12	NA	NA
1986	187	12	10	12
1987	178	10	9	8
1988	200	8	11	10

TABLE 11.1 *(continued)*

Year	Total	Blacks	Asians	Hispanics
1989	215	3	13	9
1990	161	8	6	3
1991	244	7	6	6
1992	191	9	11	2
1993	130	5	5	7
1994	127	4	4	4
1995	110	5	6	2
1996	123	6	8	1
1997	122	8	8	7

Source: S/EEOCR/Department of State

Howard is ideally suited to become an important center for the study of international affairs and a source of personnel for the Peace Corps, the Agency for International Development, the State Department, the United States Information Agency,—yes, even the Central Intelligence Agency. If Blacks don't accept the challenge of doing some of the extremely important work in foreign affairs, I can guarantee you that others will. African Americans have something valuable to say, our challenge is to say it where it counts—inside government—not outside on the streets, or in cocktail lounges or on campuses.

Thomas Wolfe said you can't go home again. That is not true. Every time I come back to the United States from an assignment, I come home to Howard. Howard's challenge to me continues. Every time I am here I can sense earlier versions of myself and I feel that they measure me and I want to assure you their standards are high. I hope I have challenged you to look at yourselves critically and to begin to set standards for yourselves that you can be proud of when you come back to Howard. I hope my part of the Howard legacy will be in good shape when you inherit it.

NOTES

1. The following is an email response from Ambassador Palmer to the editor on January 28, 1998, that we both thought would complement the text:

> Your substantive comment that I should have more to say on racial obstacles is noted. I'll give you some examples. However, the greater problem with the Foreign Service is its up-or-out values. It harks back to Calvinist and Puritan predestination types of values: the right stuff and all that. Horatio Alger—"Sink or Swim" concepts. I was born in the Depression and most folk born then were rather hard-

shelled and rugged. Remember that sports medicine is a recent concept. I played four years of football and basketball and got hurt once and walked home on a sprained ankle from football practice.

We knew the deck was stacked but we played the cards we were dealt. We didn't expect fairness; if anything, we expected to be cheated. Jack Kennedy said it and we knew it: Life was unfair. Racism and prejudice are not recent inventions.

When I entered the State Department in 1957 there was still an unwritten rule that Blacks ate closer to the steam-tables in the cafeteria and Whites ate out toward the windows where there was both light and some ventilation in the days before air-conditioning. My wife couldn't get a job at the State Department. They didn't hire Black women.

Virtually all of the Black officers then on board, 17 persons, had started their careers in Monrovia. They were deemed second-class at best. I was initially assigned to the Office of Security presumably because I was tall and burly; however, when someone with a better position for me saw my record I was removed from the clutches of Security.

It might help you to know that I clearly was someone to take seriously. A high school friend had said I was the first tough Black guy he had ever met who was not a hoodlum. I came from western Pennsylvania where I had had to fight almost every day of my life as a boy, until I got so big that folks left me alone. I walked miles to and from school every day. I was hit in the mouth by a junior high school principal who was seeking to expel me for my brains and straight back. I had sense enough not to hit him back.

I played football for a racist coach who called me Stepinfetchit and made me perform that despicable actor's role in summer football camp festivities. The poor dumb paisano ran a play at me on the last day of practice in the 1946 season and allowed me to wipe out the interference for our all-Western Pennsylvania Interscholastic League blond wavy-haired fullback, Rich Grabiak, who I smashed at his ankles in his own backfield as the shadows descended on gladitorial combat at Ramsay High School in Mount Pleasant, PA.

I had stood in lines trying to get any job I could find. What could the foreign service do to me that hadn't already been done? My cousin Howard Thomas was in the first batch of Blacks allowed into the Marines in World War II. The bastards tired to kill him in boot-camp but he emerged from the War as a Sergeant.

Do you understand? The Foreign Service was a piece of cake. But you have to remember that I was smart, tough and smooth. I quickly adapted to the culture and learned the virtues of ruthlessness.

2. Ebony, *The Negro Yearbook* (Chicago: Johnson, 1966).

ABOUT THE
CONTRIBUTORS

ALLEN CALDWELL is a Ph.D. student in the School of Education at the University of California at Berkeley. He holds a M.A. in international education from Harvard University and is a veteran of the Peace Corps. He has worked in the Ministry of Education in Guyana and as an intern at the World Bank and the Department of State.

RONALD V. DELLUMS served in the United States House of Representatives from January 1971 until March 1998, representing the Berkeley-Oakland area of northern California. Elected to the Congress from a seat on the Berkeley City Council, Mr. Dellums was elected from an overwhelmingly White congressional district, running on a campaign platform that included opposition to the Vietnam War, a commitment to environmentalism, and support for the civil rights struggles of people of color, women, gay men and lesbians, and those with disabilities.

In the House of Representatives, he has served principally on the Foreign Affairs Committee, the District of Columbia Committee, and the Armed Services Committee—now known as the National Security Committee. He served a term as chairman of the Congressional Black Caucus and has served as vice-chair of the Democratic Socialists of America.

CHARLES P. HENRY is professor of African American Studies at the University of California at Berkeley. He has a Ph.D. in political science from the University of Chicago and has taught at Howard University, Denison University, and the University of Michigan. A former chair of Amnesty International USA, he has also served as president of the National Council for Black Studies, as director of issue analysis and external affairs in the Bureau of Democracy, Human Rights and Labor at the Department of State and is currently a presidential appointee to the National Council on the Humanities. His most recent book is *Ralph Bunche: Model Negro or American Other?*

PERCY C. HINTZEN is associate professor and chair of the Department of African American Studies at the University of California at Berkeley. He has also served as chair of the Peace and Conflict Studies program at Berkeley. Hintzen holds a Ph.D. in political sociology from Yale University.

JAMES JENNINGS is professor of political science and director of the Trotter Institute at the University of Massachusetts, Boston, where he also teaches in the Africana Studies Department. He has lectured and published widely on racial politics and public policy. He has also designed research and policy evaluation studies and provided technical assistance to a wide range of national and international organizations.

KEITH JENNINGS is an adjunct professor at the American University's School of International Service and has worked as director of programs in civic participation for the National Democratic Institute (NDI). He has been a country representative for NDI in Zambia, Mozambique, Liberia, and Guyana. He has also been national coordinator of the World Council of Churches' human rights campaign on racism in the United States; regional director of Amnesty International's mid-Atlantic office in Washington, D.C.; and has held positions with the Southern Christian Leadership Conference, the National Association for the Advancement of Colored People, and the United States Student Association. Currently, he is president of the African-American Human Rights Foundation.

CLARENCE LUSANE is an assistant professor of political science in the School of International Service at American University. He has been a consultant to the World Council of Churches, the Congressional Black Caucus Foundation, and a number of elected officials and nonprofit organizations. He worked for eight years in the U.S. House of Representatives as a staff aide to former D.C. Congressman Walter E. Fauntroy, and then for the former Democratic Study Group which served as the primary source of legislative information and analysis for House Democrats. His most recent book is *Race in the Global Era: African Americans at the Millennium* (Boston: South End Press, 1997). Among Dr. Lusane's other books is *Pip Dream Blues: Racism and the War on Drugs* (Boston: South End Press, 1991). Dr. Lusane received his Ph.D. in political science from Howard University.

LORENZO MORRIS is professor of political science at Howard University. A political scientist with a Ph.D. from the University of Chicago, Morris has served as a consultant to USAID and to the Canadian Broadcasting System. He is a past president of the National Conference of Black Political Scientists and publishes frequently in the areas of racial politics and public policy.

WINSTON NAGAN is professor of law at the University of Florida at Gainesville. Born in South Africa, he was active in the struggle against apartheid and is a former chair of Amnesty International USA. He is the author of numerous articles on international law and public policy.

RONALD PALMER is professor of the practice of international affairs at the George Washington University. He was ambassador to Togo, 1976–1978; ambassador to Malaysia, 1981–1983; and ambassador to Mauritius, 1986–1989. Palmer received a NAFEO Distinguished Alumnus Award in 1988 and was cited for his service to the nation and the international community by the Detroit branch of the NAACP in 1989. A member of the Council on Foreign Relations and president of the Malaysia-America Society, he is also senior associate fo Global Business Access Ltd. and a consultant for the Business Council on International Understanding and the Thunderbird Graduate School of International Management.

CELENA SLADE works for the National Democratic Institute (NDI).

TUNUA THRASH was a John Gardner Fellow with the Greenlining Institute and is now a graduate student at Harvard's Kennedy School of Government.

RONALD WALTERS is professor of Afro-American studies and government and politics at the University of Maryland at College Park. A long-time activist on issues of domestic and international concern to the Black community his most recent book is *Pan-Africanism in the African Diaspora*.

NAME INDEX

Abacha, Sini, 147
Abrahams, General, 177
Acheson, Dean, 105, 240
Ackerman, David, 57
Adams, Alvin, 178
Adams, Grantly, 189, 196
Adams, Russell, 111
Adams, Tom, 209
Ake, Claude, 135
Alfrey, Phyllis, 201
Almeida, Juan, 67
Amin, Idi, 138, 157
Andrews, Henry, 150
Aptheker, Herbert, 99
Aristide, Jean-Bertrand (Titid), 170,
   171, 177–78, 179–82
Atwood, J. Brian, 10
Avril, Prosper, 176, 177
Azikiwe, Nnamdi, 102

Babangida, Ibrahim, 157
Baker, James, 247
Banda, Hastings Kamuzu, 157
Barnes, Harry G., Jr., 245
Barnes, Leroy "Nicky," 67
Battle, Lucius Durham, Jr., 244
Bazin, Marc, 171, 172, 173, 177–78,
   179
Bennett, William, 51
Bereuter, Douglass, 31
Bethune, Mary McLeod, 98, 102
Bevel, James, 2
Bird, Vere, 201, 209
Bishop, Maurice, 205–6
Bishop, Sanford, 26
Black, Hugo L., 105
Blaize, Herbert, 201
Blakely, Edward J., 78–79

Blandon, Danilo, 65–66, 72n. 65
Blauner, Robert, 86
Bokassa, Jean Bedel, 157
Bolen, David, 247
Boley, George, 143, 150
Boswell, William P., 247
Botha, P. W., 124–25
Bradshaw, Robert, 210
Bramble, Percival, 209–10
Bramble, William, 201
Bricker, John, 105, 114–15n. 26
Browne, Robert, 18, 105
Brown, John, 165n. 22
Brown, Ron, 7
Brumskin, Charles, 156
Bunche, Ralph, 2, 4, 6, 95, 97–98,
   100, 101, 113n. 2, 240, 241
Burnham, Forbes, 189, 205, 210, 211
Bush, George, 19, 55
Bustamante, Alexander, 196,
   200–201
Butler, Uriah, 196–97
Byroade, Henry E., 244

Cabral, Amilcar, 6
Caldwell, Allen, 6, 11, 37
Calero, Adolfo, 65
Capper, Arthur, 102
Caputo, Dante, 171
Carter, Jimmy, 108
   and Haiti, 178, 179, 181
   and Liberia, 150–51, 152
   and Third World nationalism, 205,
      207, 208
Casey, William, 128
Cashmore, Ellis, 85
Cassin, Rene, 106
Castells, Manuel, 58, 59

255

SUBJECT INDEX